SURVIVING IN SCHOOLS
in the 1990s

Strategic Management of School Environments

James R. Tompkins, Ph.D.
Appalachian State University
Boone, North Carolina

Patricia L. Tompkins-McGill, Ph.D.
Consultant and Writer
Cedar Hill, Texas

UNIVERSITY
PRESS OF
AMERICA

Lanham • New York • London

Copyright © 1993 by
University Press of America®, Inc.
4720 Boston Way
Lanham, Maryland 20706

3 Henrietta Street
London WC2E 8LU England

Library of Congress Cataloging-in-Publication Data

Tompkins, James R., 1935–
Surviving in schools in the 1990s : strategic management of
school environments / by James R. Tompkins and
Patricia L. Tompkins-McGill.
p.   cm.
Includes bibliographical references and index.
1. Special education—Administration.   2. School management and
organization.   3. School environment.   4. Classroom environment.
5. Classroom management.   6. Problem children—Education.
I. Tompkins-McGill, Patricia L.   II. Title.
LB2806.T66   1993   371.9'042—dc20   92–33169 CIP

ISBN 0–8191–8919–7 (cloth : alk. paper)
ISBN 0–8191–8920–0 (pbk. : alk. paper)

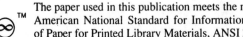 The paper used in this publication meets the minimum requirements of
American National Standard for Information Sciences—Permanence
of Paper for Printed Library Materials, ANSI Z39.48–1984.

Dedication

This book is dedicated to our parents, John P. and Dorothy Dee Longan and Leo and Cecilia Tompkins; to our children, Tim and Mark; and to Fritz Redl and David Wineman, who originally taught us about these ideas. They all inspired us to care about children and their teachers.

We also dedicate the book to the great professionals who influenced us profoundly over the past thirty years, personally and professionally, and deepened our understanding of therapeutic milieu and Life Space Interviewing. They include: Bruno Bettelheim, Eli Bower, Larry Brendtro, Eve Citrin, Bill Cruickshank, Dick Cutler, Stan Fagen, Carl Fenichel, Norris Haring, Frank Hewett, Nick Hobbs, John Johnson, Peter Knoblock, Nick Long, Bill Morse, Elton McNeil, Ruth Newman, Abe Nicolaou, Mary Lee Nicholson, Joe Noshpitz, Jim Paul, Bill Rhodes, Al Trieschman, and Mary Margaret Wood.

Acknowledgments

We owe an enormous debt to Fritz Redl and Dave Wineman, and to all the other pioneers of these techniques cited throughout the book.

We are grateful to Appalachian State University graduate student-teachers for contributions of their experiences with students while exploring and experimenting with Milieu Therapy applications in their public school classrooms. Teachers who shared their experiences with children and with us are Carol A. Nelson, Karin Nelson, Brenda Gilcrest, Marilyn Barnhill, Kathy Wyckliffe Powell, Sarah Upchurch, and Mary Ann Radke. The illustrations of encounters with children and youth are essentially the original teacher documentations. The authors have, however, edited and introduced new or revised narratives relative to the conceptual content of Milieu Therapy and teacher experiences.

William Krupicka provided a substantial contribution in reviewing the literature on the Life Space Interview. Debbie Jean Lyerly provided new material, editing, and bibliographical assistance on therapeutic relationship issues, and illustrations of the advantages of implementing Milieu Therapy practices in public school programs. Susan Roberts was instrumental in the idea of exploring a partial review of the literature on structure. We also wish to express our appreciation to Mary Callaghan, Teddy L. Grabowski, and Laura Tucker for their contributions on social cognition issues, education of adolescent youth, and the importance of structure.

Finally, thanks are due to Bill Morse, who consistently encouraged us to go ahead with this endeavor and gave us some early feedback about the first draft of the manuscript; to Jim Paul for his continued encouragement; to John McGill for his computer expertise, which made the production of this manuscript possible; to Edward Flynn for his editorial assistance and input; and to Frank Costenbader, Secretary/Treasurer of TREC, Inc. (Treatment, Rehabilitation and Education for Children), for partial support for the authors to get together to work on the manuscript.

CONTENTS

Contents

Contents

Contents

Contents

As a nation, we have provided a quantity of education unlike that of any other nation in the world. We can be justly proud of this. Now we must also attend to the quality of education. A child's mind is a terrible thing to waste, and the deterioration of student learning environments results in an extravagant waste that no nation can long afford (Erickson 1977, 121).

Preface

Every school building, classroom, and playground is an environment exuding qualities that can be sensed immediately. Is the milieu of the school healthy or is there a feeling of dis-ease? Does one feel security or fear, joy or dissatisfaction, growth and expansion or shrinking and deterioration?

School personnel must concern themselves with children's feelings and behavior as well as with their academic development. The school milieu must reflect the hope that children are malleable beyond the limits assigned them by pessimism or despair and that the world, despite its incomprehensible variations, still does not exhaust the possibilities of human resiliency. Whether through Milieu Therapy, Social Cognition, Behavior Therapy, or Affective Education, there are dozens of opportunities every day within the life space of a classroom to teach lessons of both feelings and behavior while enhancing the learning environment of every student.

The creation of an environment which deals with the whole child in a growth-enhancing manner is known as implementation of a therapeutic milieu. The use of Milieu Therapy techniques in the residential care of emotionally disturbed children has a rich and long history, but teachers, counselors, administrators, and others in the public schools may not be aware of the generic values of these practices or of their potential for use in school situations.

Due to vast economic, demographic, and societal changes in the United States during the past forty years, public schools now face unparalleled challenges. Regular educators find themselves faced with more and more challenging children in classrooms, many of whom need special help to achieve basic skills and minimal social adjustment. Special educators, trained to develop programs for highly divergent youngsters, may not have had the opportunity to review interventions other than behavior modification. For these educators, we hope to open vistas which are both historical and contemporary.

It is our thesis that the Milieu Therapy and Life Space Interview techniques which have proven beneficial in working with emotionally disturbed children can also be used to advantage in any public school classroom. Teachers and other school personnel will find this approach effective in dealing with children in the school environment, and children, even those who are difficult to manage, will benefit when these principles are applied. The use of these techniques, along with other management tools, will support transformation of school environments toward more healthy, nourishing experiences.

In this book, we explain how Milieu Therapy can be successfully used by school personnel along with existing methods and approaches. Major approaches in education are compared with the milieu approach. We include recommendations for meeting the emotional (affective) needs of students and intervening verbally, through the Life Space Interview, when they have problems. We discuss the powerful influences of relationships, of structure in the classroom and in the school, and of groups. We also reflect on historical precedents for therapeutic milieu services and refer to legislation, research, and practices which have an impact on education today.

Drawing from the fields of social work, psychology, and other human service disciplines as well as from education, we take into account the child, the teacher, and the entire school environment. We breach regular and special education differences to influence a collaborative engagement in the education of children. The extensive references and supplementary readings represent a wide spectrum of approaches reflecting almost one hundred years of thinking and practice in work with children and youth. This material offers students and practitioners in education and other fields a broad, comprehensive view of history, theory, and practices in the treatment and education of children and youth.

We include reports from the experiences of educators who applied Milieu Therapy and Life Space Interview principles while working with children from preschool age through adolescence in the public schools. Classroom incidents are described by teachers, accenting the power of sound psychoeducational and psychosocial practices in education. Teachers' reports illustrating the use of these techniques are taken from material written over a ten year period. While all contributing teachers have given permission for their work to be used, we have not cited them individually in the text or in the references; instead, teachers' contributions are treated as one body of material, appearing in the text as indented quotes without citations and listed in the bibliography as "Teachers' Experiences". We have also changed children's names in order to protect the anonymity of all involved.

The philosophical position underlying this book is associated with psychoeducational approaches and with ego psychology flowing from the psychodynamic model. However, those with other philosophical orientations can integrate and make use of therapeutic milieu practices without sacrificing their professional identities. The practices we advocate here can and should complement other treatment approaches without violating practitioners' values. Behavioral approaches are not excluded, nor are the techniques which we propose contradictory to other approaches.

While there is heated debate and little agreement about whether a specific philosophy, curriculum, or approach is preferred in the education of troubled children (Grosenick, George, & George 1990, 73), the behavioral perspective has been pervasive in schools for the last two decades. Nevertheless, schools have continued to use other approaches, with programs based on eclectic, pragmatic combinations of elements reflecting behavioral, psychodynamic, or psychoeducational positions (Grosenick, George, & George 1987, 161-163). "Only the most mechanistic behaviorists felt that it was useless to talk with students about feelings and goals and only the most doctrinaire psychoanalytically-oriented educators insisted that present environmental contingencies were unimportant in the determination of present behavior. Most practitioners acknowledge that combined approaches recognize that human behavior is more marvelous and complex than any theoretical model and provide for flexible adaptation of the intervention to match the characteristics of individual students" (Wood 1979, 12-13).

The application of the concepts of Milieu Therapy in schools is certainly not a magic solution to programming for children. We acknowledge that there are constantly huge discordant forces at work and that these are often counterproductive. Redl's unforgettable experience illustrates this point.

> On one occasion we set off for camp by bus with a load of very aggressive and disturbed youngsters. The group included a little girl who looked like a little angel.
>
> She may have been little, but she was not an angel! Her mother came to send her off and informed her in a loud voice: "Be sure to be a good girl and mind everything that these nice people tell you." Then, *sotto voce*, leaning down to the child, she said, "But remember you are my daughter and don't you take no shit from nobody." And I can assure you, she didn't take no shit from nobody, including me! The child was oppositional from the word go! (Redl 1976, 17-18)

Still, a structured, supportive milieu with careful design of activities and high expectations of achievement and socialization helps children become self-confident in school work and in relationships (Kauffman & Wong 1991, 232). One teacher reported an extraordinary healing influence for a young and very troubled child.

Jody had experienced severe trauma as an infant. He was born to a schizophrenic mother and found naked at age 2 1/2 in a closet, filthy and with bruises on his body. He had been peeling paint from the walls and eating it. He was given food and bottle, but was never held.

Jody and I were involved in housekeeping play. He was holding a baby doll and wrapping a blanket around it. We had built a small house to play inside. Jody played appropriately for a few minutes. I was the mother, Jody was the father and this (the doll) was our baby (Jody assigned the roles). He handed me the "baby" and I rocked the baby in my arms and fed the baby a bottle. Jody immediately screamed, "Put that bad boy in the closet, turn out the lights, do not hold that bad boy, never, never, never!" He calmed down and said, "Why do mommies do that?" Before I could respond to Jody, he ran around the room screaming that he would beat me, hurt me, and that I would die in the closet. He screamed to me that I was bad too and that he was afraid I would lock him in a closet.

This scene scared Jody to death. He was terrified of the trauma of the past. He was terrified of himself and his reactions, and he was terrified of me. Knowing that Jody couldn't hear me through his screams, I put the "baby" away and walked toward the futon which we used for relaxation. I sat on the futon and waited for the screams to cease. Then Jody calmed down and sat on the floor approximately ten feet away from me. He sat with tears streaming down his face in silence. I spoke softly to Jody: "You have had some scary thoughts and feelings. Let's rest on this futon and we will talk about this when you're ready and we are relaxed." He came and lay down beside me on the futon. We rested.

Obviously, Jody was still unable to cope with the devastating effects of his past. He had been unsuccessfully placed in several foster homes before finally being adopted by loving parents. No one had discussed the trauma of his first two years with him. I realized that, before he could improve, he must come to grips with his earlier experience.

I told Jody that the behavior of his [birth] mother was a result of her illness and that he didn't have to fear her anymore. I reminded him that he was now with loving parents. He had a home and a room of his own and toys, animals, friends. I explained that he was now being taken care of by his new parents and that we would not treat him with violence and anger. He understood and remembered incidents of his past, even though they were fuzzy. He said that he knew that we loved him and that we would help him to do better in how he acted with toys and people.

Milieu Therapy and it's associated techniques can fit in public school classrooms, can enhance the lives of children and adults there, and can provide opportunities for children in trouble to survive, learn, and remain in school.

CHAPTER ONE

THE IMPORTANCE OF PUBLIC SCHOOLS

School is a unique environment in the life of youth. At school, our nation's young people spend a large part of their waking time during some of their most formative years. There, many day-to-day dramas of living are played out. School is one social institution that holds children captive for a time. Whether students succeed or fail in school seems to correlate with whether they succeed or fail in later life. The school milieu and how students regard their experience there have a decided impact on their perceptions of self and reality, mastery of skills, socialization, and, ultimately, their adjustment.

The environments surrounding children are crucial in developing, maintaining, and altering their self-concepts. "Of the three environments where they spend many hours--school, home, and neighborhood--the school is the only environment that is professionally monitored. The school has vast resources with access to the self through the social components, the wide variety of learning experiences which can be introduced, and the presence of a sensitive, caring adult who is in charge" (Morse, 1985, 9).

Learning is a primary developmental task during childhood and adolescence and is crucial to self-esteem and emotional development. It builds and supports the child's sense of self and feelings of belonging, helps students set realistic goals, builds confidence, and increases the drive for further knowledge (Long, 1986; Haring & Phillips, 1962; Redl & Wineman, 1957). The process of learning weaves cognitive as well as instinctual and affective events into an inextricable design; while the preponderance of one or the other of these factors has fascinated us in the past, ways in which we may best weave them together to encourage learning in the classroom have not been emphasized (Redl, 1969a; Paul & Epanchin, 1991, 4).

Pupils need more than intellectual understanding of the world of ideas; they need to understand and interact effectively with the world around them. The responsibilities of education are broader than teaching academics; they may include promoting positive mental health, developing lifelong leisure-time skills, providing vocational training (Davis, 1989, 444), and facilitating useful social skills. Students have social or group needs--to belong, to be accepted by peers, to be understood, to express themselves, and to possess self-esteem and status. They have basic emotional needs that also affect learning: needs for affection, nurturing, privacy, creativity and growth, security, risk-taking, and exploration (Luft, 1970, 86-87; Stainback, Stainback, & Wilkinson, 1992, 6-10).

When we recognize the complexity and importance of children's needs and their bearing on classroom behavior and learning, the lives of both students and school staff are enriched. Because school personnel are directly involved in the lives of children for a great part of the day, week, and year, they have unique opportunities to observe and help them to grow and adjust.

The teacher's task is to develop an atmosphere conducive to fresh perceptions, increasing pupils' readiness for unaccustomed ideas and attitudes. New knowledge must be assimilated with what students already understand; they can accomplish this best through participation that enables them to be contributors to the group's goals and procedures, a part of the class instead of passive observers (Luft, 1970, 88).

Public schools offer natural groupings with both adult and peer role models available in the setting. Opportunities to learn and enhance socialization skills abound, and the impact of school experiences on a child can go in many directions. Children can be placed with peers who provide models for appropriate behavior. Physical education and other activities give children the chance to play together (Kratochwill & Morris, 1991, 284-285). "The child folk dances with others (a social experience), is involved with teachers and peers (a relationship experience), becomes more body aware and controlled (an identity experience), [and] . . . may become skilled enough to perform (an ego building, legitimate self-display experience)" (Morse, 1985, 170). Involvement in chorus groups requires cooperation, determination, and practice in following directions. Art classes supply opportunities for creative expression. Shop or occupational classes provide hands-on training that fosters success and self-esteem. Children can develop vocational skills required in obtaining jobs. Schools can help develop cooperation, leadership, good sportsmanship, temperance control, and assertiveness (Morse, 1971, 5-7).

In school, all children confront the ego task of behavioral control (Redl & Wineman, 1957, 27). Some children in schools present greater difficulties than others. Schools must deal with these children, regulating the degree of stress that they experience through the careful selection of material, through gradation of steps to ensure success, and through ending demands for perfection. School should be a place of work and creativity, of fun and play. School is a social context through which both bullies and scapegoats can learn from their peers as well as from authority figures in a realistic environment (Cheney & Morse, 1980, 295). There is no question about the impact of a school in the lives of its students. The question seems to be how to make the cognitive and affective domains work together to support, socialize, and educate children.

THE CHALLENGE TO SCHOOLS

Our world is caught in a whirlwind of accelerating social change and is beset by social crises of ever-increasing dimensions. Social change is so rapid that key social institutions are failing to provide for the fulfillment of the broad range of needs necessary for individuals to develop their human capacities to the fullest. People are losing their sense of compassion, a vital ingredient in fulfilling our social needs (Tompkins & McGill, 1989, 41).

Although responsibility for developing compassion is accepted in theory, it is defaulted in practice. Emphasis on developing the mind to the exclusion of the heart and soul is camouflaged by abortive attempts to introduce mental health programs into the schools. This failure to meet real needs becomes greater at successive grades of schooling. This shortfall is not entirely of the educators' making. Society freely assigns responsibilities to schools but is delinquent in making the necessary financial, physical, and human resources available to meet them (Tompkins & McGill, 1989, 41).

The public school can, by design or by accident, magnify problems that children are already experiencing. When a child fails to discover love, acceptance, and opportunities for more successful adjustment in public schools, any existing sense of inadequacy is reinforced. Children may become combative or withdrawn in response to the school's magnification of their failures. School-based attitudes, techniques, and procedures can interrupt such negative reinforcement, however, and schools can implement preventive management strategies to sustain difficult and desperate children as well as those who are merely getting past the bumps of everyday life (Biber, 1961; Kipfer, 1961; Cutler & McNeil, 1962; Newman, 1963; Tompkins, 1965).

Almost a century ago, William James (1899) told teachers that the science of psychology had little to offer that would aid them in their daily work. Teaching, he claimed, is an art, while psychology is a science. Since then, the volume of research and publication has increased tremendously, but teachers have not found an abundance of knowledge they can use; they stand pretty much as they did then--on their own (Luft, 1970, 79). Perhaps the real art is the blending of what the social sciences and other disciplines have learned with traditional educational practices in the classroom milieu (Bower, 1990, 15).

Teachers choose their profession because they want to enhance the learning, development, and lifelong potential of their students. They enjoy spending time with children. Yet during the past two decades teachers, like other professionals in human services, have been seriously challenged. Schools have become overcrowded, support personnel such as social workers, psychologists, and counselors are scarce, and demands on teachers' time for auxiliary activities are disproportionately large.

As generations of youth respond to societal problems such as increased abuse and neglect, dysfunctions and dissolution of families, poverty, homelessness, hunger, drug and alcohol abuse, lack of health care, unemployment and underemployment, and the decrease of social programs, school professionals are, more and more, seeing students whose behavior is out of control or who are so depressed and withdrawn that they cannot learn or interact. School personnel recognize that many of their students' problems are not primarily educational in origin. Academics will not be important to a student who is experiencing the absence of a parent, a pregnancy, a friend's run-away or suicide, drug addiction, or any of the other multiple problems current in our society. The best academic curricula available will not address these problems.

Teachers are frustrated because they perceive environmental odds too great to overcome through traditional educational methods (Davis, 1989, 444). "Let the teachers teach," we say. But first, children have to be ready to learn. Children and teachers cannot be expected to succeed in schools unless they receive the support necessary to break down those barriers to learning that exist in families, communities, and schools. We must refurbish an innovative track to healing and successful achievement.

Students with exceptional needs have been labeled and placed in "special" programs (e.g., "remedial," "disadvantaged," "special education"). Catchall categories have existed for those students with problems who did not fit into other, neater categories, and the number of children in categories such as "emotionally disturbed," "socioemotionally impaired," and "learning disabled" continues to increase.

Despite the labels applied to children to get adequate assistance for them and their schools, these students have one thing in common: they are viewed as differing from the established norm of a particular educational system at a given time. Such social stigma plays a role in the lack of appropriate services for these children. Indeed, such a stigma may bring to mind again the tragedy of the *Titanic*.

> At midnight April 14-15 the shortage of lifeboats on the *Titanic* was academic; the question was, who would get to use them? The White Star Line always claimed that the only rule was, women and children first; there was no distinction, the line insisted, between first-, second-, and third-class passengers. Yet there remained those uncomfortable statistics: Fifty-three percent of first- and second-class passengers saved, but only 25 percent of third class. Ninety-four percent of first- and second-class women and children saved, but only 42 percent of those in

third class. In first class just one child was lost, while in third class, 52 out of 79 children were lost (Lord, 1987, 165).

Special educational programs have developed for those "second- and third-class" students who do not fit the "normal" mold, but many mildly handicapped students (e.g., learning disabled, educable mentally retarded, and some emotionally disturbed children) may in fact be misdiagnosed curriculum casualties who have been referred to special education with "negative school labels" (Blackman, 1989). Responsiveness to students' needs, not special classrooms, is what is needed (Tucker, 1989). Many of these students could perform adequately in a regular classroom if given strong support from school personnel and other students, and their problems could be ameliorated without special education placements (Reschly, 1988, 459; Simpson & Myles, 1990, 1, 8).

Changes in federal laws for special education students are also placing increased demands on schools. The least restrictive environment provision of Public Law (P.L.) 94-142 favors educating children with handicaps in regular environments (Danielson & Bellamy, 1989, 448). Regular Education Initiative (REI) advocates maintain that there is no student who cannot be served in a regular classroom, if necessary supports are provided (Tucker, 1989, 456); they want the general education system to assume unequivocal, primary responsibility for all students in our public schools, including those with identified handicaps as well as those who, while not "labeled," have special needs of some type (Will, 1986).

There is intense debate in educational circles about the REI, producing frustrating dilemmas for many special education teachers and administrators being asked to alter some very basic philosophical and education beliefs and practices. Special education teachers and directors may feel guilt, anger, and suspicion, while at the same time they feel threatened with losing an established professional identity. There is genuine concern, too, that regular education is still not ready to meet the needs of students with special needs (Davis, 1989, 443; Cook & Friend, 1991, 25). But the "wedding" between regular and special education has already taken place, even though formal invitations were not sent and neither discipline was an enthusiastic participant. Now the real question is, how do we make this marriage work? (Davis, 1989, 441; D'Alonzo & Boggs, 1990, 22; Halpern, 1992, 209-211).

Despite P.L. 94-142 and the Regular Education Initiative, there has been little change since 1976-77 in the segregation in school of students with handicaps. Though regular classes now contain more handicapped students, this most likely reflects the number of students being labeled as "learning disabled" rather than an increase in mainstreaming (Danielson & Bellamy, 1989, 448). The REI debate reflects a basic issue--how can schools better assist students who require special attention, intervention, and support to enjoy a better quality of life? These quality-of-life issues are based on human needs and should be much more significant than political or legal considerations (Davis, 1989, 444; York, Vandercook, MacDonald, Heise-Neff, & Caughey, 1992, 257).

More and more teachers find themselves facing students who need assistance beyond traditional curricula if they are to thrive in schools. As implied in REI proposals, regular classrooms must begin to adopt more sophisticated treatment and educational interventions for more divergent students and tap the potential of classrooms for the development of healthy environments and influences in schools (Vergason & Anderegg, 1991, 5-6).

Most regular educators, already feeling overburdened and criticized for their perceived lack of response to more broadly based issues, such as rising illiteracy, increasing dropout rates, and declining student achievement test scores, view increased special education mandates as intrusive and unrealistic. Not only must they cope with public pressure to improve the overall academic performance levels of their students, but now they also must attempt to fit difficult-to-teach students within their classes. School principals feel overwhelmed and confused by the REI movement because they have not received proper training to assume these responsibilities along with the many other demands and pressures being placed on them in these calls for educational reform. To add to the stress, many parents are becoming more vehemently vocal in their criticism of education, both special (Davis, 1989, 442) and regular.

All teachers confront behaviors that reflect children's development, home influences, situational and social pressures, and fears and anxieties about new learning tasks and requirements. All children, handicapped or not, react to these influences and circumstances. Troubled children, with their adjustment problems, find it all the more difficult to function in the life space of the school and classroom. They have greater needs for more sophisticated programs (Lawrence, 1988, 349; Myles & Whelan, 1991, 8-10).

"Emotional disturbance" and "socioemotional impairment" are labels describing handicapping conditions in children and youth that, though not as visible, are as real as a physical impairment. Some of these students are called "mentally ill," "socially maladjusted," or "behaviorally disordered." There are many definitions of emotional disturbance in the literature. Their common features are that several aspects of the following characteristics are reflected in these children's behavior. These indicators are markedly serious and chronic, and these children exhibit high rates of unacceptable behavior.

- They are at the average or above average level of intellectual functioning.
- They are failing most academic subjects, usually falling two or more years behind in academic achievement.

- They are socially alienated. They have few social skills and enjoy few or no meaningful interpersonal relationships.
- Their behavior is so seriously inappropriate that it interferes with their own (and often other children's) learning progress.
- Their behavior may get them into trouble with the law or other authorities in their lives and contribute to their isolation from their peers and adult support systems.
- They are often depressed, but their depression may be expressed as angry, hostile, acting-out behavior as well as the typical withdrawn behavior usually associated with depression.
- Their self-esteem is low.
- They may have psychosomatic complaints.

The scope of this problem in schools is complicated. Numbers of emotionally disturbed children reported in public schools have increased from year to year--there has been an increase of 33.2 percent since 1976-77. Very few children with this label are placed in regular classes---a lower percentage than for all handicapped children as a whole. Many are in separate classes or drop out of school. Children with this label are often regarded as most in need of services and very few exit the education system needing no special services (U.S. Department of Education, 1987, 29, 30-31, 41-42; Danielson & Bellamy, 1989, 451; Tompkins & McGill, 1989, 38-41; Paul & Epanchin, 1991, 16-17 and 37-38).

No one really knows how many troubled children there are in the United States. Because there is lack of agreement on the definition of socioemotional impairment, the reported incidence of these children may go up or down depending on the definition used (Morse, 1985, 52). Often these children go unreported, especially as adolescents. The most conservative estimates of emotionally disturbed students in schools are 2 percent. Some studies suggest that 10 to 12 percent of school age children and youth have social and emotional problems significant enough to warrant planned professional help. Incidence reports of behavior disorders by teachers range from 2 percent to 69.3 percent of a given child population, with almost 8 percent characterized as moderately or severely disturbed (Tompkins & McGill, 1989, 38-39; Paul & Epanchin, 1991, 16-17). According to a National Needs Analysis conducted by the University of Missouri, Columbia (Huntze & Grosenick, 1980, 20-25) the prevalence of persistent handicapping mental health problems among children ages 3 to 15 ranges from 5 percent to 15 percent.

What is known is a set of alarming statistics. Children and youth between the ages of 10 and 17 commit more than half of all serious crimes in the United States (Raiser & Van Nagel, 1980, 516; Wicks-Nelson & Israel, 1991, 175-176). In 1984 alone, 1,537,688 youngsters under age 18 were arrested and brought before juvenile courts in the United States for a variety of offenses excluding traffic violations (Morgan, 1985, 221-223; Epanchin & Paul, 1987, 264-265). They represented 17 percent of all arrests made in 1984, and most were not held in custody very long. "The adjudicated and released delinquent and the socially maladjusted child who has not arrived in the court system will continue to disrupt schools. Mildly or moderately emotionally disturbed students will continue to demand too much of a teacher's time and attention because of their low tolerance for frustration, their immaturity, inadequacy, and inefficient learning" (Raiser & Van Nagel, 1980, 516).

Each year at least one million children in the United States are abused by their parents or caregivers, and approximately two thousand of them die. Estimates regarding sexual abuse of children in the U.S. range from 45,000 to over one million cases annually. Large numbers of children and adolescents use alcohol, marijuana, barbiturates, tranquilizers, quaaludes, stimulants, cocaine, and LSD (Tompkins & McGill, 1989, 39).

The U. S. Office of Education's estimate of over one million troubled children is the most conservative. Of those, only about 300,000 receive public school services. The shortage of teachers for these students is now a national crisis. To serve only those children identified, over four thousand specially trained teachers are needed, and this projected figure does not account for needed teachers for the more than 700,000 unidentified or unserved disturbed children. There is a continuing loss of personnel to teach these children--an attrition rate of 22 percent (Lauritzen & Friedman, 1991, 13) to 60 percent has been reported by some states. Repeated input from school districts indicates that many principals in charge of school programs for behavior disordered children are not supportive of such programs; they misunderstand and resist them and generally view them as an administrative headache (Tompkins & McGill, 1988).

Behavior and discipline problems in schools have become epidemic, spreading far beyond those children who have already been labeled or are in special education. Concerns in schools about children's behavior have moved from gum chewing and noise making to drug and alcohol abuse, assault, arson, pregnancy, suicide, and robbery. Children who are not considered as having special needs also may exhibit unacceptable behavior and social and affective difficulties requiring management in micro-settings across the entire school environment. So-called "normal" students have notable though episodic behaviors that appear like temporary disabilities, such as regression to younger developmental behaviors or acting-out fears and conflicts through aggression or other unacceptable behavior. Regular teachers must deal with a wide spectrum of student problems in their classroom, but they lack the training or support that would aid them in this endeavor. Rather than improvise, these teachers need to be able to individualize significant program approaches that meet the needs of their special clientele.

It is important for educators to understand the power of a benevolent school climate. Classrooms, corridors, offices, and playgrounds all have an atmosphere, consciously designed or not, that can either reinforce acting-out behavior or support the healthy growth and socialization of children. A calm, healing environment will allow children who need controls to find and internalize them, and children who are withdrawn to blossom.

We take for granted that teachers are well informed, particularly in their fields of specialization. Knowledge already gained and the ability to acquire new knowledge on an ongoing basis are basic to a teacher's work. The more subtle skills required to work with classes of young people are less well understood and appreciated. Alone in the classroom, teachers have little to guide them except what they know, observe, understand, sense, and feel. Even though superiors, colleagues, parents, and the community are looking over teachers' shoulders, rules and plans of the school can seem quite remote and abstract when pupils are reacting intensely, with strong curiosity, or apathetically at any given moment. Teachers must trust their own senses and observations, recognizing the realities of group life as well as the complexities of individual personalities. If teachers are well aware of their impact on others, they can work to influence the class in a desired direction. If they are not self-aware and sensitive to the motives and behaviors of their students, they may work hard and yet defeat their own purposes (Luft, 1970, 83).

As symptomatic behaviors of children increase, scores of other critical issues go unattended. Troubled children need assistance beyond typical therapy approaches, and schools are asked to assume more and more functions traditionally assigned to other institutions.

As a major socializing agency in the community, schools recognize that their responsibilities are broadening. Even instilling commonly accepted values is a legitimate school function, but most schools do not have the resources for accomplishing these functions. To do this, they need the infusion of conceptualizations from other disciplines as well as strong financial and service support.

Schools must provide adequately for the emotional and moral development of children while developing their cognitive abilities. A pro-active approach must replace the current reactive climate that requires development to go sour before resources are focused on behavioral redirection. While the "common cold" of development is developing into pneumonia so that it can be treated, children and youth are being lost, and the cost is inordinate.

WHERE WE HAVE BEEN

Historically, many public school classrooms have been without resources to take therapeutic advantage of children's natural growth patterns or expressions of children's distress. Teachers have been expected to teach skills and content at the same time as they are fostering adequate adjustment in the child and altering school policy and family dynamics (Cutler & McNeil, 1962, 16; Tompkins, 1965, 11). Teachers have had difficulty in discovering the management tactics necessary to respond to troubled children. Teachers are not trained in clinical work or group therapy, and their work is independent of the work of individual psychotherapy. Techniques for "preventive intervention" have often been the missing link in public school programs (Tompkins, 1965, 4).

During the 1960s, there was a growing conviction that the school had an important contribution to make to the field of mental health. Education was recognized as man's oldest and most effective tool for shaping future generations and for perpetuating a particular society. Psychoanalytic thinking and education, though seen as partners, really did not understand each other and therefore did not cooperate. Consequently, in an effort to blend mental health and education, there was a trend to recruit and train large numbers of persons for on-the-line preventive work in mental health in schools. This recruitment was consistent with the historical trend in the field to assign public schools a special opportunity and responsibility in preventive mental health activity. The decision to invest more energies in the training of specialized mental health personnel and less in direct services to children was predicated on two factors: a recognition that the manpower shortage was the most serious problem in the mental health field and a conviction that classic one-to-one psychotherapy was often not the most appropriate treatment for the moderately disturbed child in the classroom, even when the appropriate personnel were available (Tompkins, 1965, 8-11).

But transplanting mental health programs to the public schools was not the answer to some clearly recognized problems. Removing children from the classroom for a special kind of treatment that was supposed to make their lives in the classroom more successful didn't work. Clinical "mental health" jargon was perpetuated that had little meaning in schools. Power issues developed about who was really responsible for the management of the children, (the educator or the mental health system?), with resulting interprofessional conflict. Concern arose about the domination of mental health professionals in education leading to loss of attention to basic educational issues, and teachers lost the opportunity to feel adequate in dealing with their charges (Cutler & McNeil, 1962, 17).

Also, the economics of most schools did not then, and do not now, permit having mental health specialists on a stand-by basis. Because children do not have problems by appointment, perhaps it would be most helpful and effective to have basic skills available whenever the child is facing difficulty by teaching such skills to the essential on-the-line worker--the teacher. The classroom had to become the locus for dealing with these problems, for it was there that the child's problems found their most natural and usable expressions (Cutler & McNeil, 1962, 17; Tompkins, 1965, 10).

Morse (1961, 331; 1965, 396) concluded that there would never be enough specialists to handle all the mental health problems in the schools and that teachers would have to be trained to do some of the work. Some of the impact of mental health professionals in the schools had been negative, and although training designs were inadequate to give teachers diagnostic and management skills, specialists' functioning did not seem in keeping with the overall educational milieu. Perceptions of the role of the teacher offered a useful beginning point.

Teachers, in this transition, faced a heavy and frightening responsibility. The teachers' role was to handle adequately the problems their students presented. Teachers had to meet this expectation, not only for the children's sake, but for their own comfort and, sometimes, safety. They found themselves poorly prepared. To meet this challenge, there was a move in the schools to integrate techniques learned from residential treatment of seriously disturbed children into the schools for more practical general use. Therapeutic milieu practices and the Life Space Interview as a way of talking with children about problems as they arose were natural partners that teachers could use to design a healthy environment in public school classrooms.

THERAPEUTIC MILIEU

An important skill needed by all teachers is the ability to design an effective environment for the school program and to interact effectively with children in a noncritical, accepting, and open-ended manner (Fagen, 1981; Heuchert, 1983; Morse, 1963; Redl, 1969a). Such interactions facilitate learning, encourage overall development, and create an environment in which immediate behavior problems can be managed well, thus enhancing student/teacher enjoyment of the classroom environment.

"Children with emotional, behavioral and/or learning problems need much more than specific intervention strategies provided on a piecemeal basis. They need a total intervention aimed at every facet of their lives, their environments, and yes, their ecosystems" (Hewett, 1981, 3). Public schools using therapeutic milieu principles regard every aspect of children's lives in the school. The milieu is the matrix in which recognition of the value and dignity of children is evident. Children become the measure of all program elements and, with all their limits, needs, and interests, the ongoing and underlying theme. Milieu Therapy is the organization of the school environment to have a healthy impact on the child. The totality of the child's experience is considered in creating a safe environment that is structured to foster relationships and activities (Hewett, 1981, 3; Colman, 1992, 73-74).

Originally conceived by Bruno Bettelheim (1949) and elucidated by Redl and Wineman (1957) and others, Milieu Therapy was intended to expose a child or groups of children to total environmental design for treatment. The milieu was designed and manipulated with the aim of producing personality changes (Cumming & Cumming, 1966, 5) to meet the special socialization and learning needs of children with serious socioemotional impairments. The environment was designed to nurture, to gratify needs and desires, to encourage and sustain interpersonal relationships, and to help children learn self-regulation and impulse control. Children had the opportunity to master life situations--both inner and outer forces--undistracted by concerns about their basic needs, which were recognized and met in the milieu. As they learned to trust in consistent gratification of their needs, they were also confronted with the strength and comprehensive structure of an environment that could neither be destroyed nor controlled by "magical thinking" or misbehavior (Bettelheim & Sylvester, 1949, 54). Thus they learned that they could safely and effectively have an impact on their world, and that their feelings and wishes did not lead to disaster.

Environmental design and creation go far beyond choosing where furniture is placed and what is put on the bulletin board--it requires that the atmosphere be created with as much care as is used to sterilize an operating room. Just as postoperative infection can undo the effects of an otherwise successful operation, failure to maintain scrupulous psychological hygiene endangers attempts to influence behavior (Redl & Wineman, 1951, 44).

Milieu Therapy works through amelioration of a child's previous experiential deficiencies and builds on the child's strengths. No action or practice is too trivial to be considered in proper maintenance of this "good place." Milieu Therapy at school identifies the major elements of the classroom and other school settings and analyzes how they act on one another and how each must be adjusted in order for the best of all possible worlds to be attained in fostering the child's socialization and learning.

While therapeutic milieu techniques were developed for troubled children, they can be of immense benefit to all children and to teachers who wish to create a climate that is conducive to growth and learning. A therapeutic milieu will naturally transform children, acting to prevent potential problems as well as helping to ameliorate those problems that are present.

THE LIFE SPACE INTERVIEW

The Life Space Interview (LSI) is a structured, planned, deliberate way of talking effectively with children about their problems and feelings. The use of this specialized verbal exchange is an important element in a therapeutic environment. It is used for problem solving (Brendtro & Ness, 1983, 177-178), for control and disciplinary purposes, or for understanding more completely how the child feels and facilitating mutual insight into his or her behavior. It helps children to understand and cope with a specific current event that they can not handle on their own (Heuchert & Long, 1981, 5). It is a "here and now" intervention, focusing on a clear issue or behavioral incident in the direct life experience of the child at the moment of its occurrence or as close to the time of the problem as possible. Because problem situations in the child's day-to-day life have strategic therapeutic importance when they can be dealt with immediately (Vernick, 1963, 465-469), the interviewer engages a child at the very time and in the very place, on-the-spot and in the child's life space, that the troubling event occurs.

The school milieu is an ideal setting in which to use the Life Space Interview. Teachers' utilization of the Life Space Interview in schools seems a natural supplement in programming for children in trouble (Tompkins, 1965; Redl, 1969b; Long, 1990a, 10; Wood & Long, 1991). It is a generic technique that can be used with any child in a school setting. The key to improved school mental health, Morse (1961, 331) believed, "is the classroom teacher's increased ability to deal effectively and hygienically with the day-to-day life events." The Life Space Interview gives the needed focus. While the teacher is not expected to become involved in deep therapeutic interviews, there is much to be said for verbal discourse, on the spot, at times of crisis in day-to-day interaction with children. The Life Space Interview can be used in schools to ease, work through, and learn from critical events transpiring in the classroom (Morse & Ravlin, 1979, 338) or elsewhere in school. It capitalizes on occurrences in the immediate life-space of the child and facilitates intervention into problems in a child's life by a person who has direct life-experience meaning for the child (Wineman, 1959, 4). Morse found that "the Life Space Interview embodies a theory and method uniquely suited to the teacher's responsibilities in group management, social adjustment, and social learning. Hence, it is seen as the prototype of adult-child interaction both for generating control and for working through social and personal situations which develop in almost any classroom" (Morse, 1961, 331).

The technique of Life Space Interviewing does not replace the total range of techniques for managing and changing behavior; rather, it supplements them. Life-space theory does not argue that traditional methods are not effective, but rather that the Life Space Interview can be used as a powerful adjunct to these methods or can be used by itself to help troubled children with troublesome behaviors (Wineman, 1959, 4).

The Life Space Interview is based on noncritical therapeutic principles and is ongoing in children's everyday environment. The tools comprising the full range of the Life Space Interview are designed to help children get over common rough spots ("Emotional First Aid") or gain insight and motivation to develop more satisfactory ways of responding to problems ("Clinical Exploitation of Life Events"). If they are understood and adapted to individual needs and specific school settings, the methods and techniques of the Life Space Interview can help school personnel deal constructively with a variety of problems. The LSI can provide not only increased understanding of children and youth in schools but also insight into the professional problems, and their possible solutions, of teachers and administrators (Newman & Keith, 1963, iii; Gardner, 1990, 111; Long, 1990a, 15).

In the Life Space Interview, the teacher enters the immediate life experience (or "life space") of the child and deals with a crisis whenever it occurs (Redl, 1976, 56; Wood & Long, 1991). Many children do not remember the details of events long enough and may, indeed, develop distorted recollections too quickly for next Wednesday to be soon enough to talk to them about last Friday's behavior and feelings. Some children do not understand cause and effect or time relationships. If past and future do not mean much, the "now" is the essential consideration.

The Life Space Interview was developed as a systematic array of responses to disturbed children. The combination of individual psychotherapy and therapeutic milieu practices was often insufficient in the comprehensive care of children in treatment. The Life Space Interview supplemented treatment efforts occurring outside the classroom. While the school counselor, an outside therapist, or others may engage children in "50 minute hours" or other means of assistance, they may never see either the crises or the opportunities for intervention in the child's everyday life space.

Although the Life Space Interview originated in work with emotionally disturbed children, it is readily adaptable to many settings. Using the Life Space Interview in the school setting capitalizes on its more generic qualities to help children through the usual crises of living and growing up. Cutler and McNeil (1962, 17) found the use of the "Emotional First Aid" strategies of the LSI during moments of high stress an effective tool in preventive and remedial mental health efforts. The natural first aid station is in the classroom and school, where the teacher is most available. Significant alterations in the child's basic approach to the world can be brought about by direct life space management techniques. In school, manifestations of a child's problems are likely to be at an action-behavioral level, and the child is developmentally open to acquiring new social tools. Through use of the LSI, the child is offered new opportunities for alternative problem-solving methods.

Teachers testify to the efficacy of the Life Space Interview in public school classrooms. Patricia Tompkins (1965) described, assessed, and evaluated a year-long in-service training program that taught LSI and therapeutic milieu techniques to public school teachers. The study focused on teachers' feelings and attitudes about the Life Space Interview techniques as they used them, as well as behavioral changes observed in the children during the time the LSI was used.

Children's personal difficulties as well as problems with peers, adults, learning tasks, and school rules were studied. After learning and using LSI techniques, teachers perceived fewer of these difficulties in children. They saw it as a valuable tool to increase their effectiveness in handling behavior problems with fewer punitive methods and to aid them in a greater understanding of children's problems.

Teachers found the LSI easy to understand as well as to teach; most felt they could explain and demonstrate the technique to their student teachers. They felt that they understood the technique sufficiently well to judge its effectiveness in handling the behavior problems of children (Tompkins, 1965, 42-63).

A most dramatic result of the study was reduction in the teachers' perception of stress in their role in the school. Teachers reported that the use of the LSI increased their self-confidence and enabled them to handle behavior problems according to the individual needs of the children. Teachers' feelings of guilt, frustration, and inadequacy dominated before the training program. Teachers were overwhelmed and demoralized by sudden changes in the school population that had occurred because of integration efforts and by the daily management problems they faced. The training program was seen as therapeutic and supportive for the staff: teachers' feelings about themselves became more positive. Teachers felt that they had become more sensitive to the needs of the children and their methods of handling children had improved. They reported less guilt and frustration and they saw themselves as more calm, self-confident, and fair (Tompkins, 1965, 56-63).

NEW USES FOR OLD TOOLS IN THE 1990s: BEYOND BEHAVIORISM

In the past two decades, practice in education has swung heavily toward behavior modification techniques, sometimes without considering factors outside of the overt behavior that may be contributing to problems. As teachers and students have struggled merely to survive in schools, understanding of environmental influences and emotions has often been lost. Resources that were once used in schools for mental health services are now being used in remedial programs such as special education, and prevention efforts in schools have become almost nonexistent.

There is now renewed attention to broader efforts on behalf of children. Although behaviorism still remains dominant, humanism and holistic approaches are no longer frowned upon (Morse, 1985, 341-342). Teachers, "on the line" both literally and figuratively and discouraged with present methodology in education, are looking for new approaches and are willing to reexamine some previous approaches for their current usefulness. There is agreement that no single school of thought provides answers for the many situations a teacher must face and that narrow intervention strategies that force all children into the same mold may not be successful or comfortable for either students or teachers. While the behavioral approach has been a rallying point in intervention, many professionals feel there should be a blending of this approach with other approaches of the larger therapeutic community (Farkas, 1980, 364).

Wider perspectives are needed to meet successfully the challenges of the 1990s in schools. It is time to experiment with new paradigms for education that consider social, political, and economic influences on current educational environments; these may differ drastically from current practices (Skrtic, 1987; Edgar, 1988).

The fields of education and psychology are now adapting many techniques in altering children's behavior. Psychopharmacology, dynamic behavioral modification techniques, and intervention in individual, group, and family settings are being integrated in practice. Leading behavioral scientists suggest focusing on many facets--affect, sensation, imagery, cognition, and interpersonal relationships, as well as drugs and diet--in dealing with the problems that now overwhelm the schools (Morse, 1985, 162).

EMPOWERMENT OF TEACHERS

For any technique to be useful in classrooms or other settings, teachers must be empowered to learn, use what they learn, and create an environment and responses to children that are relevant and meaningful. For successful change to occur, a facilitator of change must find a sense of self-efficacy, believing in the possibilities that lie ahead enough to maintain motivation and investment in the change effort (Bandura, 1982).

"Teacher empowerment" has become a buzzword in education circles today, but much of the empowerment discussion proceeds along "one, very narrow axis: a continuum limited to strategies for redirecting the political and administrative traffic flow from 'top-down' to 'bottom up', with the clear implication that teachers are at the bottom and the avowed purpose is moving them closer to the top" (Greer, 1989, 294).

While power ladder issues cannot be ignored, the question of empowerment of teachers may really not be an up-and-down issue, but a lateral or "center out" one, with the concern being not the teacher's climb up or down the power ladder, "but teacher/child relationship as a kind of center of gravity, around which the resources and interactions of a healthy educational system revolve, like the planets around the sun. Thus, the closer to the child, the greater the field of force and the more power there is for rearranging the surrounding 'planets'--things like particular teachers, various specialists, principals, other administrators, and superintendents. [This way of looking at empowerment would help] peel off the layers of cliched rhetoric and restore to the discussion a relevancy that many teachers can understand, almost instinctively" (Greer, 1989, 295).

Real teacher empowerment begins in the trust between the teacher and the student. Trust is the foundation for effective instruction. The professional concerns educators share, the structure and quality of the learning environment, the training teachers must have to meet the needs of their students, and the administrative structure required to support everything else are secondary. "In a 'center out' model, the teacher is by definition a 'full partner' because it is the teacher's relationship with the child that comprises the core of the system, orders its elements, and holds them all together" (Greer, 1989, 297).

CONCLUSION

The public school is a critical life space. It reflects the continual interaction between inner and outer forces which comprises an individual's psychological world at any given moment (Apter, 1982, 49). It is a natural socializing influence as children interact with others over sustained periods of time. It can play a major role in preventing emotional problems and undesirable behavior.

Although abrasive influences prevail in many schools, these can be reduced. Attention can be paid to opportunities to teach social skills, to demonstrate the satisfactions of both work and play, and to present strong but benign authority relationships (Morse, 1971, 4). School personnel can support students' capacities to understand themselves in relation to place, time, peers, and adults. We can help children differentiate and distinguish themselves from one another in their growing individuality. We can contribute to an atmosphere of tolerance that reflects individual needs and is communicated through stable, uncamouflaged relationships and structured, predictable activities. Such an environment is nurturing for children and teachers alike.

Because the classroom is a place where school-age children spend much of their time, teachers are in a critical position to guide children in a healthier direction. If teachers are recognized as one of the closest and most pervasive influences in students' lives and then are empowered through recognition of the central nature of the teacher/student relationship, through administrative support to the teacher, and through professional development that includes immediate strategies for at-risk children and preventive stress management (Greer, 1989, 294), they can, indeed, make a difference. At the same time, they will experience fewer stresses themselves if they are given the support needed for them to continue to transcend both the day-to-day problems and the broad changes that are occurring in schools.

A diffuse atmosphere will exacerbate students' behavioral and psychological disturbances. Some children will come to schools troubled and will need special help in their day-to-day interactions. The role of the school is to create a climate that is supportive of the normal student, preventing future problems, as well as therapeutic to the disturbed youngster. The people serving in schools and how they interact with each other and with students determine a school's effectiveness (Skrtic, 1987, 18; Davis, 1989, 443).

It is not students and teachers who fail, but the "system" that has failed both (Davis, 1989, 444). Still, public school personnel must believe that things can be made better for these children and that effecting change is within their power. Teachers and other school personnel can create positive adjustment opportunities for children in schools. Milieu Therapy principles offer "climate control" for the life space of the classroom. The Life Space Interview offers a framework for how to interact with children beyond mere suggestions to accept the child, love the child, discipline the child, or other generalizations. These techniques, benevolent for the treatment and education of children, can aid children and teachers on their journey while blending with other useful techniques and theories.

Emphasis on the "whole child" through a family- and child-based philosophy should be fully integrated into approaches to education. Teams of professionals in education and other human service professions must design solutions that are comprehensive in scope, encourage greater cooperation and coordination among various service providers, and link the school, the home, and the community. Now is an appropriate time to renew therapeutic milieu practices and Life Space Interviewing techniques and use them more widely in public schools.

CHAPTER TWO

A HISTORICAL OVERVIEW OF MILIEU THERAPY

Manipulating the environment to foster and sustain adjustment for troubled people has a rich history. Facilities to treat or educate the so-called mentally ill have progressed beyond the primitive function of isolating their clients from the world around them. The historical roots for the gradual reinterpretation of what constitutes productive and humane treatment for patients shows, through a two hundred year history, the reconstruction of the milieu for salubrious effects on the patient.

MORAL TREATMENT APPROACH

The historical precedents for the idea of therapeutic milieu emerged at the end of the eighteenth century and during the nineteenth century as part of a cry for humane treatment for those adults and children incarcerated in asylums for the insane. Primary figures in this movement were Philippe Pinel in France, William Tuke in England, and Benjamin Rush in the United States. Influenced by the ideology of the Enlightenment, they believed that social or biological conditions caused mental illness. They rejected the previously accepted idea that emotional disturbance was God's will.

These pioneers, along with Dorothea Dix, Samuel Howe, Horace Mann, and others, advocated the position that humane treatment could have a positive impact on those with mental illness and also would benefit handicapped individuals such as those with mental retardation. They worked for improved environments for people who were seen as different--cleaner places to live, better diets, medication, reduction of brutality, and the use of kindness and consideration that fostered a family atmosphere. Thus, they laid out the philosophical tenets of moral treatment that would change the Western world's attitude toward emotional disturbance. The purpose of this approach was to establish order in the patients' lives through programs of daily care (Rhodes & Head, 1974; Reinert & Huang, 1987, 55-56).

Philippe Pinel (1745-1826), a physician and mathematician, was in charge of La Bicetre, a custodial institution for men located in Paris, in 1793 at the close of the French Revolution. La Bicetre was a notorious asylum where the insane were shackled to the walls of their cells, abused by the attendants, and given only a minimum amount of nourishment (Davidson & Neale, 1978; Fraser, 1974; McDowell, Adamson, & Wood, 1982). Believing that "the mentally ill were simply ordinary human beings who had been deprived of their reason by severe personal problems and that to treat them like animals was not only inhumane but also obstructive to recovery" (Calhoun, Acocella, & Goodstein, 1977, 18), Pinel unchained the patients, replaced the dungeons with sunny rooms, banned mistreatment by the attendants, provided a better diet, and opened the doors to allow the patients to walk about the hospital grounds. In place of primitive treatments, Pinel's approach involved not only talking with the patients and listening to their problems, but also reading and work therapy (Calhoun et al., 1977; Fraser, 1974; Apter & Conoley, 1984).

William Tuke (1732-1822) attempted similar reforms in England. Disturbed by the conditions in a British asylum that led to the untimely death of a fellow Quaker, Tuke persuaded others in the Quaker community that humane treatment in an open environment was needed to care for their mentally ill brethren. With their help, Tuke moved a group of mental patients to a country estate, the "York Retreat," in 1796. A quiet, supportive religious setting was provided, where the patients talked out their problems, prayed, worked, rested, and took long walks through the countryside (Calhoun et al., 1977; Cullinan, Epstein, & Lloyd, 1983).

Benjamin Rush (1745-1813) and others became concerned with the plight of the mentally ill in America. In 1796, a special wing opened at the Pennsylvania Hospital, where Dr. Rush was superintendent. Rush, insisting on more humane treatment for the patients, was most concerned that the hospital hire kinder and better quality staff (Calhoun et al., 1977; Davidson & Neale, 1978; Fraser, 1974; Apter & Conoley, 1984).

During the first half of the nineteenth century, when this philosophical orientation known as "moral treatment" prevailed, at least 70 percent of those hospitalized for a year or less in America and Europe improved or actually recovered (Calhoun et al., 1977, 15). As success was achieved with humane treatment throughout the civilized world, the insane came to be regarded as normal people who had lost their reason as a result of being exposed to severe psychological and social stresses, called the moral causes of insanity. Moral treatment was aimed at relieving patients by friendly association, discussion of difficulties, and the daily pursuit of purposeful activity, order and predictability in their lives (Knoblock, 1983, 120-121).

This mode of treatment was an early prototype of Milieu Therapy, in that the disturbed person's life was regimented through regular habits and work in the specially molded environment of the asylum (Fraser, 1974, 246). The effectiveness of moral therapy, coupled with changing attitudes toward the mentally ill, led to the establishment of private and state-supported institutions throughout the United States in the first half of the nineteenth century. Rural settings were preferred for their therapeutic value. Instead of being cared for in the home community, the mentally ill were taken to isolated locations, where they lived in large groups.

In the United States, this evolution of treatment was further altered by the growth of industrial cities populated by masses of immigrants. Many of the new immigrants, unable to adapt to the stresses of living in industrial cities, found themselves incarcerated in the state asylums. By 1850, the state mental hospitals had become facilities where relatively inexpensive care was provided for a patient population drawn primarily from the lower classes. Families with better economic resources preferred to send their relatives to private hospitals.

THE MEDICAL MODEL

The state mental hospitals grew in size and number, becoming overcrowded with patients who were poor, seriously disturbed, and chronically ill. The calm, tranquil atmosphere necessary to moral therapy was dispelled by overcrowding and the characteristics of the patients. The stigma of mental illness, treatment, and institutions began to grow.

These huge, isolated fortresses seemed to conceal some dark horror and the mentally disturbed were again seen as freakish, dangerous, and alien (Calhoun et al., 1977, 16). The personal touch prescribed by Pinel, Tuke, Rush, and others gave way to custodial care. The public again viewed emotional disturbance as a lifelong affliction, with those afflicted put away and forgotten.

Speculation about the cause of mental illness shifted from psychosocial to biological emphases. The problem was seen as in the person rather than in the environment or the person's interaction with the environment. People were now "sick." Those working with the mentally ill became more concerned with their physical well-being than with the environmental influences contributing to their condition.

By the latter part of the nineteenth century, moral therapy had been abandoned. The treatment orientation had shifted: creation of a therapeutic environment had been replaced by what has become known as the "medical model." The original intent of the therapeutic rural setting of these institutions was lost to the secondary isolation of the places, allowing the public to feel they were "doing something" while allowing them to deny their own fears and maintain their own beliefs concerning mental problems. The isolation of the public institutions was comforting, and the "out of sight, out of mind" attitude of the public took institutions and their treatment methods out of the public view (Newcomer, 1980, 318-319).

TREATMENT OF CHILDREN

In 1729, Ursuline nuns in New Orleans founded the first orphanage in the United States, beginning residential care for children in the United States (Lewis & Summerville, 1991, 895). Children with problems received much the same treatment as adults. Those with severe difficulties were incarcerated in the state institutions unless their families were wealthy enough to seek private care. Less troubled children were cared for in private homes in the community. If children were poor and causing havoc in the local community, they were likely to be placed in reform schools or other institutions caring for children that had developed along with mental hospitals.

The moral treatment movement had little influence on these institutions. Instead, the reform schools provided a harsh, primitive environment, where the emphasis was on discipline and adherence to strict routines. Conditions were often terrible, and children were abused or, at best, neglected (Wooden, 1976).

As the unique needs of children were slowly recognized, pediatrics, child psychiatry, and specialized treatment practices in residential settings gradually developed (Lewis & Summerville, 1991, 895). Though some institutions have now changed from medical models emphasizing custodial care and hospitalization to settings that use behavior modification, many still have not fulfilled the functions of nurturing, rehabilitation, and education for which they were created. Institutionalization, especially for children, has deleterious effects upon the patients' functional abilities as well as upon their emotional and psychological adjustment.

Smaller, more therapeutic community programs are preferable to institutions, providing better therapeutic, educational, cultural, and recreational opportunities. An innovation toward decentralizing institutions was the cottage plan, in which small groups of children lived in secure, homelike cottages on a campus in simulated family situations. Self-sufficient units were grouped into villages with schools for educational or vocational rehabilitation. Cottage personnel were trained to use behavior management techniques, and temporary stays replaced indefinite institutionalization. This type of environment reflected a therapeutic milieu (Abate & Curtis, 1975; Knoblock, 1983).

THERAPEUTIC APPROACHES TO CHILDREN

Nearly all the states enacted compulsory school attendance laws between 1852 and 1918. These laws eventually led to the idea that no children could be excluded from education, despite their problems or needs. Special classes were created, and orphanages, institutions for the retarded, homes for delinquents, and special schools of all types were established. Treatment for emotionally disturbed children did not develop until the late nineteenth century (Rhodes & Head, 1974; Reinert & Huang, 1987; Davis, Myers, & Sarbo, 1989, 55-56).

Slowly, the belief that the problems of emotionally disturbed children are inherent in the children themselves has given way to a consideration of their environment. In intervention strategies, accordingly, the total community is taken into account, for there is now a recognition that much human disturbance is related to community and environmental influences.

Other developments in the treatment of mental illness occurred elsewhere toward the turn of the century. In 1881, Sigmund Freud (1856-1939), a clinical neurologist, opened a practice in Vienna. During the first quarter of the twentieth century, Freud's theory of the psychosexual stages of development became widely known. Freud's psychodynamic theory had a major impact on the treatment of the mentally ill, becoming the foundation for one of the main schools of thought regarding the development of mental illness. Subsequently, the idea of using the environment as a primary therapeutic tool for helping troubled individuals revived and applications of this approach were made to emotionally disturbed children.

Psychoanalytic Approaches

"Psychoanalysis has made an impact on the philosophy of education in practice and in theory. The most radical and experimental schools of the century have been guided by psychoanalytic concepts, aiming in the main to provide an environment of freedom and honesty in which children may escape the psychic distortions that produce neuroses in adults" (McClellan, 1967, 246). Psychoanalytic approaches were developed for use with adults, but despite certain technical difficulties, Anna Freud, Selma Fraiberg, Melanie Klein, Susan Isaacs, and others were able to apply these principles to children and thus support the relationship between treatment and education. Analysts, parents, and teachers had many common goals, and each contributed to the same process. Several notable educational endeavors reflected these approaches. A few are discussed below.

Beacon Hill School: According to Lord Bertrand Russell (1872-1964), the school was an agency for the inculcation of intellectual and emotional freedom. Russell, who regarded the sexual and political enlightenment of children as the prime duty of education, believed that it was necessary to get outside the ordinary school system to engage in education. His Beacon Hill

School (c. 1927-1934), continued by Dora Russell until 1943, was one such effort. Although Russell accepted the basic premises of psychoanalysis, Beacon Hill was not a therapeutic center for disturbed children. Russell's school was a forerunner of special programs, but its purpose was to establish for children conditions of absolute intellectual honesty and the maximum possible degree of personal freedom so that the intrapersonal dynamic processes of development could occur with a minimum of crippling after effects (McClellan, 1967, 243).

Summerhill: Although A.S. Neill (1883-1973) was influenced by the psychoanalytic school, he rejected its clinical and analytical techniques. Instead, freedom as a normal condition of life was the basis for the central teaching procedure at his school. Neill's unique contribution during his Summerhill, 1921 program was proving it possible for normal and seriously disturbed children to live in freedom, especially in matters of psychosexual development. Neill was influenced immensely by Homer Lane's extraordinary genius in teaching intractable children and reeducating disturbed adults (McClellan, 1967, 243-244).

The Children's School: Now the Walden School, the Children's School was established in 1915 by Margaret Maumberg (1890-1983) in New York. A notable early center for psychoanalytically based educational procedures, it provided an environment of honesty and freedom. In Europe, schools such as the Malting House School in England and the Kinderheim Baumgarten in Berlin were also devoted to psychoanalytic principles. In these schools there was a deliberate attempt to disseminate the effects of psychoanalytic pedagogy. Therapeutically oriented, these schools had a benign, permissive milieu. Some took the position that self-regulated children could and would learn academically when and as they needed to learn. Susan Isaacs (1885-1948) made careful observations of the intellectual processes in children's learning but never tied together her study of sociosexual development and her study of intellectual growth.

August Aichhorn (1878-1949): A notable application of psychoanalytic theory in the treatment of children was developed by August Aichhorn, an educator who, following World War I, became the director of an institution in Austria for delinquent children aged fourteen to eighteen. Aichhorn believed that the deviant behavior of troubled children was rooted in either overindulgent love or lack of love from their parents. He asserted that reeducation was not possible until the youths developed a strong positive feeling for the people in their environment (Aichhorn, 1935, 149).

To meet the needs of these dissocial youths, Aichhorn created an environment that was enjoyable to live in, consisting of reliable friendliness and kindness. Demands for achievement were not made until the youngsters had formed a strong positive emotional relationship with a friendly adult with whom there was no past or strong cathexis. Once this identification had been achieved, it was then used to help the youths attain greater integration within their personality, more self-control over impulsive behavior, and more maturity (Alt, 1960, 45).

Aichhorn gradually directed the youths' energies into socially acceptable channels. One of his methods was to assign work tasks that provided the opportunity for investing energy in useful behavior. Aichhorn used daily routines and conflicts to achieve therapeutic and educational purposes. Assuring the youths of his interest and affection and creating an environment calculated to please them, he made use of the relationship to help them retrieve a neglected part of their development and make the transition from their earlier unreal world of self-indulgence to one of reality. Aichhorn was "painstaking in his avoidance of brutal severity. Punishment was meted out only on the basis of an accurate evaluation of the psychological constellation [of the individual] and after detailed explanation of the punishment's reason and purpose" (Pfister, 1949, 36).

Bruno Bettelheim (1903-1990): During the 1930's, Anna Freud arranged for an American child suffering from infantile autism to live with a couple in Vienna while a colleague treated the child. The foster parents, the Bettelheims, restructured their home life around psychoanalytic insights to meet the little girl's physical and psychological needs. They worked with her for over seven years, until Hitler invaded Austria. This experience was the beginning of Bruno Bettelheim's involvement with total treatment milieu (Bettelheim & Sanders, 1979).

In 1944, following his release from a Nazi concentration camp in Europe, Bettelheim emigrated to the United States and became director of the Sonia Shankman Orthogenic School of the University of Chicago, where he had the opportunity to restructure this residential program. His work was among the first projects designed to set up and study a treatment and school program for autistic children. Acknowledging August Aichhorn's earlier efforts, he attempted to sensitize the child to interpersonal relationships. Bettelheim and a colleague, Emmy Sylvester, named their technique "Milieu Therapy."

Bettelheim and Sylvester (1948) identified children for whom Milieu Therapy was indicated as children whose ability to maintain contact with parent figures had been catastrophically destroyed or those who lacked the tools for establishing contact because they had never experienced personal gratification in any interpersonal relationship. According to Bettelheim, the cause of children's problems was in the family relationship; treatment should therefore include removal from the family and the severing of family contacts for a total restructuring of the children's environment. Bettelheim viewed such placement as long-term, meaning at least several years.

Bettelheim followed orthodox psychoanalytical procedures in the treatment of these children. His approach centered around encouraging free expressions of emotions, with an attempt to interpret the meaning of the avenues of release and thus gain a better understanding of the children's disturbance (Haring & Phillips, 1962; Morse, 1985).

Bettelheim's original concept of Milieu Therapy was to expose a child to total environmental design for treatment. The very attempt to treat children in and through environmental settings opened a wide avenue of therapeutic enrichment while requiring knowledge of ego control mechanisms, their areas of disturbance, and techniques of supporting and repairing them. Children in this environment were required to face the realistic consequences of their acting out and were protected from their own potentially self-destructive behavior. Bettelheim believed that all children with major emotional illnesses suffered from severe ego disturbances and that helping them master life experiences that would lead to ego growth would alleviate the problem. Bettelheim thus set out to develop a milieu that would adjust completely to the children's existence (Bettelheim & Sanders, 1979).

Bettelheim felt that absence of interpersonal relationships was the cause of these serious deviations in the children's personality development. He noted that personality disturbances are observed in children who are without meaningful interpersonal relationships--for instance, children who have long lived in institutions or those who are exposed to noxious foster home or family settings (Bettelheim & Sylvester, 1948, 192). He believed that, before children would be able to establish any true interpersonal relationships, unconditional gratification of their needs and wants would have to be provided by others. Also, the children would have to grow to trust their ability to master their impulses.

Bettelheim reported that 85 percent of the children who remained in the Orthogenic School over a prolonged period recovered sufficiently to live independently. Most were able to graduate from college and hold responsible positions in society (Bettelheim & Sanders, 1979, 216).

While we can learn much from Bettelheim's model, and his clarity in describing Milieu Therapy, his theories and approaches have some drawbacks. Usually, it is not possible to provide the highly intensive and controlled approach which Bettelheim achieved. One of the major bases for his theories was that the patient must be separated from family and community, so that the environment could be controlled to the extent that he required. Even if this isolation is feasible, it is not, in most instances, desirable. Certainly, in the public schools, isolation in such a controlled environment is not possible.

Fritz Redl and David Wineman: In the early 1940s, Fritz Redl at Wayne State University in Detroit became interested in setting up a treatment milieu to help "children who hate." In 1942, Redl and his associate, David Wineman, founded the Detroit Group Project, a residential treatment program providing group therapy to aggressive children referred by other agencies. This service was later extended to offer 6-8-week coed camp experiences for children 7 to 15 years of age during the summers of 1944 through 1947. The clinical insights gained from these experiences led to the opening of Pioneer House under the financial sponsorship of the Junior League of Detroit, Inc., in September of 1946 (Redl & Wineman, 1957, 34).

Pioneer House was a small home located in a private neighborhood near Wayne State University. Ten boys between the ages of 8 and 10 were admitted to Pioneer House and five remained for 15 to 18 months. The shortest length of stay of any boy was 1 1/2 months. These boys were carefully selected on the basis of their intelligence, health, socioeconomic background, and degree of disturbance. Only those who could live in an open environment--one where there was contact with the community-at-large, interaction with the neighbors, attendance at public school, and outings--were served (Redl & Wineman, 1957, 48-49).

Criteria for selection were delinquent or predelinquent behavior patterns. The children were characterized by "severely crippled ego-functioning with an amazingly effective set of defenses against any adult attempts to help them" (French, 1952, 53). They were highly impulsive, destructive, aggressive, and often uncontrollable--truly "children who hate" (Redl & Wineman, 1957).

The treatment program offered at Pioneer House was structured to provide a psychologically sound milieu much like that described by Bettelheim. A protective climate was created to afford unconditional gratification and tolerance of symptomatic and regressive behavior, with attention to avoiding any sharp clashes with the socioeconomic life-styles of the residents. Programming for ego support and the clinical exploitation of life events were mainstays of the program.

Redl and Wineman defined 22 specific functions of the ego and the defensive techniques a disturbed ego will employ against the changes the clinician or educator is trying to bring about. They believed that children who hate suffer from specific disturbances of their control systems--that is, their egos and superegos. To help them, it was necessary to have a precise picture of just what ego disturbances and superego misdevelopments existed, which ego functions were still intact and which were disturbed, and which defenses the children had developed to ward off the impact of the world around them. Then the task became one of providing a supportive design to strengthen deficient ego functions and a counterdelusional design to dissolve their defenses (Redl & Wineman, 1957, 74; Morse, 1985, 12-16; Rosenberg, Wilson, Maheady, & Sindelor, 1992, 234-235).

Pioneer House was set up to provide a warm, inviting physical and psychological atmosphere, but also an environment not so different from the residents' previous life-styles as to feel alien or frightening. Furniture, toys, and other objects were selected that conveyed the message "use me." Space was made available for boisterous play as well as quiet activity. Flexible routines were established to provide clear expectations yet allow the children ample time to follow them. To convey the message that the adults wanted the children to have fun, the program of activities consisted of those the children enjoyed. The role for the adult was that of "protector"--to protect each child from fear of the other children, from fear of losing control, from fear of interference by parents or others outside the treatment environment, and from the fear of the whole group getting out of control. The adults intervened when needed but in a way that let the children know it was their behavior that was unacceptable and not them as persons. Love, affection, and happy, rewarding program experiences were provided at all times without conditions. The child was allowed to escape any group activity that became too threatening. No form of physical punishment was permitted. Care was taken to avoid any experience the child would find traumatic. Group size was kept small, with regrouping possible at any time. Enough staff members were always on hand to carry out program activities as planned or to change them immediately, depending on the needs of the children at any given moment. An ample supply of materials and props was always available. Finally, the development of group-emotional ties was encouraged (Redl & Wineman, 1957, 281-316).

These pioneers prescribed specific ways to assure planned activities that were supportive, evaluating activities according to whether they achieved their goal without doing damage to the individual or the group. They recommended techniques for the management of surface behaviors and for therapeutic exploration of life events, further defining therapeutic milieu and developing the techniques of the Life Space Interview.

CONCLUSION

The pioneers discussed above have shown that benign environments can help children. More recently, Carl Fenichel at the League School in New York City; Fritz Redl, David Wineman, and Nick Long at the National Institutute of Mental Health; and Nick Long, assisted by Jim and Pat Tompkins and others at Hillcrest Children's Center in Washington, D. C., are among those have practiced and further defined therapeutic milieu concepts. They and others cited throughout this book have shared a host of techniques that can be applied in a variety of settings, including the classroom, to help children on their way to enhanced growth, development and learning.

CHAPTER THREE

COMPARISONS OF MILIEU THERAPY PRINCIPLES WITH OTHER THEORETICAL APPROACHES

Many approaches are used in public schools to socialize and change children's unacceptable behaviors. Program and treatment designs range from permissive or therapeutic approaches to more traditional, structured, educational programs. Approaches in remedial education have sprung from several theoretical orientations, of which the dominant ones are psychodynamic, behavioral, or ecological. These approaches can be differentiated through statements about the cause of disturbance.

Advocates of the psychodynamic approach see the disturbance as in the child and, in search of causes of the disturbance, have historically implicated parents and their child-rearing practices. In this approach, (Cullinan, Epstein, & Lloyd, 1991, 148-149), the growing child's development is seen as racked with unresolved conflict and anxiety. The treatment approach, accordingly, is aimed at resolving these internal problems.

Proponents of the behavioral approach view emotional and behavioral disturbances as learned maladaptive behaviors. Because behaviorists do not see early life experiences as relevant to behavior, the focus in treatment is the child's current observable behavior rather than some inferred internal disturbance. Behaviorists recommend an approach that increases the probability that adaptive behavior will develop while decreasing the probability that maladaptive behaviors will occur (Morse & Smith, 1983, 15; Cullinan et al., 1991, 149).

Educational ecologists see emotional disturbance as a phenomenon created by an interaction between the child and the environment. Discrete sociocultural forces strongly influence the child and his or her behavior. Disturbance is a result of a mismatch between children and the social context in which they exist. Thus, the proposed strategy for change is to approach the child as well as the environment (Morse & Smith, 1983, 56-57; Cullinan et al., 1991, 149).

Several educational interventions have emerged from these theoretical positions and will be discussed in this chapter. Comparisons of the various approaches will be made, showing that Milieu Therapy and Life Space Interviewing, coupled with other approaches, sustains a creative blend of techniques, producing an alloy of programmatic practices.

THE PSYCHODYNAMIC MODEL

The psychodynamic approach provided the initial framework in the 1950s in programming for children with severe emotional difficulties. Psychodynamicists, who emphasize the importance of ego functions, see early experiences with a pathological environment as causing unconscious internal conflicts in the child, which, if unresolved, might lead to extreme aggression or withdrawal as a means of dealing with anxiety. They see disturbed behavior as the product of conflicts between the impulse system (or id) and the control system (or superego) that the mediating ego cannot integrate and handle. If impulses overcome controls, the child's behavior may become aggressive and unpredictable. If the control system is too demanding and impulses are constantly quashed, the child may become inhibited and withdrawn (Reinert, 1980, 39-42).

Some theorists take a view that removes the onus from families, acknowledging an interaction of individual and event in etiology of disturbance. Inherent predisposition of the individual, the severity of the "stressor" (Selye, 1974, 24) or trigger event(s), and the age at which continual stresses are experienced are all seen as factors in whether and to what degree disturbances may manifest themselves. Stressors contributing to problems in children may include rejection, hostile criticism, frustration of basic needs, humiliation, neglect, aggression, battering, or abandonment. Thus, emotional distress may be tied to early family relationships or to other life circumstances (Fishman, 1991, 55-56).

Psychodynamists believe that school problems are simply repeated manifestations of these early disturbances. Troubled children are frequently not conscious of the motivation for their inappropriate behavior, nor can they consciously control the behavior that these circumstances have produced (Apter & Conoley, 1984, 193). Interventions attempt to help the child develop more effective controls or learn to express some impulses appropriately.

The Psychoeducational Approach

In the psychoeducational approach to intervention, the psychiatric and educational emphases are balanced, interwoven, and equal. Educational decisions, made with consideration of underlying motivation, emphasize creative projects, individual differences, and a benign but not permissive atmosphere (Morse, Cutler, & Fink, 1964, 28).

Influenced by the psychodynamic model, psychoeducationalists see all behavior as meaningful and motivated, reflecting conscious and unconscious factors indicative of past experiences and early environmental influences that persist into the present (McDowell et al., 1982, 45). A dynamic relationship between drives (impulses) and resistance to them is drawn.

This model fuses education with therapeutic support as children learn to understand and cope with their feelings. The term *therapeutic*, used by the psychoeducator, refers to the process of helping disturbed children develop self-understanding and self-directed behavior from both an educational and treatment perspective (McDowell et al., 1982, 240). Because underlying causes of behavior are considered more important than the behavioral symptoms, treating and changing behavior without first investigating the underlying causes is inappropriate. Central to the model is the assumption that the same behaviors can have many causes, while the same cause can be expressed through many behaviors.

Cheney and Morse (1974, 307) described the psychoeducational approach as a "restorative curriculum that capitalizes on the latent self-corrective capacities of the disturbed child to enhance emotional growth and mental health." Because there is a need for a highly organized program of education and training that can bring order, stability, and direction to minds that are disorganized, unstable, and unpredictable (Fenichel, 1966, 9), the environment is structured to meet the needs of children at their level.

In the psychoeducational approach, the individuality of the child is emphasized. The development of an educational plan is based on the psychological makeup of the troubled child. Conflict, implicit in all behavior, can be used to learn new means of dealing with stress (Fagen, 1981, 9-10; Fagen, Long, & Stevens, 1975, 331). Some major principles underlie this approach:

1. The teacher's goal should be to establish a positive relationship based on empathy, understanding, and genuine caring (Rich, 1978, 5).

2. There must be sensitivity to the student's interaction with the teacher, other school staff, peers, the curriculum, and other aspects of the school's climate in order to develop a supportive educational milieu.

3. Each member of a group contributes to group behavior.

4. Learning is invested with feelings; learning style is individual to each student.

5. The student's current level of functioning directs teacher effort (Long, Morse, & Newman, 1980, 447).

Some other observations about the psychoeducational model are important for the teacher. Children should not be punished when they misbehave, since they cannot always control their behaviors. Teachers should be taught not to personalize hostility directed at them, because it likely has little to do with the child's actual feelings for the teacher. And teachers should expect to see inconsistencies in children's external behaviors (Newcomer, 1980).

The psychoeducational model considers basic needs as motivators in personality development. These include the need for a well developed, positive self-image, the need to feel loved and to feel that one belongs, physiological needs, safety needs, and the need for self-fulfillment (Zabel, 1991, 11-14).

While the psychoeducator uses the tools of education and remediation and works in a school setting, the teacher in this model does not focus exclusively on increasing cognitive ability and academic skills. An equal emphasis is on affective development and on learning to understand, cope with, and "control" one's feelings. The teacher uses the everyday events in the child's life in the educational setting to promote appropriate expressions of feelings and personality development. Interpersonal and physical/educational environments are manipulated to sustain maximum emotional support for the child.

In summary, the psychoeducational approach considers both intrapsychic and educational matters in making educational decisions. Awareness of unconscious motives and underlying conflicts is maintained. School experiences are pleasant and meaningful for the student. Group processes and crisis situations should be used to develop insight. Thus, the teacher should establish an empathetic relationship with the student, and, although the teacher must enforce limits, flexibility is important (Brown, 1981, 10; Cullinan et al., 1991, 151).

BEHAVIORAL MODELS

Behavioral approaches have emerged in recent years as the treatment of choice in many settings for severely disturbed youngsters. The basic tenet of the behavioral theories is that behavior is learned through reinforcement and can be shaped and changed through similar means. Behaviors associated with pleasant activities or consequences are most likely to be repeated and sustained. A behavior that is followed by a desirable consequence (positive reinforcement) or by the removal of an undesired consequence or unpleasant stimulus (negative reinforcement) will increase or become more likely to occur. Conversely, behaviors are less likely to recur when followed by an undesirable or unpleasant consequence, the withholding or removal of a desired consequence, or better yet, ignored (no reinforcement) (Zabel, 1991, 14).

The initial task of the behaviorist involves assessing the particular behavioral needs of the child. Baseline data must be collected to determine the frequency of those behaviors one wishes to change (targeted behaviors), as well as the context in which those behaviors occur. While standardized assessment instruments can provide information regarding the particular skills that a child has and a comparison to those of other children, baseline data provides information, collected when the program begins, upon which intervention strategies are based. These data also provide a basis from which to measure the effectiveness of intervention strategies. Frequency of the occurrence of the target behavior can be measured and compared to baseline data as the intervention program proceeds.

Once baseline has been established, it is necessary to analyze the undesirable behaviors and those desirable alternative behaviors that one wishes to foster. The effects of various factors in the environment on the child's behavior must be determined. What immediately precedes the target behavior? What happens just after the behavior occurs? One must also determine what each child perceives as desirable or undesirable consequences. What may be rewarding to one child may be a neutral or even negative experience for another.

The behavioral approach requires a highly structured program to which the child is expected to attend, comply, and respond. One very important element of this approach is instructional control (i.e., compliance and attention). Instructions must be clear, consistent, and brief, and the environment must be free from extraneous stimuli (see, for instance, Hewett, 1968, 51-58). Training sessions are short at first but gradually extended.

When a new skill is taught, immediate reinforcement of each desired behavior occurs. Later in the teaching process, the reinforcement can gradually be delayed and become less consistent. If attention is reinforcing some maladaptive behavior, systematically withholding attention (planned ignoring) at each occurrence of the behavior becomes the treatment of choice. The behaviorist makes an effort to pay attention to the child when the undesirable behavior is not occurring. The child often actively resists this process, and one sees a definite, but temporary, increase in the targeted behavior or the intensity of the behavior in the initial stages of implementing such a plan. Barring unacceptable levels of self-injurious behavior, aggression, or destruction of property, it is best to continue the ignoring program, even in the face of this increased negative behavior. An abandonment of the procedure would be seen as desirable by the child, and the undesirable behaviors would be reinforced.

Social reinforcers such as affection, praise, and attention can be powerful reinforcers for appropriate behaviors. Used in tandem with another reinforcer, they can increase its effectiveness. When concrete reinforcers such as food or tokens are used, they should gradually be replaced by social reinforcers so that ordinary social interactions and reactions will eventually be the cues to which the child is responsive.

Shaping is an important technique that springs from behavioral theory. Starting with a response already existing in the child's repertoire, the teacher identifies some behavioral steps toward a desired skill. Only after the child acquires stable performance at each step is another introduced. Failing to master any step along the way, the child must return to the preceding step to regain stable performance before advancing toward the goal. This technique also is called "errorless learning." It gives the learner reinforcement through continued success. When stable performance occurs on the target skill, the shaping procedure is complete.

Shaping can be useful in teaching many skills including language, self-help, motor, academic, pre-academic, and prevocational skills. When a particular behavior has been learned through shaping procedures, it can be linked with other behaviors to form a behavior chain under the control of a single instruction. A prompt can be used to guide the child toward the desired response to a directive, thus maximizing the child's opportunities for reinforcement. Prompts may consist of giving the child the correct response, physically assisting (i.e., placing the child's body, hand, mouth, etc., in the correct position to do the activity), modeling the desired response (i.e., instructor performing the expected task), or giving cues that suggest the desired behavior. When prompts are no longer needed, they are "faded" (i.e., become less obvious and intrusive until they are no longer used). Then, only the training directive remains.

Through a combination of shaping, prompting, and chaining procedures, an effective training program can be developed that is consistent across the various environments a child encounters. Consistency is essential for target behaviors, goals, and procedures to be carried out. A team approach, with communication and continued training opportunities among people in all aspects of the child's environment, is vital. While negative reinforcement may sometimes be used, ethical behaviorists do not advocate the use of punishment.

ECOLOGICAL MODELS

The proponents of the ecological approach see children's problems as products of all the forces or influences, supportive or restrictive, existing in the environment. Educational ecologists abhor the labeling of deviant children. Looking at discrete sociocultural forces outside the child and the interactions between the child and the environment, they define emotional disturbance within the ecosystem as results of mismatches, or lacks of "goodness of fit" (Fagen & Long, 1979, 68-69) between children and the social contexts in which they operate (Morse & Smith, 1983, 57-58). Such environmental variables as school size, the schedule of a school day, or the arrangement of equipment or materials may have powerful effects on behavior (Fagen & Long, 1979, 68-69). Thus, emotional disturbance must be reconceptualized in terms of the environment and the social context in which it occurs if the greatest potential for interventions is to be maximized. Behaviors must be viewed in terms of the environments in which they occur, and programs should move from the focus on disordered behavior and instead attend to the disordered ecosystem in which the child must function. Intervention cannot occur in isolation from the total environment, and programs cannot continue to focus solely on the child and his or her specific behavioral deficits (Noel, 1982, 23-24).

Hewett (1985) indicated that stress, caused by poor person-environment fit, is essentially the cause of deviant behavior. This idea is a unifying one, particularly for those convinced that the time has come to adopt a systems, ecological, or milieu perspective.

> Persons fit their environments when their characteristics (e.g., attractiveness, behavior, abilities, needs) match up reasonably well with environmental expectations; and environments fit persons when the rewards or motivators available for meeting these expectations are in line with the person's needs and interests. Stress occurs when persons are in environments where there is a mismatch between expectations and personal characteristics. There is also stress when the reinforcers available do not match up with the personal needs or when punishment is experienced because of failure to meet environmental expectations. Such stress may be tolerated for long periods of time, modified by changes in the person-environment relationship, or eventually lead to physical illness or emotional disturbance. (Hewett, 1985, 2)

Much of human disturbance is relative to the community and the culture. Ecological psychologists suggest that the behavior of children can be predicted more accurately from knowing the situation children are in than from knowing the individual characteristics of the children. They stress that interventions designed to eliminate disturbance must focus on altering the system in which disturbing behavior occurs (Hobbs, 1975, 339).

Ecological interventions have in common the goal of adapting the fit between the setting and the person to establish harmony and balance between the child and the surrounding subsystems of the environment. Such interventions operate on the belief that taking the child out of the environment makes it impossible to face or deal with the problem because the problem exists within the environment of which the child is an integral part.

In this approach, there are no "bad kids" and no behaviors that are essentially disturbed. "Badness" is relative to the goodness or badness of an environment for a particular child, or the goodness or badness of the child for a particular environment. Interventions do not focus on one set of variables to the exclusion of others; rather, problem behavior is viewed as a global interaction between the individual and his or her environment. Ideal intervention measures are those that enter the actively disturbed situation, identify the point of convulsive encounter between the child and the surrounding human community, then trace the problem to its cultural source in the surrounding context both in terms of people and the cultural practices and influences of the microcommunity or ecological unit (Rhodes, 1970, 309-314; Epanchin & Paul, 1987, 24).

An ecological analysis undertaken in the natural environment may suggest that to change the crucial interactive relationship, changes need to be made in the child, in the environment, or in both. Having arrived at a diagnosis by collecting information about which niches in the child's environment are positive and which are negative and on the antecedents and consequences of the problem behavior, one can plan and implement interventions. These may take the form of alterations in the classroom structure, counseling for the parents, therapy for the child, or other modifications in the school or service network (Swap, Prieto, & Harth, 1982, 70-98). Actual procedures vary depending on the target of the intervention (child/setting) and on the theoretical perspective of the intervenor.

"Much of developmental psychology, as it now exists, is the science of the strange behavior of children in strange situations with strange adults for the briefest possible periods of time" (Bronfenbrenner, 1979, 19), but ecological psychologists have typically avoided the use of experimental methods involving controlled manipulation of isolated variables. They stress careful description of the environment and naturalistic methods of studying behavior in its situational context.

Because the ecological perspective encourages the development of interventions that reduce interactive disharmony by focusing on the child and the environment simultaneously, it allows integration of practices from diverse theories: sociological, behavioral, organic, and psychodynamic. This orientation asks a wide range of questions about a particular behavior, thus providing a more flexible view of disturbance and encouraging broader approaches to intervention.

Rhodes (1967, 449-455) summarized the goals and impact of the ecological perspective by saying that the emotionally disturbed child affects and is affected by his or her community and that this reciprocal relationship should be taken into consideration in any attempt to describe or treat the disturbance. Changes in environmental components such as physical objects, people, events, or locations may change the child's relationship to the environment, producing either positive or negative changes in behavior. Therefore, focusing attention on the child to the exclusion of family, school, and community can make identification and remediation of difficulties almost impossible.

Apter and Conoley (1984, 190-191) put forth several arguments for adopting an ecological basis for programs:

1. Traditional children's mental health programs have been unsuccessful in reducing the numbers or the severity of emotional disturbance in children.

2. The child is seldom, if ever, the whole problem.

3. Assessment, planning, and follow-through need to be much more functional and comprehensive.

4. Because the ecological orientation stresses the importance of looking at the entire system surrounding the child, it is important to respond to the needs and concerns of significant others in the child's environment

5. Coordination of efforts between professionals should be emphasized and linkages between the various aspects of each child's world (parents, siblings, neighborhood peer groups, church and school) should be seen as critical elements in the development of successful programs.

6. Ecological intervention also may have positive impact on others, thereby contributing to prevention efforts.

Ecological theory has been criticized for advocating too broad a base for intervention. Services may not be available in all the areas deemed significant, and schools may find it difficult to include all the elements of an ecosystem considered critical. Moreover, ecological theory has not answered enough questions about how conditions in school environments may contribute to deviance by inappropriate demands on an individual child's abilities and tolerances.

Still, educators can assume the role of ecological intervenors, not only in the classroom but in other parts of the child's ecosystem as well. Thus teachers, administrators, guidance counselors, school psychologists, social workers, other service providers, and families can collaborate to become more responsive to the needs of the child.

THERAPEUTIC MILIEU CONCEPTS

To teach children to live successfully, there must be a focus not only on what society expects of them but also on what they enjoy and what will one day make life meaningful and help them be at peace with themselves and with one another. Bettelheim (1950, 35, 41) believed that the aim of any psychotherapeutic procedure was to help disturbed children strengthen their egos and acquire adequate mastery over the inner and outer forces in their world. Milieu Therapy also acknowledges that the environment plays a major role in children's development and thus gives attention to the total milieu and to the child's interaction with it.

The goals of the therapeutic milieu are directly tied into positively altering the inter- and extra-personal deficiencies that children exhibit. A major purpose of the milieu is to provide the child with new and more adequate possibilities of personal relations that will help the reconstruction of the child's inner world. One must consider how the child perceives surroundings as well as how the surroundings and individuals in it perceive the child (Bettelheim & Sylvester, 1948, 191-206). Personal security, adequate instinctual gratification, and group support all sensitize the child to interpersonal relations (Redl & Wineman, 1957, 296-297.) In a total treatment design, every phase must be not only supportive of the basic treatment, but must become an integral part of it (Redl & Wineman, 1957, 283-284).

Information concerning a child's home life and relationships with parents and siblings are weighted factors in understanding the child. How the child is perceived in the home, any healthy or unhealthy relationships with family members, and how behaviors are handled in the home environment are of great importance. This information, which can be useful in developing a therapeutic milieu for the child, also can be helpful in efforts to impact or restructure the home environment. Thus, an important aspect of therapeutic intervention is to be able to view the child as a person with specific environmental factors acting upon him or her.

In the therapeutic milieu, children may gain insights into their behavior and more realistic understandings of their environment. A child entering a therapeutic milieu can be viewed as a child changing from an environment that was rough and stressful into a situation that is smooth and easy, representing the combined effects of internal and external factors acting upon the child. These factors, when supportive of a child's development, create a level of life stress with which the child copes successfully (Cheney & Morse, 1974, 295). With new tools of understanding and insight, children can continue in or return to home situations with skills that are appropriate both to them and to those around them.

COMPARISONS

The ecological approach alerts the educator to the possibility that there may be environmental influences on a vulnerable child that sustain the child's unacceptable behavior. Ecosystems such as the classroom, total school milieu, neighborhood, community, or family may have supportive or deleterious effects on the child. Special educational and socialization procedures for the child may improve systemic disharmony or interactive mismatches.

Psychodynamic and behavioral approaches are often considered to be of opposing philosophies. The nature, timing, and goals of the two seem to be at odds. The behaviorist perspective is realistic, objective, and external. The analytic view is idealistic, with the perspective and cognitive abilities and views of the perceiver forming the basis for the existence of the external world; subjective, with experience seen as unique, private, and unable to be generalized beyond the individual; and introspective, with constructs formed by taking the subject's point of view into account (Messer & Winoker, 1980, 818-827).

These views result in differing emphases on tasks and the assessment of outcomes. Differences are also apparent in the view of human reality and possibility for change. The view of the psychodynamic model embraces an attitude of curiosity, adventure, and openness to new developments, for it views life as essentially lonely, conflict-ridden, and difficult.

The behaviorists take a more pragmatic stance through strict adherence to the scientific method, with emphasis on specific, measurable, realistic goals determined at the outset of therapy. Behaviorism also contrasts with psychodynamic intervention in its emphasis on brevity and economy of intervention. Analytic therapists seek out ambiguities and paradoxes, while behaviorists focus on specific, somewhat discrete problems, strategies, and outcome criteria. In the analyst's perspective, conflict is inescapable. It is inherent in human existence and can only be partially mastered. The behaviorist views conflict as centered in situations and believes that it can be eliminated by effective manipulation of those situations leading to solutions free from guilt and anxiety. The psychodynamic approach leads to introspective reflection and inquiry, sometimes painful, whereas the behavioral approach leads to somewhat painless action to alleviate human suffering.

Both learning and psychoanalytic theories reflect deterministic views of behavior dealing with goals, plans, and purposes as products of the experiential histories of individuals. But psychoanalytic theory, developed within a clinical context with emphasis on the explanation of deviant behavior, frequently does not make the clear-cut distinction made by learning theorists between maturation and socialization in learning (Tompkins, 1980, 26).

A synthesis between psychodynamic and behavioral practices has been sought. Attempts to integrate the two approaches range from application of behavioral language to psychoanalytic theories, to designating techniques for particular pathological syndromes, to weaving principles of both approaches into the fabric of the same treatment (Messer & Winoker, 1980, 818-827). Many of these attempts have been met with indifference or confusion. Purists from all schools of thought have remained rigid in their beliefs about the causes of problems and subsequent treatment approaches. The old "nature v.s. nurture" controversy rages. Is the problem in the individual or in the environment or, as is now generally agreed, a product of the interaction between the individual and the environment? Nevertheless, modifications being made in both schools of thought suggest a closer alliance and the use of more eclectic intervention techniques.

Both Freud (psychoanalytic) and Pavlov (behavioral) discussed reactions to traumas or danger signals that could become chronic and undifferentiated from the original experience, but Pavlov saw the danger signal (or conditioned stimulus) eliciting, by a process of simple substitution, reactions that were previously produced by actual trauma. Freud, on the other hand, saw a danger signal producing any of an infinite variety of reactions, wholly unlike the reaction to actual trauma, with the first response not completely overt, but rather an implicit state of tension that he called anxiety. Seeing much in common between these views, Mowrer (1939) recast Freud's views on anxiety into stimulus-response terminology.

The psychology of learning was developed in the tradition of psychological experimentation emphasizing carefully controlled laboratory methods. Miller and Dollard (1941) subsequently developed a social learning theory based on the work of Clark L. Hull, whose own work was probably inspired by Pavlov who, with Skinner, was a well-known pioneer in behavioral theory (Tompkins, 1980, 27-28). Later, learning psychologists and psychoanalysts emphasizing the role of unconscious processes in the personality began to borrow ideas from one another (Sarason, 1966).

Milieu Therapy tends toward the eclectic, taking useful practices for intervention from various approaches. The structure and consistency called for by behaviorists is certainly useful in Milieu Therapy. Therapeutic techniques such as "planned ignoring" are consistent with behavioral theory, and the behavior of the child rather than the cause of the behavior is one central concern. Ego psychology and psychodynamic approaches have also played a large role in the concepts upon which Milieu Therapy is based, with the role of the unconscious recognized and theories of ego development and ego strength central to Milieu Therapy techniques.

Consider the following statement by a teacher who was beginning her first experience using therapeutic milieu techniques.

> I went into my student teaching and my first classroom ingrained with behavioral modification theories. My employment of a behavioral program during student teaching was accepted slowly but successfully. When I accepted my first paying job as a teacher in a self-contained classroom for emotionally disturbed children and the principal said the kids needed structure, I naturally pulled out my "bag of behavioral modification techniques." When my kids arrived so did my token programs. The contingencies and rules were defined and the race was on. Behaviors increased, but I'd been taught to expect

that. Persistency and consistency were the by-words, my professors had said. I persisted and was determined to be consistent. The kids continued to laugh and say, "Oh, poor teacher--only damn teacher dumb enough to use a token. Hey, teach, what's a token?" I plugged on and they laughed but something very strange took place. Behaviors improved as did work output. The kids still laughed, though. They worked hard to get their tokens but never accepted the rewards I offered. Should I have known better than to put such "strange gratifications" and very unusual programs into my "therapeutic milieu" public school classroom? Yet, I can't help but feel that the strangeness of the program in addition to their embarrassment for me was the very thing that made the program work. And I realized that a relationship in a therapeutic milieu had been created.

Milieu therapy speaks of long-range therapeutic aims in mind with every plan for and technique used with a child. The educator who must deal with a child and his or her behavior daily often traditionally approaches a child's behavior from the standpoint of more immediate results. One student teacher who struggled with this apparent contradiction realized that Milieu Therapy offers support for immediate intervention techniques based on long-term therapeutic goals: she did not have to wait until ego problems were resolved to gain some relief from children's negative behaviors.

Both Milieu Therapy and ecological theory heavily emphasize the interaction of the child and the environment. Both see the milieu as all of that which is outside the individual. Both include other people as critical milieu ingredients and see group efforts, including peers, parents, and professionals, at the very foundation of effective programs.

Thus, individual psychology and educational and behavioral techniques are not at odds with concepts of Milieu Therapy. Instead, Milieu Therapy offers support to teachers in their use of other techniques that may increase their usefulness. Background and training offered to students in both psychodynamic and behavioral techniques, in individual psychology, and in Milieu Therapy and Life Space Interviewing techniques may be heralding a new era in education (see Grosenick, George, George & Lewis, 1991, 91).

CONCLUSION

A review of professional comments about common public school practices indicates there is abundant overlap of philosophies. Most theoretical perspectives discuss the need for individualization, positive interpersonal relationships, structuring environmental influences in a therapeutic way, building self-esteem, and benign communications techniques. These are many of the essential ideas in Milieu Therapy.

Classroom teachers working with difficult children cannot base their intervention on their own comfort or philosophical bias. The needs of each child must be primary in these choices, and teachers have to do what works! Human beings have a great deal in common, but it is their uniqueness that must be addressed--the individuality of each as unmatchable as fingerprints. Individual psychology reflects a blend of developmental and learning psychology with attention to both the affective and cognitive needs of children (Morse, 1985, 4).

There is increasing awareness among professionals from every discipline that there needs to be more emphasis on helping the individual and less on championing theoretical models (Beare, 1991, 217). "The shortcoming of the single-theory approach is that no single school of psychology provides answers for the many situations a teacher must face" (Morse, 1985, 4). As teachers try to secure equality of consideration for all children, different approaches based on individual needs will be more widely used; when each child's individual needs are equally considered, equality is achieved.

It is easy to be seduced into a confrontational position when siding with a particular approach. Teachers are asked to decide among various theories and avoid a muddy orchestration of all the possible approaches. What a teacher requires to survive and provide competent services, however, is resourcefulness in program development, with emphasis on comprehension of the nature of the pupil's self--its evolution, its current structure, and its amenability to change (Morse, 1985, 38-39).

Hewett (1987, 61-63) said that for decades it has never been very clear just how one creates a therapeutic classroom, a therapeutic curriculum, or trains a therapeutic teacher. Teacher training strategies struggle with various positions. Some years ago one of the authors participated in a project designed to present various theoretical points of view to teacher trainees. The project consisted of a series of videotapes that showed a variety of behavior problems erupting in a classroom. Following each problem, two experts associated with contrasting points of view analyzed the problem, offered an explanation for its occurrence, and then suggested a possible intervention. In one videotape, the author was identified as a behaviorist and paired with an ecologist. Not only did the two agree with each other on practically everything they said, but both suggested psychodynamic interpretations and interventions.

Careful practical applications of many theories can be combined and educators can achieve clarity in programming for children. Milieu Therapy appears to be an appropriate means of achieving this unity. It's techniques do not favor one approach at the expense of another, nor is it intended to replace any other method; rather, it combines and expands techniques that can add to the tools already being used in our efforts to work successfully with children who are not "labeled" but who will flourish in a nurturing climate as well as with those who are disturbed and disturbing. With a wider range of tools from which to choose, we can better match the program and the strategies to the child and create a truly "special" education.

CHAPTER FOUR

MANAGING CHILDREN'S BEHAVIOR

The person who is on the scene with the surface behaviors of children faces a problem: How does one interfere with inappropriate behavior and survive symptoms while still using the situation toward a positive end? The technical implications of such a situation transcend the primary concerns of psychiatry. No matter what may be therapeutically desired, many life situations arise in which the immediate behavior of the child needs interference for reality reasons. Planned, positive interference techniques can be used as tools in their own right. Redl and Wineman (1957, 232-237, 395-397) gave the name "individual antisepsis" to such techniques.

Teachers know that participation in even the best of activities may have marginal or unseen effects on children, and that those effects are communicated through wild, out-of-control, or too withdrawn behavior. Training and practice are highly desirable in the use of some Milieu Therapy and Life Space Interviewing techniques, but many teachers do not have these opportunities. Most of the techniques described in this chapter are those that many teachers use, consciously or not, and they can be deliberately used without extensive training. They are easily adaptable to the public schools, as the following examples given by teachers who used the techniques in the schools testify.

The many "antiseptic techniques" discussed in this chapter are important corollaries of Milieu Therapy and Life Space Interviewing. Other techniques for managing behavior as outlined by Redl and Wineman (1957, 395-486), such as regrouping, restructuring, and limitation of time and space, are discussed elsewhere in this book.

PLANNED IGNORING

One antiseptic technique that the educator can employ is that of planned ignoring. This involves the skill of an adult in assessing surface behavior and in limiting interference to only those behaviors that carry too heavy an intensity within themselves or to those that would not stop without intervention (Redl & Wineman, 1957, 400). As one teacher illustrated:

> Every morning without fail Casey greeted me with a "Good morning, you g.d. mother f..... ." My only reply was "Hello Casey." It would have served no purpose to get defensive about his remark. I feel 8 a.m. is too early for tantrums. His morning greeting finally became more sociable, with a mere "hello."

SIGNALING UNACCEPTABILITY OF BEHAVIOR

At times, it may be enough for the adult to give a clear signal, in a friendly way, about unacceptability of behavior. This signaling will block the rising disorganization that may be occurring in a child's behavior (Redl & Wineman, 1957, 400). One teacher reported:

> I have found that getting eye contact with a child, a stern look, a shake of my head, a raised hand, etc., are very effective means of signalling a child and consequently stopping or preventing negative behaviors from occurring.

INCREASING PHYSICAL PROXIMITY AND TOUCH CONTROL

Teachers know that stages of excitement, anxiety, or restlessness are occasionally taken care of simply by increasing the physical proximity between child and adult. When children's controls are slipping, the greater the distance between teacher and child, the more difficulty the child has in coping with frustration or impulse onrush. For some youngsters a simple geographical proximity is enough (Redl & Wineman, 1957, 405-411). One teacher gave this example:

> Charles' attention span was very short. I found, though, that when his attention began to wander, he would snap back to task the closer I moved to him.

Sometimes, direct physical contact is needed. Redl and Wineman (1957, 405) call this technique "touch control." Another teacher illustrated:

> Michael will often become a non-singer in the middle of a song or music time. A hand on his shoulder is often enough to get him going again.

Touch control, when used in an appropriate and timely manner, can help avoid frustration and the aggression of children produced by more intrusive interference techniques. This can be a tremendous advantage in preventing more serious behavior infractions (Redl & Wineman, 1957, 405-411).

DIRECT ADULT PARTICIPATION

The ego-disturbed child needs adult assistance in reviving and maintaining of interest far more than other children do, but adult participation in activities usually provides cohesiveness and stimulates interest from children, even those who are not labeled as disturbed. Because this demand for continuous adult vivacity can be fatiguing and a serious strain on adult nerves, the availability of enough sufficiently rested adults is an absolute necessity for work of this type (Redl & Wineman, 1957, 410). One teacher illustrates:

> I have on many occasions received questionable comments from colleagues when I play games along with my children. They wonder about my "dignity" and becoming too friendly with the kids. The other day I was playing with the boys (four-year-olds) during free time. One thing led to another until all of us were rolling and tumbling on the carpet. The boys were thrilled to pieces and had enormous fun. Afterward I was completely drained. Staying excited and being an "actress" to 27 four-year-olds is very emotionally draining. Some days I feel the "camera" is always on.

HYPODERMIC AFFECTION

Hypodermic affection is the term given to the provision of additional quantities of affection to help the ego or superego retain control in the face of anxiety or impulse onrush. At Pioneer House, a direct affectionate relationship was constantly maintained by the adults with the children (Redl

& Wineman, 1957, 412). As a teacher reported, this technique is a natural for application in a public school classroom.

> Each day we try to provide a lot of extra physical attention, usually in the form of holding, with the four-year-olds who seem a little insecure that particular day. During opening exercises, I noticed that Nicki had a very long face and sad eyes. I called her over to my desk to ask what was wrong. I put her on my lap and rocked her while she tearfully told me, "I want my Mamma." I said, "I know you do, Nicki, but Mamma's at work right now. Do you know that your Mamma wants you to stay at school today and have fun with the boys and girls?" I just held her for a while and then added, "You'll stay here for awhile and be my special buddy, won't you?" She shook her head "yes." After a few more minutes I walked back to her place with her. She was fine the rest of the day--all she needed was a little extra love and reassurance.

TENSION DECONTAMINATION THROUGH HUMOR

One teacher states that she was pleased to learn that this was a technique Redl and Wineman (1957, 414) suggest, because, during her first year of teaching, she had "patted herself on the back" for discovering this technique and having much success with it.

> Eddie had been the victim of too many humorless teachers. His so-called antics were in reality not that disruptive. Classroom teachers would become furious with comments Eddie made [but] his classmates loved them. The teachers had helped him to develop a vicious cycle: silly Eddie-angry teacher-silly Eddie-angry teacher. His low ability plus his non-conforming behavior had landed him in the self-contained Educable Mentally Retarded classroom. After I began teaching, he was to be my first pupil. The first time he "cut up" in my class, I laughed. After getting to know him over a couple of weeks, I found out he really was a very funny kid. He soon learned that I was laughing with him and that it was o.k. to be funny once in a while. By the end of the year, Eddie became much more conscious of the socially appropriate times to be funny.

HURDLE HELP

As Trieschman (1970, 2) pointed out, children's development fluctuates; there are ups and downs as they acquire self-worth, competence, and an ability to deal with frustration. At times of particular stress, they may lose control. Youngsters usually throw their most vicious or dangerous temper tantrums not out of a clear sky, but when they run into an obstacle on the way to an attempted goal. If the teacher can sense the oncoming outburst and provide the youngster with immediate help, the outburst may be avoided.

Trieschman described the stages of tantrums and suggested adult reactions that can prevent or deal with full-scale blowups. Tantrums build from the child's vague sense of discomfort, expressed by "rumbling and grumbling"; progress through deliberate, outrageous acts (such as throwing or breaking things) that indicate the child has lost control of his or her behavior and needs the restraining influence and help of an adult (Help! Help!); move to expressions of rage (such as threats or name-calling) when the child is assured that the adult is in control; to being oppositional in the extreme (No! No!), denying or opposing every adult suggestion; to placid, sad, withdrawn behavior with only occasional outbursts of negativism; and, finally, the post-tantrum stage, when children seem tired and guilty and may even reproach themselves aloud or become too withdrawn.

Teachers can be aware of each child's pattern of build-up and help the child contain the problem by talking about it or expressing feelings in another way. Best is early detection and prevention, as one teacher illustrated.

Sam was reading a story to me. The teacher aide was helping a student work a math problem. Johnny was struggling with a written assignment. He began to argue to himself about the work. With both instructors busy, there wasn't anyone available to help him. He started rocking his chair back and forth. He threw his pencil across the room. He turned his desk over and kicked his chair a couple of feet. All of this could have been avoided if a staff member had been available to approach him before he exploded. The problem of his written assignment and his impasse with it could have been discussed calmly and quick assistance over this "hurdle" provided, avoiding the violent explosion of behavior.

While ignoring is the first line of defense against maladaptive behavior, when a tantrum is underway that can't be ignored, the immediate task of the adult is to calm and control the child in such a way that the child knows that the adult is in charge and he or she is safe. Holding the child physically (discussed at the end of this chapter) or giving directions loudly, clearly, and repeatedly may be useful. It is pointless to argue with, threaten, or try to reason with the child at this point (Trieschman, 1970, 2). When the oppositional stage is reached, it is appropriate to tell the child that one is angry and doesn't like what the child is doing--children can understand and imitate reasonable anger more easily than unlimited patience and complete passivity in the face of fury. Legitimate options also may be sought by adults at this point, such as "When you're calm, we can talk about what you want." Conveying understanding to the child that he or she really wants to be in control ("You can be your own boss again when you say 'no' to all this yelling and shouting") may help, but telling the youngster how much you want to help him or her will not help at this stage. When the tantrum is subsiding, withdrawal of the child should be respected, but stay with him or her, talking in brief, calm sentences. Reassure the child that the tantrum is over, but don't ask searching questions or try to start a conversation. Finally, in the post-tantrum stage, children can learn alternative ways of coping with anxieties as adult and child describe their feelings, behaviors, and what can be done next time instead (Trieschman, 1970, 3). This last step is the beginning of or may lead to a Life Space Interview, discussed in a later chapter by that name.

INTERPRETATION AS INTERFERENCE

Redl and Wineman (1957, 420) saw interpretation as an effective interference technique by which youngsters are helped to understand the meaning of a situation that has been misinterpreted or to grasp their own motivations in issues. Interpretation in this sense is not meant to be a treatment technique; it is purely an interference technique that helps a youngster correct confusions that he or she had about external situations and internal motivations and reactions. As one teacher noted:

> I returned to my student teaching classroom from a job interview and found my supervising teacher holding Scott. I knew something was very wrong but all I got from my supervising teacher was "Do something!" Scott was running around the room shouting "I hate you, I hate you!" and "Leave me alone; just go away." At first I didn't understand, because over the semester Scott and I had developed a very positive relationship. I tried to talk in a soothing voice about the good times we'd had. Still his only response was "I hate you." Finally it all clicked. I said "Scott, I don't believe you hate me. I think you like me a lot but you're very angry because I went to a job interview. You know that means I won't be here forever, but we've always talked about that." He pulled his coat over his head and I stuck my head under it too. I said, "Scott, you don't

have to act like this. You've come so far while I was here. Goodbyes are hard for you and me. Scott, I'm not leaving because I don't care about you anymore; only because I'm graduating from college." I told him we still had weeks together and I'd come back after Christmas to check in on him. Once he understood why I was leaving his behavior quickly moved back toward the positive.

IMPULSE DRAINAGE

One function of program in a therapeutic milieu is that of impulse drainage. Redl and Wineman (1957, 329) attempted to help children by creating program structures that would provide a chance within program patterns for the discharge of the impulses that might otherwise have overwhelmed the child. The program sanctioned or made provisions for a harmless discharge of impulse pileup. If a program provides this, the goal of impulse drainage must be primary, with goals of educational learning or practice of social skills secondary. A teacher illustrated:

> During student teaching I usually read to the boys following lunch. Generally, this worked very well--they were relaxed and quiet. Usually I read from their social studies text--they found it very interesting and much less cumbersome than reading it alone silently and "doing questions." The topic had been Colonial America. Finally, we came to the inevitable topic-- slavery. (The only Black in the room was my supervising teacher, who suddenly came to my attention!) I read of the slave ships and the treatment of the slaves as they came to America. Scott, Mark, and Richard were wide-eyed at the descriptions. Darren giggled along for awhile before he cut loose with bellows of laughter and proclaimed, "Just to think them damn niggers are packed in like sardines, and all they eat are beans. Them niggers farted their way to America."
>
> Needless to say, the other three boys went wild and all began to imitate Darren's images. My supervising teacher quickly left the room. I suggested we read no further and that we could draw pictures of today's story. The boys giggled some more but really worked hard to produce some good pictures. Darren's pictures fit his earlier sentiments to a "T." I never could have continued reading and fairly expected the boys to gain composure and listen again. The art activity provided an atmosphere where giggling and talking were appropriate. It also

gave them an acceptable medium to express their feelings. I did not plan the activity to see if they could adequately portray slave ships. By the time they had finished their drawings, the humor of the situation had been dropped--they had then moved successfully to the next activity.

Here is another example of how a teacher used programming for impulse drainage.

With my four-year-olds we had a program called "Animal Island" each morning. The kids look at a big book, listen to a tape, and answer comprehension questions. On this particular day the kids were extremely "antsy." I concluded the lesson after a page or two and suggested we listen to some music. I put on a Hap Palmer record that encourages a great deal of movement. Then I stepped back from the group and "let them go." Having listened to the same record many times previously and working with me through the stated movements, the kids initially fell into the same routine. However, as a few kids dared to "cut up" with the record and the others realized I didn't mind, they all followed suit. They had a rollicking good time--got rid of all their extra energy--and began to sit down one by one. When all the die-hards had sat down, I took off the record and suggested a story. The story was very successful.

DIRECT APPEAL

Some teachers find that by directly appealing to students, behavior problems can be stopped. Of course, without a positive relationship between teacher and child this technique is valueless. But within the context of a good relationship, this can be a good antiseptic technique (Redl & Wineman, 1957, 429). One teacher offered the following example.

During May of my first year of teaching, I developed flu symptoms during the day. Determined to stay as long as I could, I told the kids to take it easy today because I was sick. They really tried. About 1 p.m. I was really showing the effects of my illness. Eddie told me "Hey, teach, why don't you go home-I'll keep this class for you." I was very touched by his concern.

And another teacher also testified to the effectiveness of direct appeal.

This year the teacher in the engineered resource room has used me for some crisis intervention work with her children. This teaming of services is something we have independently worked out. Her children work for points in a very structured system. A boy named Everett would often refuse to work if she did not respond immediately to his need for help. His idleness prohibited him from earning points. In his anger toward her he often lost points for defiance. So, I was called in.

One morning in particular he clammed up and refused to do anything. When I arrived, I asked, "Mrs. J. picking on you again?" No response. So I continued: "Everett, you know Mrs. J. really likes you, but you have to do your own work. Right now she's being observed (by the peer review team) and I'm sure she's a little tense too. You're making her look bad, but even worse, you're hurting yourself by not getting your points. I know the work is hard sometimes. Mrs. J. will help you, though. Give her a break--she can't always be right with you; there are nine other kids in there. Besides, lots of days Mrs. J. doesn't feel well; she's going to have a baby, you know."

Everett turned away and began to cry. I asked him to go wash his face and said that I would go to class with him to be his special help. We went in together and with my direct help Everett slowly began to work again. We quickly went through three worksheets in his packet. Then I asked if he'd go on alone and let me check my class. He said "Yeah, they might need you now." Everett did fine the rest of the morning. In fact, he earned around 36 points; 16 more than the required 20. With a little help, Everett's morning in the Resource Room had been saved.

INTEREST CONTAGION

This technique makes use of the effect that the interest of an adult or a small number of youngsters sometimes has on others. Effective programs aim to develop the child's interest in them. The interests and moods of adults as well as those of other children may have a positive contagion potential (Redl & Wineman, 1957, 410). A teacher noted:

Many times I have called aside a handful of kids and got them all stirred up and involved in an activity. Their excitement will then spark the others and get them involved too. My own mood and interests (as a teacher) also play a part in the creation of interest involvement.

BUILDING SATISFACTION IMAGES

The buildup of satisfaction images is a valuable resource in a therapeutic milieu. The Pioneer House staff named all their games and activities so that the children would identify with them on later recall, and teachers report the use of "name giving" arouses the children's initial curiosity about an activity. Between activities, a child's interest can be maintained through what Redl and Wineman call "promotional buildup" (Redl & Wineman, 1957, 372). As one teacher said:

"Touch time" with kindergartners always evoked a positive and motivated response from the children. They loved the opportunity to touch the bean barrel, sand, satin pillows, furry rugs, and other objects provided for tactile stimulation and identification. While some tactilely defensive children initially resisted this learning experience, they soon came to identify "touch time" with a pleasurable and non-pressured time that became fun!

Building satisfaction images is not always easy, but it is most often possible. A teacher reported:

Through my work with disturbed and retarded children, I have found that children who are failure-prone need a lot of convincing to believe that something we will do will be fun. I have found too that at times you can "talk an activity to death." On occasion my kids have accused me of lying to them beforehand about the potential fun of an activity, especially when the activity totally failed.

DECODING, LABELING, AND REDIRECTING

Teachers need to be aware of the child's verbal and nonverbal forms of communication that provide insight into the behavior exhibited. This awareness and it's communication to the child is "decoding." For instance, "Scott, you are moving your body a lot right now and your face looks red." After decoding, labeling of the problem is made possible, e.g., "You could be feeling angry because you missed recess today." This enables the teacher to give the child some insight into the problem and lets the child know that the teacher understands and accepts the feelings of the child. After labeling and accepting the feelings, adults find appropriate ways to redirect the behavior. Teachers can help children learn ways of expressing their feelings through the techniques of ventilation ("Can you tell me how angry you feel?"), skill development ("Will you draw how mad you are now?"), and verbal insight. With ventilation, the use of words is preferred to the child's putting feelings into action. Skill development can be used to sublimate the child's feelings into an activity, which must be invested with feeling to give it meaning, interest, and purpose. Verbal insight can be obtained then by using the Life Space Interview (Long, 1969, 367).

PERMISSION AND VERBAL LIMIT SETTING

Adults often communicate either permission for children's behavior or a clear message that the behavior is not o.k. Permission is used to encourage desired behaviors or to alleviate anxiety and guilt that a child may have about behavior. A less thought of and seemingly paradoxical use of permission is to stop a behavior by openly condoning it. This use of permission is usually limited to behavior that was meant to challenge the adult. If openly permitted, such testing loses its attraction to the child and the activity may stop right away, with none of the frustration and aggression that might be tied to a more direct attempt to limit the behavior. For instance, if the child picks up something that belongs to an adult, the adult may say, "Look at it, but please be careful." Here, the purpose is not to stop the behavior, but to keep it manageable (Redl & Wineman, 1957, 459-461). Adults should limit the use of this technique to what they can really accept in children's behavior. When those limits are reached, adults must say "No!" and mean it!

For verbal limits to succeed, the basic relationship of the child and the adult must be intact. The technique is used most often when youngsters are not out of control but merely excited. In situations of clear danger when behavior has to be stopped, the technique is used more forcefully, leaving no room for argument. Sometimes verbal limits may precede or even stop with simply signaling unacceptability of behavior, with a soft "No" as a reminder. However, if used sparingly, around important issues, and without hostility, anxiety, or anger on the part of the adult, a verbal limit, accompanied by changes in tone of voice or gestures, can be extremely hygienic and also effective (Redl & Wineman, 1957, 463-464).

PROMISES, REWARDS, PUNISHMENTS, AND THREATS

The use of promises and rewards are common educational practices, but they must be used carefully with children whose basic ego functions are impaired. Since promises and rewards are "future" events, children's ability to postpone gratification and control impulses must be considered. Other issues also must be considered. Did the child meet the conditions for the reward promised? Can the child understand the relationship between his or her behavior and the reward? How will the use of these tools affect the child's self-esteem? There are pitfalls to watch for, too. Because children's behavior varies, the use of rewards may create rivalry among children. A "fatalistic and business deal concept of life" may develop. Nonetheless, gratification should be provided to children without conditions (Redl and Wineman, 1957, 468-472).

The use of punishment and threats is tricky, since they stimulate in the child additional aggressive energy. Punishment should never be used to discharge anger or frustration an adult is feeling. It is usually an ineffective way to deal with children altogether (Redl & Wineman, 1957, 473-474).

Threats differ from reminders of natural consequences of behavior; threats imply that punishment will come under certain circumstances. We do not recommend threats in any form in dealing with children. Rather, it is most effective to stay clear-headed and unhooked emotionally so that realistic consequences can be pointed out or carried out without the counter-aggression, anger, and loss of control from the adult that threats imply. The same words "If you continue throwing food, you will have a time-out" may be either a threat or a realistic reminder of a natural consequence, depending on the adult's emotional state, tone of voice, and intention.

TIME OUT

Almost all educators are familiar with or use time-out procedures with youngsters whose behaviors are not acceptable. Redl and Wineman (1957, 440-451) call this "antiseptic bouncing," noting the term "antiseptic" to be of primary importance, since "an angry adult throwing out a youngster with a display of hostility, aggression, anger, and triumph" (Redl & Wineman, 1957, 441) is a misuse of the technique. There are times, though, when removal of a child from a scene is called for as the only way to cope with behavior or as a therapeutic tool to be considered before crisis has developed. Some obvious scenarios for removal of children are when there is physical danger (a child is about to hurt another person or himself or herself) or when destructive impulses are manifesting themselves, such as through destruction of property.

Other situations that may call for removal of a student from a situation are:

- The child is overstimulated in the group and can't calm down as long as he or she remains in the situation.
- The student is stirring up the group and must be removed in order for the group to calm down.
- The child has reached a stage of excitement that must be checked.
- The student is ready to give in but cannot possibly afford to do so openly without losing face or being considered a wimp; a time-out at this point helps him or her save face (Redl and Wineman, 1957, 441-443).

In short, selective use of time-out, with the psychological hygiene and safety of the individual or group as primary considerations, is important.

Equally important are the attitudes and procedures involved in time-outs. Relationships between the adult and a child or groups of children must be protected by being sure that children know we are stopping behavior which will, in some way, hurt them--that we are trying to help them avoid worse trouble. Time-out must not be confused by anyone with punishment--that is not it's purpose. Thus, time outs must be kept free of anger, aggression, and disapproval. Face-saving rather than face-losing for the child should be the goal. Adults also should be sensitive to the effect of a child's time-out on other children and the group (Redl & Wineman, 1957, 443-445). Finally, time out of the situation should be limited to only periods of time that are reasonable, not punitive, and that are appropriate for the child and his or her developmental level. Ten minutes is usually the maximum effective time-out for a young child, and thirty minutes is a long time for even older and more "together" children.

James Tompkins (Krupicka interview, 1988) discussed time out as isolation when children are seriously out of control. Krupicka noted that some professionals suggest that when a child must be socially isolated during a time out procedure, the teacher or adult must not be present or in contact with the child; therefore, no Life Space Interview can be conducted. Tompkins replied:

> I need to say something about time out procedures or isolation of youngsters during explosive, out of control episodes. I have encountered professionals who take the position that even with seriously disturbed children in specialized settings, the child should be isolated and be by themselves. Can you imagine a severely emotionally handicapped youngster, highly disturbed, distraught, even terrified by his/her own fury and anger about

some triggering experience, dragged off and placed into an empty room, screaming, kicking, crying: absolutely devastated and now isolated with his own flood of feelings and unattended to? This kind of adult reaction appears to create a cocoon of inescapable terror for the child! Redl and Wineman and others calm the child and then take the position that this is the very time to exploit the feelings, the behavior, the incident to help children learn about themselves, see how they contributed to their difficulty, and how they might have done something differently. This is the time to glue the relationship between child and adult. This is the time to show the child that the setting is helpful, the adults are available--at the worst times-- to "educate" the child about their needs, which are often expressive of symptomatic behavior. The analogy is: A patient is brought to the hospital emergency room with a severed artery and the Doctor looks at the injury and indicates the bleeding is so serious that the patient should be isolated. That's the time for emergency procedures! So too with kids!

PHYSICAL RESTRAINT

Physical restraint of a child who is totally out of control--biting, kicking, throwing, spitting, screaming, swearing--is sometimes necessary. But there is sometimes confusion between "physical restraint" and "physical punishment." In a therapeutic milieu, these have nothing to do with one another. Physical punishment should not be used in any form under any circumstances. It is ludicrous to think that pain will teach the youngster, that character will be built through paddling, or that children feel better when they "pay" (with a spanking) for their misbehavior. No matter how mild, physical violence does not motivate a child toward being more socialized, but instead exacts a tremendous price in terms of the child's self-esteem and his or her hostility toward adults (Redl & Wineman, 1957, 453).

Physical restraint, on the other hand, involves "antiseptic manipulation" without a trace of punitiveness. Aggression and force are not part of restraint. The adult remains friendly and affectionate, talking calmly to the child. While physically holding a child, the adult does not take the destructive intent of the child's behavior personally, realizing, instead, that "the child's ego . . . obviously has gone AWOL" temporarily (Redl & Wineman, 1957, 454-455). Holding offers the child security in such a situation, and that is the therapeutic intent of the adult--assuring the child that *someone* (the adult) is in control and that the child need not, therefore, fear the rage he or she is experiencing.

The child must never be rejected or punished for the behavior that caused him to need to be held (Redl & Wineman, 1957, 455).

It is important that holding be done in such a way that neither the child or the adult gets hurt. Training in appropriate holding techniques is very useful in this regard.

While it is not easy for adults to remain consistent and calm when physical and verbal aggression are coming their way, they can become skilled in handling these incidents. Sometimes adults see behavior that has escalated to the point of needing holding as a "failure" or their part (Redl & Wineman, 1957, 455-456). But the child's behavior is the child's responsibility--not the adult's. The adult's responsibility is to respond therapeutically and constructively when such behavior does occur, in a way that maintains the critical rapport developed with the child. Offering children acceptance of their feelings (but not necessarily their behavior) and security and safety when their rage has taken over, staying clear-headed about this intent for holding, and communicating this to the child after the tantrum has ended, builds trust and rapport.

CONCLUSION

Antiseptic techniques are basic but important techniques in a therapeutic milieu. The techniques discussed in this chapter are, for the most part, easily used by anyone who wishes to have a positive influence on children's behavior. The last two techniques discussed, time-out and physical holding, require more attention and training to be used effectively. By naming and describing these techniques, Redl and Wineman (1957) have brought them to more awareness so that they can be used consciously by teachers and others in schools.

CHAPTER FIVE

POWERFUL MILIEU INGREDIENTS
BASIC COMPONENTS OF A HEALTHY ENVIRONMENT

Students will be connected to adults at school as much by the dynamics of the environment as by relationships and programs. How the milieu is structured and responds affects the types of relationships that develop (Christof & Kane, 1991, 50-51). This chapter is about designing a healthy milieu for enhancing children's normal growth and development as well as for remediating the lives of special students. Here, we summarize some Milieu Therapy principles that directly influence participants in schools and give examples of their application in public school settings. Among the specific milieu ingredients discussed in this chapter are physical setting and use of props, nurturing, child care and child advocacy, avoidance of traumatic events, avoidance of unhygienic handling, depersonalized controls, encouraging independent functioning, and acknowledging and respecting cultural differences. Other components of a healthy environment and their applications to public school classrooms will be discussed in later chapters.

Treating children in and through environmental settings opens a wide avenue of therapeutic enrichment, undreamed of before and holding implications for the total school environment. Healthy, supportive, and personalized learning environments are effective not only for enhancing the success of academic pursuits, but also in developing, sustaining or renewing satisfying attitudes and relationships, and reducing misbehavior (Redl & Wineman, 1957, 240-241, 264-265, 396; Jones & Jones, 1986; Paul & Epanchin, 1991, 294-295; Wood, 1991, 19).

Each person lives in a unique environment composed of the varying conditions in a person's life. This "environing world" (Uexküll, 1909, 173) varies from time to time and place to place. Most theorists agree that stress or distress is not so much a product of either the individual or the environment as a product of the interaction of the individual and the environment (Selye, 1974; Endler, 1975)--how a person perceives and reacts to environmental stimuli (Uexküll, 1909, 173). This unique, individualized adjustment determines what can become either a stimulus or a response, the amalgam of the two reflecting the person's inner world and the internal direction for its behavioral repertoire.

For children, the reality of the environment in time and place is subjective and based on how they are dealt with, treated, regarded, or responded to by the significant others in their lives. Some classrooms or other school climates may be dominated by the requirement for student compliance, conformity, competition, achievement, social grace, and so forth, and the environing worlds may interact in ways that produce unacceptable behavior. But carefully designed surroundings contain mediating elements that can help children learn better methods of coping with internal and social problems. If the environing worlds are specifically "hygienic," supportive, and individualized, the interaction may lead to successes and enriching opportunities for greater achievement, social grace, and loving relationships (Uexküll, 1909, 173).

All schools consist of a milieu--an atmosphere or environment--that gives immediate messages the moment anyone walks into the school. For children, every school-related experience--including the ride to school, the lunchroom, the free play period, and academic instruction--presents an opportunity for enrichment. While some practitioners have maintained awareness of the need to attend to this fact, deliberate design and creation of the school environment are not always so conscious.

The milieu is the totality of a person's environment, the whole surrounding culture, and everything that is done to, for, or by a person in any given location. The milieu also involves everything that a person is receiving through the senses, and this is continually changing (Redl & Wineman, 1957, 281-284). As one teacher put it:

> The milieu is people: children, professional staff--teachers, principals--janitors, cooks, visitors, friends. The milieu is buildings: the rooms where the child works and plays and sleeps, the playground, the path where he goes for a walk, his school. The milieu is the child's possessions, books, television, letters, conversations, and pets.

Within the milieu are subsystems and microgroups seasoned with political, personal, and professional forces; policies, rules, routines; hierarchies of power; and personal differences, animosities, alliances, and struggles. The therapeutic milieu involves a highly complex communication system for everyone in an individual's life, and this communication breaks down in a public school setting or any other situation where the whole person and his or her environment are not areas of concern. In a healthy milieu, each professional person becomes bigger than his or her craft; bigger than him or herself (Powers, 1980, 5; Ostrosky & Kaiser, 1991, 6).

No milieu is good or bad in itself. Many factors determine the effectiveness of the environment. The healthy environment is multidimensional and fluid with a variety of interfacing components. Therapeutic milieu principles, taking advantage of problems or crises in the life space of the child, conceive of the environment as a shaping tool that can be manipulated either to soften or to draw out symptomatic behavior as the situation requires. Symptoms are thus subjected to a kind of cultivation procedure by the manner in which the clinician or the teacher copes with them (Redl & Wineman, 1957, 489-491).

A healthy school milieu radiates security and protection from threats or traumatic experiences. The total school environment is designed to support children's normal development in learning and socialization. The atmosphere should sustain students' needs for positive, meaningful nurturing, which in turn will elicit from students responsive learning and social maturity in keeping with their growth and development.

The goal of consciously or specially designed climates is to help students know as much as possible about themselves--why they behave as they do and the consequences of their behaviors--and to allow them to experiment with innovative solutions to their dilemmas. The environment must provide other models for behavior that are clearly productive and gratifying. How well this goal is accomplished is determined as much by the actions of those who "live with" the students in the various programs and activities as by specific therapies.

With all students, but particularly with troubled children, the first few months in the classroom are crucial. After a possible honeymoon, or a calm initial period when inappropriate behaviors do not occur, teachers should expect and be prepared for regressions that may surface and be apparent in such forms of behavior as transference, outward aggression, and hostility, seemingly directed at the teacher. A healthy, responsive environment can be very helpful in dealing with or even preventing some of these behaviors.

TROUBLED STUDENTS

While the application of therapeutic milieu concepts is very useful in support of normal growth and development, it is essential for children in difficulty. A therapeutic climate for the more highly divergent student requires a more deliberate, individually designed program with key educational decision-makers uniformly dedicated to its implementation. Personnel in the milieu enfold the student each day in assistance and support for growing adjustments (Noshpitz, 1962, 284-296). These practices offer the maximum security possible and foster mutual trust to allow troubled children to let down their defenses and enjoy a social solidarity with others in this environment. Indeed, every student will flourish in such a climate, but children with handicaps are so vulnerable that they often *require* this type of special intervention.

A few treatment hours with a therapist are not enough for seriously disturbed students, and the youngsters themselves realize this. Anna Freud quoted an adolescent schizophrenic girl who complained that therapy didn't offer what she needed since the therapist was not with the girl the whole day and didn't see her when she was "different" (than when with the therapist) (Bettelheim, 1974, 50).

A good milieu design for disturbed children needs a greater treatment orientation, with emphasis on structure, limit-setting, group dynamics, program activities, and general physical conditions of the school. The therapeutic climate at school stresses getting along with others (social skills development) in the context of academic activities and, through the sanctuary of sustaining relationships, emphasizes children's self-concept, self-esteem, and feelings.

In the public school setting, teachers are faced with making the most of the limited time they have with students during the day. It is especially unfortunate for children with serious problems that there is often not even constant 8 a.m. to 3 p.m. contact with them. Taking advantage of opportunities throughout the school setting will require rethinking and careful study by school administrators and teachers, because it takes cooperation and adoption of the attitudes and techniques by all concerned. Such limitations create difficulties in making optimal use of the therapeutic environment within the confines of the school, as well as difficulties in enlightening the faculty and community and establishing supportive alliances. As this is a complex matter even with highly trained personnel in a residential setting, one certainly cannot expect public school personnel to implement a classic program of environmental treatment, because they lack control over other aspects of the students' environments. Still, an individual classroom teacher with skills in therapeutic milieu procedures can greatly benefit children in public school environments.

BASIC THERAPEUTIC MILIEU CONCEPTS

Fritz Redl (1959b, 721-736) delineated "twelve powerful milieu ingredients": the social structure, including a clear role distribution of the adult figures, the pecking order of the children, and the communication network; the value system of the staff, which is communicated in every way (both verbally and non-verbally) to the children; routines, rituals, and behavioral regulations (rules); the impact of the group process; personality traits of the children that affect other children; attitudes and feelings of the staff; the overt behavior of staff and others in the environment toward and about children; activity structure; space, equipment, time, and props; consideration of influences from the outside world; the system of "umpiring services" and "traffic regulations" between environment and child; and resilience and flexibility in the environment.

Redl and Wineman (1957, 35-36) identified some characteristics of a therapeutic milieu. First, the child should have complete protection from traumatic handling by any personnel associated with the program. Also, gratification through activity programming, adult love and tokens of affection should be absolutely divorced from consideration about whether the child deserves them. There should be tolerance for symptoms and leeway for regression. Finally, the program should not run too contrary to the sociological and cultural traditions of the child: staff should avoid using their own philosophical, ethical, and political convictions to determine what really does or does not have therapeutic effect.

Based on the experiences of teachers in public schools we have, in this chapter, outlined some powerful milieu ingredients.

PHYSICAL SETTING

An inner cohesiveness is attained in a healthy environment through the commitment of staff to a common psychological understanding of the children's needs, forming the basis around which the school integrates. An ongoing, active process of analysis of all aspects of the environment--from all levels of interaction down to the smallest detail of the physical setting--leads to a nurturing, integrated climate. Such a climate is particularly helpful to troubled children who, because of past experiences with mixed messages, know better than to trust what they are told. They are a bit more ready to believe the meaning conveyed by what is done and how they are approached, but most of all they believe what they can touch, smell, and see for themselves (Bettelheim & Sanders, 1979, 216-217).

Bettelheim stressed the importance of providing a physical setting that conveys the message to children that this environment will protect them from their destructive impulses, while meeting their needs. How the institution is built and furnished, down to the last detail of lighting and furniture, must convince the children that this is a place where they can afford to let down their defenses. Further, they must become convinced that their needs will be satisfied and that these satisfactions will not endanger them if they relax their controls over their anger and anxiety. But they will believe this only if even inanimate objects tell them that everything is here for them, that they are terribly important to the staff, and that life can be good, even for them. Only then can they dare to begin to trust the intentions of the setting (Bettelheim & Sanders, 1979, 220).

Redl and Wineman (1957, 284) described a physical environment that enhances the lives of children as "a house that smiles, props that invite, space that allows." One teacher reported:

> The four institutional green walls, radiators, and venetian blind covered windows found in most classrooms hardly qualify as a "house that smiles." I put much work into room decorations and action-packed bulletin boards. Even the spaces around the outside of the door display things that make all children want to come and take a peek. Furniture in my classroom is kept to a minimum. I always guarantee individual working room for each child; however, depending on the situation, I don't always guarantee one desk per child. I found that this really baffles the older child. Everyone wants a look at that "strange classroom."
>
> More than once the line of "regular ed." kids outside my door caused hassles with the faculty, especially the principal. He told those kids "no one in their right mind would want to choose to go in there." The days when I invited those kids in, they were totally thrilled. A child once told me, "You think you're so tough on kids, but you're not really." He then requested for the umpteenth time for me to take him. I can't help but feel I had indeed created a house that smiles and props that invite.

The arrangement of space is important. The design and arrangement of furniture and props in the child's environment can speak to the child of use and misuse. Care must be taken to prevent overstimulation of destructive impulses (Redl & Wineman, 1957, 433), and many teachers have found that the very physical closeness of children often creates problems that could be eliminated through the rearrangement of furniture. When desks are too close together, accidental bumping and touching can provoke major outbursts. Some teachers put a desk in every corner, providing each child with his or her own space and also allowing a group area. Space arrangements can also reinforce rights to privacy and "aloneness" by defining each child's space and telling the group that no one but that child is allowed in without permission. A child's desk or other personal space should clearly be designated as that child's private property, and teachers and children alike should respect this privacy. Likewise, the same rules may be expected to apply to the teacher's desk.

One teacher reported:

> Definition of individual and group space worked extremely well
> for me. I found it an effective method to eliminate tantrums
> due to elbow-bumping.

This teacher also observed that a cluttered room upsets children. A
neat, well-ordered environment and respect for personal space in the physical
environment will be reflected in children's behavior as they order their
internal worlds and integrate their own boundaries and limits.

USE OF PROPS

One constant in devising a growth-enhancing classroom environment
is the use of "props," which can serve as valuable aids in building satisfaction
images. Many kinds of props can be used, and teachers give numerous
examples. One teacher commented:

> In my classroom I have frequently used puppets as one of my
> props. The children now know when they see the puppets that
> something fun is in store.

Another teacher described creative uses for a variety of other props.

> I prefer to use bright colored teacher-made materials and kits
> with gimmicks. A math kit that offers a certificate at the
> successful completion of 10 cards seduced many a child into
> doing math. The day I brought my typewriter to school was the
> day many a child first began English and reading lessons. Of
> course, I often had to eliminate sentences such as "I hate you"
> to decipher the story. But the kids couldn't wait to type. There
> was much sorrow the day the typewriter broke. The use of a
> make-it-yourself filmstrip kit brought about the first successful
> team work we had that year. The kids were thoroughly
> delighted with the results of their work. My unconventional
> approaches to the classroom, the kids, the material, the staff
> itself, invited the kids to come and get involved.

NURTURING, CHILD CARE, AND CHILD ADVOCACY

The formation of strong interpersonal relationships as the basis for
successful, growth-producing classroom encounters is often strongly based on

provisions made for the gratification of a child's basic needs. The teacher's attitudes and actions in providing child care and in being an advocate for children can contribute greatly to the establishment of close interpersonal relationships that are nurturing and healing to children. Child care, in the therapeutic environment, is a function added to the basic provision of education. It is the immediate, practical embodiment of the advocate's philosophy that every child has a right to a proper environment.

Ego development in children is heavily dependent on the gratification of biological needs. For this reason as well as for the facilitation of therapeutic relationships, provision of adequate child care becomes one of a teacher's most important functions and roles. In providing for children's comfort and security in the environment, a teacher's concern and affection for the children is transmitted to them. Eventually, children will come to appreciate this attitude and even to reciprocate, although, as one teacher said:

> It was a long drawn-out process before we reached the point of any reciprocity, At first, the boys resisted my attempts at "mothering" and saw it as demeaning to them. They could stand a little cold and discomfort, but not for too long. They eventually decided it would be much more comfortable to be warm and dry. Although I did not know it then, these were most likely the precipitating factors in establishing the relationships we later had, most of which did not evolve for months to come. Gradually they began to trust me and to know I genuinely liked them and was interested in their well-being and security. They slowly began to communicate some guarded thoughts, trusting me enough to know that whatever they said, I still liked them as individuals and posed no threat. They trusted me to help them work through difficulties, although often it was not within my capabilities to give neat, pat answers. I could see them growing and maturing as they developed enough self-confidence in themselves to make more mature decisions of their own and find more acceptable ways of solving problems. I tried to be close by to listen and to guide, but not solve problems for them. As the year progressed, many of them developed enough confidence in themselves that they needed me less and less and became more independent in their actions and problem-solving abilities.

The public schools are in an excellent position to meet basic biological, emotional, and social needs of children through sensitive and nurturing responses to the need for food, the need for sleep, the need to use the bathroom, and the need to be warm, dry, and comfortable. The child alone cannot meet all these needs; support from adults and the program is imperative. This type of "child care" should be structured to have a flexible but clearly defined framework for building relationships. Adults who provide this kind of support are saying to the child, "I care about you--I like you--you are a worthy individual, and I understand and I want to help." Relationships are given a chance to emerge.

Sleep is a basic biological need that can, at times, be a major factor in working with children in schools. When children have not had enough sleep, teachers may have to make program changes. One teacher observed:

> It is incredible to me that I still hear teachers talk of punishing children who are inattentive without investigating the possible cause of that inattentiveness. The morning Penny fell asleep in class, all the paddlings, threats, removals of points, ridiculing, etc., were not going to make Penny stay awake. What she needed at that point in time was sleep. I did wake her up and take her to the hall to see if there was anything I could do. She related the tales of last night's fright at home. I then took her to the health room and put her to bed.

Another major factor in the issue of nurturing people, particularly children, is food. One teacher reported:

> We have worked into our routine a milk and cracker break twenty minutes after their arrival at school for our four-year-olds. I think it's vital we acknowledge the fact that some, if not many, kids come to school hungry. Since our school does not have a breakfast program, I believe it's our obligation to meet their needs for food. Following this break we always go to the bathroom. Yes, it can be time-consuming, but in the long run it surely shows a routine that meets the mental hygiene as well as managerial efficiency reasons for having [nurturing] routines.

Other basic biological needs are those for warmth, shelter, and clothing. Another teacher showed her sensitivity to these issues.

> Wintertime caused my greatest time of concern because it was cold and snowy most of the season. The children would arrive at school in shirt sleeves in a snow storm! Of course, the snow itself, being one of the most irresistible natural "props," beckoned them to engage in throwing it and rolling around in it. When I arrived in the morning, they were thoroughly soaked to the bone and chilled. Having limited resources at my

disposal, I became one of the best scavengers around. I scrounged through last year's "lost and found" boxes to get all the extra sweaters, gloves, hats, and jackets I could find for emergency days such as these. I was usually able to get the children dried off by the radiators in order to avoid colds and coughs that might result. At times they were so drenched they had to be taken to the nurse's office to undress and wrap in a blanket while I borrowed the clothes dryer in the home economics room to dry their clothing.

I remember that one day the home economics teacher had a guest speaker, and I was in and out with the wet clothes (I had no less than four boys in the nurse's office wrapped in blankets). The speaker was trying to deliver a lecture while the tennis shoes in the dryer were banging around. Fortunately, the home economics teacher was more patient than most, and I was not in her disfavor for too long.

I provided countless boxes of Kleenex for the sneezes and sniffles that resulted from the snowball fights and mud puddle splashings. Many days when a child was too sick to be in class but could not go home because no one was there, I again went back and forth to the nurse's office checking to see that he was covered up and warm. I would usually take the child home at the end of the day if the parents could not come for him.

Some teachers have discovered how taking care of the basic creature comforts could influence a child's behavior and perceptions.

Randy came from a dreadful home environment of physical and emotional neglect. His aunt, who he lived with, would leave him and his brother and sister outside alone in the mornings to wait for the bus while she went on to work. This left a considerable amount of time for Randy to explore the neighborhood. One morning, Randy excitedly came running in the room to show me what he had found while waiting for the bus. He emptied his pockets on the table and I couldn't believe what I saw! He had pulled up several small cactus plants by the roots and stuck them in his pockets! He wanted to put the plants in some dirt to see if they would grow. I told him we would talk about the plants later, but that right now I wanted to look at his hands. When he showed them to me, it was obvious that they were covered with needles from the cactus. After Randy calmed down from his excitement, he began to complain that his hands were "feeling funny." I tried several different methods of removing the stickers before Randy consented to letting me use a sewing needle to get them out. It took the better part of the morning to get most of the stickers out. I had to continue to take care of several infected places on his hands for the next few days. The first thing Randy would want me to do when he came in was to check his hands and put ointment on the infected places.

After this incident, I could see a change in my relationship with Randy. In the past, he had never been very receptive to my attempts at showing affection or concern for him. I felt that after this experience his perception of me changed. He began to accept me as someone who truly was interested in him and cared about his well-being. He began to respond to some affection. There were many other times when I tried to take care of Randy's physical needs, such as giving him a shower or getting him something to eat. It seemed that Randy's attitude toward himself and others could be improved by first taking care of his physical needs. I feel that these experiences were very important in helping me begin to establish a positive relationship with him. It was often clear that, before we could begin to make progress in other areas, Randy's basic physical needs had to be met.

Even at the high school level, providing for the physical needs of students is an important facet of Milieu Therapy. However, these provisions may take a different form with adolescents. As they struggle for autonomy, they are less likely to openly express dependency needs. A student might ask for help in sewing on a button, but one teacher reported that even that is rare.

They are much more likely to present themselves at my door, expecting me to notice some change in appearance. It is my happy task to provide positive feedback, usually on a new hair style, a hair cut, or a new article of clothing.

Older students have more resources and abilities to provide for their own physical needs than do younger students. Their teachers do, at times, remind them about hygiene, and girls may ask female teachers about the application of makeup and other "female" issues. Physical needs at this age may differ in their level of importance to the student.

One teacher illustrated:

> I was able to discover and meet one of Brenda's physical needs.
> She had not dressed out for P.E. all year. The coach came to
> me to find out why. When I talked to Brenda about it, she told
> me that she could not wear gym clothes that showed her legs.
> Instead of being honest with the coach, she had acted
> rebelliously and refused to participate in the class. Once the
> problem was identified, we could work together to solve it.

When positive feelings of care and concern are transmitted through
meeting students' physical needs, the child learns to trust and confide in the
adult, thereby beginning the formation of strong interpersonal relationships
upon which the success of the rest of the school program may rest.

Equally relevant may be child advocacy efforts. While child advocacy
does not involve directly interacting with students to meet their physical needs,
it does affect physical, emotional, and social needs in a strong way. Advocacy
emphasizes the rights of children to have their basic health, housing,
nutritional, and clothing needs met as well as their rights to opportunities to
develop socially, emotionally, and educationally. The purpose of child
advocacy is to ensure and protect those rights and to remind schools and
communities of responsibilities toward their own children. For many children,
these services have not been rendered but, rather, have been missed, ignored,
or denied.

Teachers can function as successful advocates for the children they
teach by creating awareness of needs--for example, by lobbying and providing
information to decision makers for developing and improving programs.
Teachers can also take direct action, such as participation in class action
lawsuits. Becoming consumer advocates, providing parents with information
on legal rights and services available to them nationally and in the community,
and helping them to exert pressure for change on those in power can also
strongly serve the rights of children.

Individual advocacy is a potent tool. One teacher reported on her
advocacy efforts in a school setting.

> Several of my actions on behalf of the students proved very
> beneficial in unifying the group. "Going to bat" for them would
> be a good descriptive term to clarify what I mean. It was proven
> time and again that if we did not stick together the forces from
> without would destroy the cohesiveness of the group and the
> relationships we had with one another.
>
> In one case, a student had been thrown up against a
> locker and shoved around by one of the faculty members. The

student trusted me enough to tell me about it, even though he was humiliated to tears and a lump was swelling on the back of his head. He could have run away from school or struck back in several ways, but instead he came to me about it.

This had happened before with other students as well as with this particular boy, and I had attempted to deal with it in several ways, all of which were ineffective. I felt it was my responsibility to do something about it since the student was powerless in this situation. If I did not take action, why should the student ever ask for help again? He would only resort to more unacceptable means of dealing with future problems. I would have proven myself untrustworthy at that point.

At the risk of further alienating myself from the faculty, I brought the person in question up on charges before the school board. He was given a warning that he would be dismissed if this sort of thing occurred in the future. This instance and others like it proved to the students that I was there for their benefit and, whenever possible, to help them out.

When this finally became clear to them, I noticed a tremendous change in their attitude toward me. They reciprocated by helping me at certain times and defending me in very difficult situations before faculty and community.

AVOIDANCE OF TRAUMATIC EVENTS

A central concept of therapeutic milieu is the avoidance of traumatic events. A program must, in its very design, try to avoid exposing the children it serves to situations that are likely to be traumatic for them. One teacher recounted the following experience.

For the past month the entire school has been involved in a candy sale. Those children who sold a certain number of boxes were allowed to put their name in the "hat" for a bicycle drawing at the close of the sale. None of our four students got very involved in the sale, though they did sell a couple of boxes of candy each. The bicycle drawing was to be held at a school-wide assembly toward the end of the day. Three of the boys had no interest in the assembly--as Scott said, "I don't give a damn who wins the g.d. bike." Richard, however, was determined to attend the assembly because he just knew he'd win it. We all tried to explain to him he had not even sold enough candy to be eligible for the bike. He countered with his fantasy that "just maybe."

Ideally, Richard probably should not even have gone to the assembly. As the hour grew closer, his determination to win and to go grew. Together, he and I went. Once inside, he declared, "I ain't no baby. Go sit somewhere else." Anticipating imminent trouble, I located myself discreetly in the row behind him--within arm's reach. As I predicted, he did not win--but he remained calm. Children and teachers begin filing out of the auditorium, and all hell broke loose with Richard. He began beating the chair in front of him and screaming, "G.D. people, don't give a f--- about poor little kids! Hell, the bike's mine!" I was able to move up next to him and quietly talk to him until he was back in control. It took a little maneuvering to keep everyone else moving but then, in the end, I could assure him they hadn't stopped to stare.

This teacher was able to support the child in spite of a traumatic event she could not protect him from, and to avoid another event (being stared at while having a tantrum) that might have added further trauma.

Another teacher stayed calm as a child became overstimulated and worked his way into a potentially traumatic episode.

The mall was filled with Christmas decorations and animated displays--talking bears, talking chipmunks, large Christmas trees to delight the hearts of young children--and, of course, there was Jolly Old Saint Nick. Another teacher and I had taken six children to the Mall. We had had a lovely day. The children had followed most of the rules and there were no catastrophes. We were admiring the animated displays and the children were enjoying talking back to the bears and asking questions. We wandered around and the children wanted to return to the talking bears. As we approached the bears, we saw that "Bears Are Sleeping." There was no one inside the house to talk for the bears. We turned to walk away and all of a sudden I heard Phillip talking for the bears. Somehow he managed to get inside without any of us seeing him. Standing next to the rail was a lady and a small boy with glasses. Phillip sang "Santa Clause is coming to town." He received no positive responses from his audience. As the lady and small boy walked away, Phillip screamed, "You jerks! What do you want for Christmas, Four Eyes?" He climbed out immediately, begging not to be punished. He seemed to be embarrassed. He said, "I just wanted to get inside so bad. I'm sorry." We talked about it for a moment and Phillip reassured us that no way would he do it again. Later, consequences were developed for him. No big deal!

Some emotional problems are brought on by anniversaries or holidays such as Halloween and Christmas. Anniversaries are notorious for their ability to recall past traumatic events (such as the divorce of parents or the death of a parent) and to create ego diffusion in the present. While anniversaries and holidays cannot be avoided, teachers can offer extra emotional support to vulnerable children at these times. A teacher noted how she helped prepare a child for one of these difficult times.

As Christmas approached, all the kids began preparing the usual lists of what they wanted. At the ages of 10 and 11, Scott, Darren, and Mark could absorb a greater amount of reality than eight-year-old Richard. Supplementing Richard's fantasies about what he'd get was the fact that he also came from a very deprived home. I used role playing to help each boy realize that there had to be reasonable limits on what he wanted to "ask Santa" for. Richard persisted with a long list of expensive items--many of which were not even age appropriate. Talks of his dad's limited income, the cost of living, the great number of siblings, inadvisability of the gift, etc. had no effect on Richard. Scott, Darren, and Mark chipped in to make sure he got at least one present. My student teaching ended with Christmas break. I never heard the outcome but I feel certain Christmas morning was not all that Richard had built it up for.

AVOIDANCE OF UNHYGIENIC HANDLING

Absolute avoidance of unhygienic handling of children is a critical element of a therapeutic milieu. Any form of physical punishment whatsoever must be totally excluded; the use of a threat or promise to enhance the momentary comfort of the adult is out; and the children must not be exposed either to threats, fears, embarrassment, ridicule, or overcompetetive challenges. Strong displays of personal feelings unrelated to the child's current situation, exposure to anxiety-producing events or reminders of earlier traumatizing events, and adults talking about children's problems with other adults in the presence of the children also must be avoided (Redl & Wineman, 1957, 306).

Avoiding unhygienic handling of children is a challenge, as one teacher indicated.

> This component of a therapeutic milieu is one of the most difficult to carry out in the public school. At best the teacher can attempt to ensure this in her classroom. Parents, principals, janitors, librarians, policemen, etc. are beyond the control of the teacher. Personally, I also fell very short on reaching this goal. Additionally, four years at college made me, in part, a behaviorist and proponent of William Glasser's reality therapy. I don't feel my position needs defense. I stand by my behavior methods, my Life Space Interviews, and my attempts to make my kids deal with reality. I hope experience in the classroom and advanced training will help me to come closer to an actualization of this component of the therapeutic milieu.

The difficulties of influencing other personnel concerning treatment of a child are well known to many teachers. While teachers can do much through modeling therapeutic and hygienic handling and through advocacy efforts with other personnel on the child's behalf, unhygienic handling may nonetheless occur, and sensitive teachers will then have to help the child deal with it. One such episode was reported by a teacher.

> Randy had been at our school for a little more than two years. His previous regular classroom teachers and I had learned from past experiences that he found attending a structured physical education class in the gym with the other children a very frustrating, anxiety-ridden, impossible task. Randy's time seemed much better spent in another activity.
> This year, his teacher decided it was time for Randy to participate in P.E. class "like all the other children." Against my urging her not to push the issue, she decided to try to make Randy participate. When he refused to go in the gym, she tried to physically make him go in. When she took Randy's arm, he began cursing, kicking, and spitting at her. At this time, she sent another student to get the principal, who came and brought his paddle. He tried to make Randy go into the gym by threatening to paddle him. Randy still refused and began cussing the principal. The principal then paddled Randy for calling him a "bastard" and telling him to "go to hell."
> At this point, Randy began beating his head against the wall, became more aggressive, and seemed completely to lose control. He kept shouting, "I'm gonna blow up this school and

bring a black widow spider over here to kill her (the teacher)."
The principal sent for me. When I arrived, I had to help
physically restrain Randy to keep him from hurting himself.
When he had calmed down some, I took him to my room to try
to help him cope with the experience as best I could. It took the
rest of the afternoon to help Randy calm down. Several days
passed before he stopped talking about what had happened.

At some time, all children are exposed to wrong situations and to
wrong handling that can hardly be avoided, partly because of the happenings
of daily life and partly because of the imperfections of well-meaning parents
and educators. Teachers must often intervene in situations outside the school
setting. One teacher of a young child whose parents were divorced and who
had, until recently, been living with his father, reported the following
experience.

For three days Marty entered the classroom very depressed and
unagreeable. He refused to begin any academic assignments. He
would put his head down on his desk and cover up with his
jacket. I would not push him to perform. I would ask him what
was wrong and try to get him to discuss his problems. Marty
expressed anger against his father for moving in with a
girlfriend. Marty had been living with his mother for a couple
of weeks.

Marty was so upset over the matter that he could not
attend to academic tasks. He became physically and verbally
aggressive to his peers. He went into fits of shaking and
verbalized that he was possessed. His father was called in for a
conference. The staff confronted him about Marty's behavior
and accusations. The father said that he was not living with his
girlfriend. Marty was questioned in front of his father. He stated
that his mother had told him these things. His father explained
that his ex-wife had told him that to hurt their relationship. He
expressed to Marty that his love for him would never allow him
to move away and leave him alone. He told Marty that he was
welcome back in his home anytime that he was ready to move
back. Marty went back to class very calm and constructively
began work on his assignments.

If I had originally forced or punished Marty for not
working it would have only made his problems worse. He
needed love and understanding during this time of crisis.

The consequences of unhygienic handling with adolescents may be different than with younger children. Adolescents are older, physically bigger, and have had more years to build rage and resentment about poor handling they may have experienced at the hands of others. Hygienic handling is at least as critical with adolescents as with younger children, but adolescents may test limits in more provocative ways, making consistent hygienic handling more difficult. In this regard, it is important that teachers not expect perfection of themselves. All of us are human, have impulses and feelings, and make mistakes. Bettelheim (1950, 152) states that "at least as many good relations have been established by admitting our mistakes to the child, by apologizing to him, and by our genuine effort to make up for them, as were established by correct handling in the first place." One contributing teacher's story illustrates these points.

> During my first week, I had my most important learning experience of my first two years as a teacher. As I called the roll and began to learn who my students were, I was disturbed by the fact that one girl had not yet reported to class. I asked the group if anyone knew Angela. "Ooooh," they warned, "you gonna' have trouble with Angela." I did not think much about it until Angela walked in the next day. She grinned triumphantly, then threw an admission slip on my desk and sat down in a desk near the back of the room. I told her that I wished she would take a seat closer to the front so that I could get to know her better. She moved forward and engaged me in a hilarious conversation, and I thought we were going to get along just fine.
>
> The next day, she came up to my desk where I was answering a note from another teacher and she grabbed the note away from me. Without thinking, I slapped her hand as she jerked the paper away. She dropped it and her eyes became cold. She strode to the window and tore down the shade, complete with the wooden roller on the end. She ripped away the shade from the roller and held the thick dowel menacingly. She then cracked it over her knee, broke it into halves, and held each over her head. She moved closer to my desk where I sat immobilized, pretending to continue the note.
>
> Finally, after what seemed to be an eternity, I glanced up. Sure enough, she was still there, though I thought I saw hesitation beginning to replace the rage in her face. I took a chance and said "Angela, those sticks need to be in trash." After another 45 to 60 seconds, she threw both sticks toward the trash can with amazing force. I looked at her and said, "Thank you,

Angela." I then directed another student to actually put the sticks into the trash can because "Angela missed it by a little bit." The student did as I asked, and the bell sounded signaling the end of class.

Angela hung back, providing me with the opportunity to clear the air. I told her I was very sorry I hit her hand, but that I was so upset when she tried to take the note, I hadn't thought about what I was doing. I asked her to help me never to do anything like that again. On impulse, I hugged her. She seemed genuinely shocked and left without saying a word.

The next day, she came early to class and announced that she was going to be a sweet girl in my class from now on. I told her I really needed her help and addressed her as Miss Angela--(I certainly didn't want 170 pounds of solid muscle angry with me again). She smiled and said, "That don't sound right. It should be sweet Angela." After that, I called her "Ms. Sweet." She was true to her word and never did anything else that year or the following year that would require suspension. Moreover, her attitude was manifested in other classes. The other teachers remarked that Angela explained the sudden change in her behavior by saying that she was now "Miss B's sweet girl."

I never again broke the first rule of Milieu Therapy, which mandates complete protection for the child from traumatic handling by anyone associated with the program.

DEPERSONALIZED CONTROLS

Redl and Wineman (1957, 352) declared "depersonalized" controls a special relief in working with their boys. They found that whenever they could "depersonalize" the acting out a child was doing toward them, it was easier to deal with and to take less personally. This is a skill that requires learning, experience, and support. The experience of the teacher who told the following story is not uncommon.

My first experience with this phenomenon was a most difficult moment for me, because my immediate response to such expressions of fury was one of genuine surprise and hurt. The first episode of this behavior occurred when a particular boy, on an impulse and triggered by another student's comment, threw the trash can at me. He screamed obscenities at the top of his lungs, slammed me up against the wall, and fell to the floor, regressing to sobs. I was thunderstruck, because all the while I was across the room working with another student. It was necessary first to restrain him and then to hold and comfort him for a long while as he cried.

He felt badly after this and was very apologetic. He went out of his way to be helpful and cooperative for some time after that. This was my first experience with this sort of thing. It took me a while to realize it was not me he was angry toward, but that something had happened at home that morning that precipitated the behavior. He told me this later when he calmed down enough to talk it over.

I was, however, the recipient of his and the other students' anger on other occasions. Once I had experienced it I was better prepared for it and learned not to take it personally. I also learned the importance of telling them that I did not react personally to these instances, so as to minimize their guilt and anxiety. A certain amount of tolerance proved to pay off, and later some were able to learn new ways of dealing with their emotions rather than by explosions of temper and violence.

ENCOURAGING INDEPENDENT FUNCTIONING

Guiding children toward their most independent level of functioning is one of the biggest favors teachers can do for a child's self-esteem. Independence can be facilitated by offering challenging situations, but ones that are not too far away from the scope of children's abilities and control and with ample support available, if needed.

Program planners in special education are often criticized for overprotecting the youngsters and isolating them from the rest of the community. One teacher had the following reaction.

Obviously, the public school programs, by their sheer design, do not protect or isolate a child in the same manner as a residential treatment home. However, I do believe that many educators in the public school also overprotect and isolate children to some degree, especially those in special programs. I have heard fellow teachers state that "No child should experience failure." Personally I find this thought ridiculous. Life is not a continuous string of success stories. I believe that children do in fact need to experience failure--with ample support, of course. Success and failure must both be experienced so that the person can define what he experienced. How much more isolating and overprotecting would continuous success be? I feel we must teach children not to be devastated by failure and also how to avoid it.

Knowing the balance between doing too much for children and encouraging them to do more things on their own, however, is one of the most difficult things a teacher must learn. "The aim of [the therapy] is reachcd when new tools of mastery become integrated. Until they are one must shield the child from the impact of the forces that drove them to distorted mastery" (Bettelheim & Sylvester, 1949, 54). The balance between avoiding frustration and encouraging children toward more independence depends on their individual needs, strengths, and weaknesses. The situation and the environment must be structured accordingly. This is not always easy, as one teacher indicated:

> It was very difficult at times to let them try it on their own. However, if they could stand a minor defeat, I would let them try, remaining in the immediate proximity to offer support when I could. Some never reached the point where they would risk the defeat, and I protected them from it whenever possible; those who did were able to deal with it quite maturely when they did fail.

CULTURAL DIFFERENCES

Program planning also must make what Redl and Wineman (1957, 36) call concessions to sociological taste patterns, avoiding staff's "taste buds" as the guiding factor. Programs should not be loaded with too many elements that are new or gratifications that are strange to the child.

Teachers must be aware of cultural differences in children's behaviors and their meanings. For example, in some Native American cultures, "polite" children are frequently taught not to make eye contact with adults. Misinterpreted, this behavior could be labeled as maladaptive by adults who are sensitive to withdrawn or antisocial behavior but not to cultural norms. Needless to say, cultural differences must also be taken into account in testing and assessing children (Grossman, 1990, 363; Correa & Tulbert, 1991, 22).

CONCLUSION

Healthy school milieu practices can go a long way toward meeting students' needs, for the school day is an important time to help children grow and adjust. Such practices can enhance the lives of both students and teachers and are essential to students in trouble. While requiring concessions to psychological hygiene, a therapeutic milieu is more than a mere trapping--it has, by itself, a definite and tangible impact on the functioning of children.

The school atmosphere can emphasize good child care, rich personal relationships, protection from excessive painful experiences, and high expectations for appropriate academic achievement and social growth. For special educators and specialized personnel in schools--social workers, psychologists, school counselors--recognition of the milieu as a fertile field for growth and development can be extended to create a therapeutic milieu to support students who need specialized assistance. But applications of Milieu Therapy concepts need not be limited to children who are seriously disturbed or deprived--youngsters with other difficulties or those with none will also respond to environmental therapy. All students--not just those with deprived backgrounds or problems--will benefit from healthy environmental influences.

Many techniques that have evolved from Milieu Therapy are being used in public schools. These techniques, far from being mutually exclusive, are often combined to create the most enriching environment possible for each individual situation. The ability to conceptualize and implement various techniques is the key to using them successfully.

Educational theory and practice have traditionally honored the value of personal, individualized reactions to students, and this value has dominated over recognition of the power of environmental forces. Yet the influence of the environment is powerful. A balance must be achieved that recognizes this power without losing responsiveness to individual differences.

CHAPTER SIX

OTHER POWERFUL ENVIRONMENTAL INFLUENCES IN CLASSROOMS

In the last chapter, we discussed some milieu practices that can be used in classrooms. Other milieu components in classrooms should be considered. Activities must be planned for the enjoyment of the youngsters, to foster socialization and group cohesiveness, and to prevent acting out. Children have to be held responsible for their behavior, yet there must be some tolerance of behavior that does not damage people or property and of thinking patterns that are not too distorted (Reinert & Huang, 1987, 55-56). Transition times in the program and each student's frustration tolerance must be considered.

In this chapter, we discuss other ideas important in Milieu Therapy and provide examples of their application in public school classrooms. Teachers have found these additional tools useful. Topics discussed in this chapter include activities, programming, and restructuring; rules, routines, and structures; flexibility; frustration avoidance and budgeting; and timing and transitions.

ACTIVITIES, PROGRAM, AND RESTRUCTURING

Because gratification and stimulation must be available for each child in a healthy environment, rewarding programs and activities are emphasized. The environment has an impact on children through what they are allowed or requested to do as well as through behavioral restrictions. Lesson tasks, assigned readings, lectures, and required examinations do not, by themselves, create a climate for learning. Experiential learning is better promoted by instruction in which the students set their own pace, simulations of experiences and events, and work in small groups. As learning should be pervaded with personal involvement, it should be evaluated from the internal frame of reference of the only person who can truly evaluate it: the learner (Grossman, 1990, 110-111).

The very exposure of children to a given game, with its structure and demand for performance, may have considerable impact on at least the events of that day. How and where activities take place, and what structure, components, and feeling tone they have are important ingredients of the milieu (Redl, 1969a).

Activities, which are vehicles for interaction and communication, are key in the process of using a climate for growth. To make activities and programs meaningful, the teacher should consider the student's special interests and needs, structure learning tasks to the child's level to ensure success, and incorporate group projects and programs that will be motivating, potentially successful, and fun. One teacher of adolescents found a flexible pattern of activities and academic tasks.

> Although there has been little discussion in relation to academic learning within the therapeutic milieu from most sources, it is interrelated from my frame of reference. The activities were the daily academic activities followed by "free time" activities. There were also long-term projects followed by rewards at the termination of the project. I maintained an atmosphere of respect for learning and accomplishment and provided for some pleasure and reward for learning. Lesson plans were designed to use materials of interest. Though there was considerable structure, this was not applied rigidly since modifications and alterations were used when needed. There was adaptability of teaching style to fit the learning styles and patterns of the students.
>
> Through repeated experiences of success at each learning task, the students finally came to realize that the tasks themselves posed little threat for failure. These tasks were set up for optimum success at each individual's ability level. Once completed, they were followed by reinforcements, rewards, or "payoffs." This gave the students courage to try new tasks and to begin using new forms of mastery, minimizing the initial "learner's panic." Although at first the students did show some anxiety and reacted aggressively, this diminished after they experienced success at the tasks at hand.
>
> Within each learning activity there was social reinforcement. The "free time" activities were varied. Often the students would bring in games from home or albums they wanted to hear. This often worked to my disadvantage. If I were unfamiliar with the content or the rules of these new items, it

gave me little opportunity to plan the appropriate leverages to structure the activity for sublimation, honesty requirements, control of the props, etc. Usually these activities went smoothly and I would often sit in on the games until I felt the rules were understood by the group. After a particular experience with an album that a student brought from home that contained some rather inappropriate material for classroom purposes, I began more careful screening procedures of materials brought into class.

Programmed activities at school are designed to benefit the students, so they should not be included or excluded from activities simply because of good or bad behavior. But activities can, at times, produce frustrations or temptations for children. For instance, working with clay is satisfying for young children, but there is also a temptation to throw it, eat it, or otherwise use it inappropriately. In these cases, protective interference from the supervising adult is needed to keep an activity tied to its basic goals. Protective interference stops the deteriorating behavior without aggression from the adult. It is very useful to have extra adults to monitor activities that are rich in potential for excitement, and to help interfere and redirect in a friendly and supportive way before things get out of hand (Redl & Wineman, 1957, 369-370). Techniques such as those in chapter 4 are useful for this type of interference, but teachers need to be aware, when planning activities, that this is a consideration with students of any age. As a kindergarten teacher said:

> In my resource room I used the protection/interference technique to help ensure that 'educational games' truly were educational. The use of additional staff members has been very helpful in our program for four-year-olds. Four-year-olds have an instinctive knack for getting an activity off track.

Redl and Wineman (1957, 426) apply the term restructuring to the technique of abandoning the activity pattern in which the children were engaged when it became insufficient and then substituting for it a temporarily more desirable and well-matched activity. A teacher illustrated this technique:

> We attempted to have a movement experience activity to an "autumn" record. The record gave the children directions to do such things as "move like a falling leaf, pretend you're a tree in the wind, rake leaves, walk in a pile of leaves," etc. Our four-year-olds were much more interested in holding hands and running freely around the gym. After a couple of attempts to bring their attention back to the record, it was obvious we were

failing terribly. We took the record off and let the kids have free play. In the long run, it was much better for all of us.

One teacher learned through her mistakes how to provide a program structure that encouraged acceptable behavior in a special education class.

I made many mistakes before discovering the most effective structure for my students. My first mistake was to wear casual clothes that did not communicate the fact that I was serious about teaching. I learned that dresses and suits with skirts always dramatically increased student receptiveness to classwork.

My second mistake was to make visual aids like the ones I made for younger children in student teaching. My students let me know that they did not want anything to do with such obvious "special ed." bulletin boards, etc. (Other "special ed." stuff that could not be tolerated included field trips, picnics, and in-school holiday parties when regular classes were not allowed to have them).

My third mistake was to attempt to adapt materials and books designed for younger children because they were on the appropriate reading level for my students. Such books, etc. were met with a chorus of "Give that to somebody who's stupid." So I searched and found a fabulous textbook designed for the Educable Mentally Handicapped (EMH) high school work-study students and the reading level was 2B. Because it looked very adult, it was well received by all.

My fourth mistake was to attempt to give oral directions at the beginning of class. The students were never quite sure what I meant. I found that if I wrote the directions on the board in very simple terms, they would work hard to complete the assignment.

When I erred in judgement regarding structuring the class, I lost control of the class and they animatedly proclaimed that I did something "special ed." again. It is not easy to know when you have planned something that is acceptable. The easiest way to tell is that if you are still in control, they probably like it or are at least comfortable with it. Some of the more popular activities for my students were going to the library (other special ed. teachers did not take them), watching good correlated films, listening to situational tapes related to their classwork, and, on rare occasions, meeting class outside. Guest speakers from the community were popular, too. The most important factor that . . . I considered in programming was keeping the class quiet at . . . the appropriate times. I cannot recite a research article to document this statement, but it has certainly been nonverbally communicated to me by my principals these past years.

RULES, ROUTINES, AND STRUCTURES

Routines are valuable; they increase children's security in a setting. Simple routines such as a time schedule for certain tasks or repetition of the same or similar activities do, in themselves, have a relaxing, quieting, and soothing effect on children and are an important factor in ego-development (Redl & Wineman, 1957, 117).

Rules and routines are important parts of a therapeutic milieu, but they must be designed for the child's benefit and well-being. Meaningless regulations only serve to alienate children and adults, creating a sort of emotional institutionalization. Depersonalized rules and routines may lead to children's dependence in decision making, lack of spontaneity, and failure to develop inner controls. Many rules in schools are made to inhibit and regulate the impulsive behavior of children, who are told in many ways to stop, slow down, and control their behavior. While these kinds of rules are important in group settings, it is as important for children to know what they can do as what they cannot do (Long, Morse, & Newman, 1971, 442).

The number of rules that exist should be limited. Teachers and others should prioritize which rules are really important and should specify those that will result in consequences for students who break them. Too many rules can be overwhelming to students and adults alike. If rules are too numerous, they become obscure and meaningless, translating into the message for students that the only real rule is that they must do what the adult says. Such a message can result in a power struggle, sacrificing the lessons that rules are intended to teach and emphasizing only that adults are bigger and stronger than kids. When providing consequences for unacceptable behavior, it is important to let the youngster know that it is the behavior that is unacceptable and that he or she as a person is not being rejected and, to the extent possible, to reassure the youngster that his or her place in the program is ensured.

Rules and routines are necessary but are often viewed by the children as vicious inventions by nasty adults, designed to make life miserable for them, rather than as an unavoidable part of the relentless reality of life (Redl & Wineman, 1957, 290). Even untroubled children exhibit some resentment toward rules and routines, so the emotionally disturbed child can be expected to react in an especially negative manner. Rules and routines must make sense to the child and, as much as possible, the child must have a hand in making rules and agreeing on consequences for breaking them. Moreover, the child needs to understand the reasons for rules and realize that they are designed for his or her welfare and safety (Leone, Luttig, Zlotlow, & Trickett, 1990, 55).

A teacher of adolescents reports rules that she considers important.

> Fighting on school grounds requires automatic suspension for all involved parties. Absence from class is excused only by a school admission slip or other official excuse. Students who are tardy to class might bring an excuse from the office or other faculty member. Students will remain seated until they are dismissed from class.

Other teachers report rules they institute in their classes for older students.

> I don't allow sleeping in my class. If a student seems ill, excessively tired, or suffering from the effects of alcohol or marijuana, I send them to the infirmary.
>   A class rule (which initially may seem harsh) is that no one will be allowed to leave class to go to the restroom or the water fountain without a doctor's recommendation, except in urgent and reasonable circumstances. I learned quickly that if you let them go, it is difficult to get them back again. If a student insists on being excused, he must make up the length of the absence at the beginning of his lunch period. After the first semester, I usually am able to relax this rule greatly. Last year after the first semester, a particularly quick student asked to be excused. He seemed so desperate that I said "O.K." Immediately the rest of the class said "So you're letting us go to the bathroom now?" I had not thought about it, and it made me laugh to see how they called me on the rule. I explained that they had made great progress and I knew that now I could trust them to respect the privilege. And they did.
>   No drugs are to be exposed in my class. I tell my students that I will never check their person or property for drugs. However, if I see anything being flashed/passed around, I will report them to the police for possession. I am very glad that this rule was never challenged. The students seemed to think that it was fair.

Some teachers orient both students and their parents during the first days of school to their classroom rules. Presented in a positive manner so as not to be taken as a dare or a threat, one teacher uses this initial parent/student occasion to present the following rules:

> No weapons; come prepared with pencil and notebook daily; enter and exit the room in an orderly manner; tasks/homework will be attempted within the allotted time before free/trade periods; profanity will be avoided; no fighting; respect the property of others; and maintain your own work area.

Teachers must also consider their own comfort levels in the rules they make and enforce.

> In my class, nobody stands behind the teacher. It makes me very uncomfortable, and I lose a measure of control over any student I cannot see. And no one is to sit in the back of the room. Here again, I do not feel in control unless all students are close to the front of the room.

It is important that rules be prioritized and that the consequences for breaking the rules be known. One teacher said:

> Completion of homework is not critical because the student may have been academically derailed. However, some noticeable attempt must have been made. If homework is not "attempted," privileges are diminished in time-like elements--i.e., each student has fifteen minutes per day (one hour and fifteen minutes per week) privileges; these privileges are cut by five-minute deductions. The privileges include use of the tape recorder, phonograph, slide projector, modeling clay, or doing floral designs, dances, drawing, painting, or playing games.

In enforcing limits around rules and routines, actions speak louder than words. Rules and routines must also exist around the activities necessary to accomplish the primary goal in a public school classroom: learning. One teacher used the following approach.

> It was my responsibility to teach them while they were in class, and certain routines and structures were defined to minimize confusion and distraction. Rules were followed unless there was an emergency. They were expected to be in class on time with the necessary materials. Their daily lessons were always on the bulletin board the week before so they knew what to expect. There were new and different approaches to the materials, but

essentially the sequence was the same for each class period (e.g., math first hour, English second hour, etc.). Later in the year we used individual student contracts that each child wrote himself with guidance from me. In this way, each student knew clearly what was expected for the grade he wanted to earn. Special projects were included here to motivate the student to contract for a fairly good grade as opposed to a "D."

The payoffs were long- and short-term. The last ten or fifteen minutes of each class period were for "free time" activities. They were allowed to listen to records, go outside if weather permitted, play a quiet game, etc. after lessons were completed. I should say that at the beginning of the school year, the lessons were considerably shorter and the "free time" periods were much longer. I gradually worked up to more extensive study periods, so that by Christmas we had reached the desired lengths of time for lessons.

As shown by the above examples, teachers vary in the rules they institute in their classrooms. One teacher reported:

At first, the obvious rules were in effect in my class, such as no knives, no fighting or harassing other students, and no willful destruction of property. I believed that no matter how negative a reaction I observed in response to the rules at first, they all wanted and needed comfortable limits within the structure of the class. I tried to be firm and stick by all the rules. The students soon saw that I meant to abide by these guidelines. They were never punished in any physical or psychological ways, but they did lose privileges when they deliberately ignored the rules. They tested these limits constantly for the first two months.

Any adult who has ever tried to enforce limits with a youngster is familiar with the testing this teacher described. With troubled children, the testing may be even more fierce--these children have come to expect and feel they deserve harsh punishments and unreasonable adult reactions. When troubled students are new to a program, it may be meaningless to give them explicit reassurances that their actions will not lead to punishment, retaliation, or betrayal. This approach only leads to reinforcement of the youngsters' previous and existing attitudes. They will attempt to test the limits of their environment until they learn by new experiences that they may discard their old fears and already proven defenses (Bettelheim & Sylvester, 1948, 191-206).

All children will test limits to see if adults "really mean it," but adolescents will outdo themselves with this testing. Caught between childhood and adulthood, they need and "want" the security of structure, yet they resent an authority's interfering with their budding sense of independence. Adolescents who have not yet built good inner controls or who have had painful experiences with authority figures will be particularly slow to trust adults' judgments and accept their rules. One teacher recounted how she and a student discussed the student's enormous battle to reject authority figures and rules. The student told the teacher of an incident that occurred while she was confined in a residential setting. She had been in many physical battles with peers, and her counselor daily expressed the need for her to accept the rules concerning fighting. The counselor proposed a bargain, to which the student agreed; if she could maintain the "no fighting" rule for a week, she would be treated to a movie of her choice with a friend of her choice. During the last day of this bargain, she was hassled by two of her peers who had somehow found out about the movie arrangement. After the verbal abuse did not cause her to breach her agreement, the two instigators began physically pushing her from one side of the room to the other.

> At this point, she exploded. Though she tried to explain that she did not initiate the altercation, that she truly tried with all her controls to avoid striking back, and that she only struck back to defend herself, the counselor took none of her arguments into consideration. She would not be allowed to go to the movies, and not only that, but now her free activities were also suspended for a week. This was one of numerous episodes that led this girl not to respect rules or their executors. She viewed all adults to be unrealistically harsh in punishment, unfair and unfeeling, inhumane, with phony values and the lack of ability to listen. As she spoke, I saw a lifetime of hate, loneliness, fury, bitterness, and despair in her 14-year-old eyes. At that moment I wanted to hold her close and assure her that her perception of the world was grossly disfigured, but I felt that she would not tolerate such infantile treatment and remained glued to my seat.

New students in a class may upset the rule-abiding routine that has been established, renewing earlier testing of limits that had occurred. As one teacher of adolescents noted:

> One particular student joined the program well into the bottom half of the second quarter. At this point, the "seasoned" students were academically inclined (after many, many problems

and derailments). Seeing the entire class following all the rules seemed to offend this newest addition to the group. Her immediate attitude was one of hostility and defensiveness. In-class tasks were most often difficult for her to attend to. After I had gotten the group on direct course (the veterans began without hesitation) this student pulled out an album cover and proceeded to "doodle" on it. I placed my chair beside her (close enough that our shoulders touched). She pretended not to notice my presence. I began asking her about the album cover and the group it depicted. "That's my favorite group. I saw them perform last summer in Pennsylvania. Did you see their television special?", I asked very excitedly. My newest student was shocked out of her wits. Needless to say, we found our first commonalty. From this point, we began our relationship, and I was careful not to allow an interchange of roles of student/authority. But I was cautious to give her some degree of control and to show the main concern was for her and her needs.

The teacher in this incident understood that a student who gains satisfaction from a relationship with the teacher is more likely to be motivated to learn, change, and grow. She also knew that all academic work must be highly personalized to fit the interests, needs, preoccupations, and life expectations of each child. The problems of a student can often be used very successfully as a basis for beginning an academic program.

Although typical disciplinary techniques at the secondary level are detention and suspension, one of our contributing teachers soon discarded both of these with one exception; the universally unaccepted fighting in class always resulted in 3-5 days' suspension. Punitive techniques, she found, not only created more discipline problems than they solved, but they seemed to destroy the positive aspects of the teacher-student relationship.

Routines with adolescents should be appropriate for the age level of the students, though they can be as simple and structured as those for younger students. As one high school teacher reported:

The students daily must get out a pencil or pen, go get their books and folders, take out the first worksheet, and begin classwork. I then go to each student and make contact. After fifteen minutes, the class becomes teacher centered. We read orally, listen to any related audio-visual materials, and have a class discussion of the topic or related subjects. The class discussion is the most valuable portion of the class for me because of the feedback I receive from the students. It is hard at first to convince students that class discussion is "work." Five minutes before the bell, materials are replaced and students are seated for dismissal. Students have to know what to expect in order to settle down into a workable class routine. They want to know how far they can go, and what will happen if their actions conflict with the established rules and routines. It is only when limits on behavior are defined that security in the setting is achieved.

Another teacher of older students described the following routine:

Our normal day is begun with mathematics, reading, English, etc. Each subject is conducted no longer than fifteen minutes. Homework is essential to daily tasks as one automatically ties in to the other.

Some routines in the public school are determined by the administration, and a set schedule must be followed for P.E., library, lunch, and even group bathroom times. The public classroom teacher, unlike the personnel in treatment homes, often cannot demand that the mental health of children take precedence over administrative criteria. As one teacher said: "Quite obviously, the numbers are against you in the public school. Even if your classroom contains four to ten students, the 650 plus children in school outweigh the limited number of children served in a residential home." Nevertheless, teachers can control to some extent the format in which rules and routines are enforced.

FLEXIBILITY

Flexibility in rules is important. Rules that are dictatorially made and rigidly enforced may only reinforce the problems that a child is already having, whether these problems are manifested through withdrawal or acting out behavior. Teachers need the flexibility to make and enforce rules selectively, depending on the situation and the student's individual needs within the milieu. One teacher found a way to use rules and routines flexibly.

I have always tried to provide my students with an outline of what we will be doing. After briefly stating my long-term goals for them, I then focus on immediate goals. I believe that it is important for the child to know what kinds of things I have planned to help meet the set goals. I have found that children can react more positively when they know what activity will be next. (The most positive reaction can occur when the students are involved in planning the routines or making the rules that they will follow).

Sometimes children become overwhelmed if they are presented with the complete list of the day's activities; I have heard more than once "I can't do all that." But if I tell the children "after break we will divide into groups for a while, then we will all come together for music," they can handle it. They know two steps ahead what we'll be doing. They may not know that if the small group activities "bomb out" we may quickly move on to music. They do not know that, depending on their reactions to the small group activities, music may be quiet singing or an active dance session. They do know, however, that music will follow the small group activities.

Planned programming should be flexible enough to meet the individual needs and special circumstances of the child as they arise (Redl & Wineman, 1957, 318). Whatever the expected program may be, changes that become necessary must be possible at any time under all circumstances.

My students, ages four through thirteen, have always done better if I follow a daily routine. After using a routine for awhile, I presumed the children were bored and so I'd create an "upside down day." That almost seems too calm a description for what the kids go through! They can really go "bananas." It's not hard to figure out why--they are simply insecure. Whether the return to routine is immediate or the next day, it is certainly welcomed by all.

A teacher working with troubled children must be ready to intervene in a situation and give a flexible response to avoid creating more anxiety for the child. One teacher's experience illustrates how flexibility was incorporated into daily program planning for a particular young kindergarten student.

Part of my class routine every morning included what we called the "morning circle." We would sit in a circle and do some of the following activities: recite the Pledge of Allegiance, change the weather chart, recite the days of the week, and talk about special events coming up. The "circle" usually ended with some kind of group language development activity--or reading a short story and discussing it.

Most of the children seemed to enjoy this time and had little trouble sitting in their seats and attending. Randy was the exception. He did not want to participate and became very anxious and frustrated when we tried to coax him into joining the group. On the few occasions when he did sit with us for a few minutes, some kind of disruptive behavior usually occurred (kicking or hitting others, making loud noises). I decided we had to try a different approach with Randy. When we would begin "morning circle" time, I would take Randy over to another table in the room. I would give him several choices of activities to choose from that I knew he enjoyed (doing Legos, puzzles, clay). He could choose any of these activities, but he had to work quietly and not disrupt our "circle time." Giving Randy choices of activities seemed to work well most of the time. This seemed much more gratifying to him than trying to get him to join our group every morning. Later in his development, Randy often became interested in what we were doing and would come over and join our "morning circle." Even when he didn't join in the circle, he would often say something during the day that made me realize he had listened to the circle activities. Flexibility was an essential ingredient in planning an appropriate program for Randy.

Another teacher reported flexible rule enforcement based on individual needs.

The time period from 8:00 a.m. to 8:30 a.m. was used as a planning period for me. During this time I had three of my children in the room. The children could use this time to finish homework or start on assignments. This particular morning Michael came angrily into the room. He slammed the door, kicked Andrew and picked the chalk up and threw it across the room. The "tornado" hit without warning. Michael was told to go to time-out to calm down, which he did. I went into the time-out room to talk with him five minutes later and the whole story poured out. He had awakened late and the morning routine turned into chaos. His father yelled at him. He did not eat breakfast and he had to wear "this dumb shirt" that he did not like to wear.

I sympathized with him and talked for about thirty minutes. The other children had begun to arrive so my aide had taken over for me and settled them into the assignment. Michael and I ate breakfast in the time-out room together. This turned out to be a very pleasant experience. Michael and I now eat breakfast together most mornings, or at least drink juice. It gives us time to talk alone.

Another teacher illustrated the need for flexibility with some children in order to individualize the antiseptic handling called for in a therapeutic milieu.

> In our four-year-old program we have a period called "Opening Exercises." During this time, we welcome all the children, say the pledge, sing a song, learn the days of the week and then have our milk break. For most of our children this is a very enjoyable time. Their self-confidence is built as well as their skills.
>
> For William, this was one of the worst times of the day. The approach of this time brought floods of tears. While my team teacher led the class, I sat with William. Initially, we went out of the room; then, we came back into the room but away from the group, then closer to the group, then in the group with me, and finally, in the group without me. It took nearly two months, but we made it. By then, no one would ever have guessed the now-confident William had such earlier problems.

FRUSTRATION AVOIDANCE AND BUDGETING

Avoiding frustration and budgeting that which cannot be avoided is a major task for teachers in a therapeutic setting. It is essential to avoid exposing youngsters to organizational structures that are beyond their readiness and expectations that are too frustrating to their actual needs. It is also essential to take advantage of chances to gradually increase challenges and to give ample support to children in meeting more difficult and complex situations. Considering the low levels of control which many youngsters exhibit, the primary purpose of program planning may sometimes be to insert activity structures or enjoyment patterns into their lives in such ways that frustration is avoided or budgeted. Because competitions and frustration are often closely related, competitive activities early in the program should be mild with potentially satisfying and successful outcomes (Redl and Wineman, 1957, 333). One teacher described the need for negotiations with other school personnel around this issue.

> The year I had my self-contained Emotionally Disturbed class I had some trouble making the principal understand why my P.E. program could not conform to his rigid standards. Many things caused the necessary non-conformity. First of all, I had two girls out of ten kids. The boys ganged up on the girls. Then there were the two very small third-graders among the fifth- and

sixth-graders--size was an important limitation. Of course, the fact that I had only ten kids eliminated many team and group games. Most importantly, I believed their recess had to be a release of energy. Competitive games only added to the classroom problems. When my kids began "Monday night quarterbacking" yesterday's Candyland games, I got the idea that even mild competition needed to be closely monitored.

Some teachers find it difficult to balance a need for frustration budgeting on the one hand and the multiple demands of a teacher's role on the other.

We are constantly bombarded by the field representative on the latest "individual program activity" or materials that "ensure success." Individual Education Plans, Public Law 94-142, and college professors continue to convince the teacher that both individual programming and success-oriented activities are indeed necessary and beneficial. But frustration avoidance and frustration budgeting are realities in special education classes. Both in education and fun activities this idea has much value.

Many teachers use frustration avoidance and budgeting in the classroom frequently and instinctively, especially in relation to the learning process.

In order to reduce frustration in the classroom I have utilized many techniques. When Warren, Richard and others swore they could not do something, my initial response was "fine." I simply backed them up to a level at which they could succeed with sometimes nearly no effort. Then I quickly worked them back up the "ladder." This way, they experienced much success and I began to prove to them that they could do the work. The more challenging problems were meted out in very small doses. As they were successful with these small doses, I began to play a game with them. I really seduced them into doing more work by suggesting "too much of a good thing could be bad" or "we'd better not do any more" (paradoxical intention). Often this made them curious or made them want to prove to me they could go on. Of course, praise was generous as was my support. I felt very proud the day a stubborn Eddie worked and reworked a math sheet ten times--often through a few tears and outbursts--until he could prove to himself and me he was capable of "solving" on the sheet. To ease Charles' frustration with writing I would bargain, "You write two sentences and I'll write two." The thoughts and words were his but occasionally the handwriting was mine.

Another teacher used games as a way of avoiding frustration at learning tasks.

I have had various groups of lads who would "turn off" and "bomb out" if I used worksheets or task cards to teach math. So I devised a dice game to do the job. We usually had about five to six kids in the resource room at a time and I let the whole group play. Though math was never mentioned, the kids were indeed doing math. We used two or three dice, depending on the background of the group. As each child rolled the dice he had to add, subtract, multiply, and divide, or perform a combination of operations depending on the skill needed. To eliminate the connotations of math, all work was done in their heads. If their answer was correct, I wrote it down and kept a running total that served as their "score." The highest score won.
    The kids loved it. The task was one the children could do with minimal frustration and it certainly was challenging in the long run. It required them to use old skills as well as develop new skills.

Another teacher described an example of how frustration was avoided:

Randy had reached a stage in his development when I felt he might be ready to participate in a card game with other students in the class. We called it "concentration." Pairs of matching picture cards were randomly laid facedown on the table. Players would take turns, turning two cards faceup. If they matched, they could keep the cards. If they didn't match, the cards would be turned facedown again. The player with the most pairs of picture cards won.
    I soon discovered that Randy became very frustrated when he had to wait for his turn, and if he could not find a "match" early in the game. After his first or second turn, he got up from the table and began to stalk around the room saying "you made me play this dumb game and I ain't playin' it no more." I decided to try to lower the frustration level for Randy by modifying the game somewhat. I talked him into coming back to another table and playing the game with just me. We played using only five pairs of pictures, and Randy beat me. We

then played the game with one other student. We kept the number of picture pairs small (6-8) so that Randy would not have to wait long for his turn. This also made it easier for Randy to remember where the pictures were, so that he could feel successful at the game. Later in his development, Randy enjoyed playing this game with two or three students and using a larger number of picture card pairs.

I also learned that, in working with Randy on academic skills, frustration avoidance was very important. For example, if he were given a page of math problems, even though they were on his ability level, he would say, "You know I can't do them," and would get up from the table and walk away. If I gave him only about five problems to work at one time, he would usually try to solve them. Frustration avoidance seemed to be a constant consideration in planning a daily program for Randy.

TIMING AND TRANSITIONS

Other critical elements in program planning within a therapeutic milieu are timing and transitions. Activities and programs need to be well timed--neither too long nor too short--and sequenced. Consideration must be given to the type of program activity selected, the transition from one activity to the next, and the sequence of the activities. Gauging the optimum time for different types of activities and the sequence of activities becomes one of the most important parts of the program plan (Redl & Wineman, 1957, 119; 359-360).

The element of timing must be considered in terms of both individual and group psychological elements. Often it is beneficial to break down the total activity into small time units. It is imperative to maintain flexibility in order to meet emergency needs as they arise. Children's behavior often reflects the difficulty of transition periods. Because an activity has ended does not mean that the pattern in which children are engaged also stops at the same time. The main function of adults may not be to plan for the next activity, but to plan for helping children to cope with impulses and frustrations that were stirred up by the previous activities and to move more smoothly to the next activity. While transition from one activity to another can present quite a problem in children's lives, the easing of transitions is not difficult to integrate into a public school classroom. Children need to be prepared for the transition from one activity to another, and for the ending of any activity (Redl & Wineman, 1957, 361). A teacher discovered how to help young children cope with this phenomenon.

To help ease transition from one activity to the next with our four-year-olds, we always let them know what's coming and how soon. While we always alternate active and quiet activity patterns, we have found that the kids often need a couple of minutes free time--language or movement--before they are ready to begin again.

Especially with my four-year-olds, I have found that "relying on structural support" is a valuable technique. After waking up from their naps the children are often slow to respond to the next activity. We have found that having prepared examples of the activity ready for them to view will get the ball rolling. Just as I prepare them for the daily transition from one activity to the next, I prepare them for the closing of the activity. Statements like "We have time for two more songs" or "Coloring time will end when I return from the restroom" conveys this to the younger children. With older children (five and up) I have found that setting a kitchen timer provides such warnings.

Another teacher found a way to help an individual student with transitions.

Randy seemed to have a very difficult time going from one activity to another, especially when coming to my resource room from the regular classroom or returning to the regular classroom. At first, I was so engrossed in planning activities for him to do while in my room that I neglected the transition period. I did observe that Randy had an especially difficult time getting started on any task when he first came into the room. Often he would ignore requests from the teacher or aide to sit down and get started on an activity. Usually, he wanted to walk around the room and sometimes he disturbed the other students.

One morning he came in and began to walk around the room. He ignored the aide's request to "please come and sit down." He went over to Jeffrey's [another student's] table and said to him, "Dummy, look at that paper. You can't do nothin' right." They began to argue and the whole class became upset. I decided then to plan something different for the next day when Randy came in.

Because he was required to sit for most of the time in the regular classroom, I decided to give Randy a chance to move around when he came to my room. When he came in, my aide or I would take a few minutes to stop and talk with him. This helped us to get a feeling about how things were going with him. Then we would take Randy over to an area of the room where we would have two or three activities set up for him. These activities allowed him some freedom of movement, such as playing with toy trucks or cars or building blocks. After having a chance to play with such activities and "explore" in his area of the room for about fifteen minutes (sometimes longer), Randy usually was ready to sit down and engage in a more structured activity.

Even the transition of going to the lunchroom was difficult for Randy. Leaving the regular classroom and going to the lunchroom seemed to be a very difficult, frustrating time for him. He seemed to find waiting in line and eating with such a large number of people almost impossible to handle. Usually this frustration resulted in unacceptable behavior in the lunchroom. To try to help Randy cope with this situation I started going through the lunch line with him and sitting with him during lunch. The first few days we sat alone at a table near the rest of his class. Later, we sat at a table with his classmates. After Randy became more accustomed to the lunchroom setting, he was ready to go through the lunch line alone and sit with his peers.

CONCLUSION

Careful manipulation of ongoing activities for children can be therapeutic. Programming, rules and regulations and their flexible use, frustration management, and careful maneuvering of transition times will enhance children's potential for academic and social success, enabling both teachers and children to enjoy themselves as much as possible. The therapeutic potential of these arrangements seems to augur a better school experience for children and teachers alike.

CHAPTER SEVEN

ENTRY AND GROUPING IN SCHOOLS

The entry of a student into a program or classroom is a critical time, since the youngster forms an impression of the school and the people in it during the first few days. This impression will lay the groundwork for the development of relationships and the child's response to the milieu.

Once the child has entered school, considerations for the group he or she will be in will be critical to the success of the school placement. Teachers who understand how groups form, their developmental processes, and how to maintain good psychological health in groups will be best prepared to use these critical components of the milieu to advantage.

In this chapter, we discuss initial entry procedures; placement, grouping, and regrouping; group psychological hygiene; group developmental stages; group process, and group dynamics.

INITIAL ENTRY PROCEDURES

Entry time is an extraordinary opportunity to smuggle into children's experiences a notable therapeutic influence. Children often have considerable anxiety about the first days of school, and the adults' considerate handling of this potentially stressful period of time may bring relief from anxiety--for both children and adults. Here, the stage can be set to maximize for children a sense of emerging safety through the efforts of caring and supportive teachers (Tompkins & Pace, 1991).

Teachers can gain much information during entry interviews at the same time that they are orienting and reassuring new students. Issues to be dealt with during entry are: How well is the child dealing with stress and reality? What information can he or she offer about prior experiences in other classes and with other children and teachers? and, How effective were prior management and remedial efforts?

Bettelheim (1950) noted that a child initially needs some time without a large amount of pressure to feel out the people, spaces, and routines of the new environment, to gain confidence and a sense of competence in dealing with the day-to-day flow of life in that place. When a child feels anxious or threatened, overly aggressive or withdrawn behavior may result. Entry interviews can help reduce the child's apprehension about a new situation, thus helping the child to contain behavior and laying the groundwork for early relationship development. Good initial procedures have solid clinical rationale for anxiety reduction and for eliciting children's disclosures about their feelings, past experiences, and resistance to the new situation. Furthermore, the entry interview provides teachers with a means to obtain critical impressions to guide them in designing child-specific learning and behavior programs. Finally, the entry procedure, through program descriptions on rules, schedules, grouping, etc. (Tompkins & Pace, 1991), can help teachers establish clear expectations (for themselves and for the children) about new academic and management approaches.

Some initial questions or inquiries, couched in conversational style as ground-breaking overtures, may include how many schools the child has attended, the name of the last school and teacher, and the last grade the child was in. Even while gaining information, questions can be phrased so that the child is also given information and reassurance in the process, through beginning the question with a statement such as "Most kids are pretty nervous when they're starting a new class," letting the child know that they are not unique in their anxiety and that the teacher understands their feelings. Questions which find out the child's style and preferences about peer relationships and socialization strengths or vulnerabilities can be asked. Such questions, beginning with the understanding generalization discussed above, might be "In every class, certain boys and girls like other boys and girls better than others. They have friends and some kids are not their friends. Tell me who your friends were. How did they act--treat you? Tell me about a boy or girl not your friend. How did he or she treat you?" (Tompkins & Pace, 1991).

In the interview process, information also may be obtained about the child's influence, power or dominance behavior, and how he or she perceives the peer pecking-order, e.g., "What happens when you ask another kid to play a game with you or borrow something?" The child's reactions to teachers as a whole and prior experiences in relation to teachers may become obvious through questions such as "Some teachers are understanding and helpful--others are not so kind and get angry with kids. Tell me about a teacher who is nice. How did that teacher act or treat you? Tell me about a teacher who was not so nice" (Tompkins & Pace, 1991).

Initial interviews also can elicit information about how the child sees himself or herself as a pupil or learner ("What subjects did you study in your other class? How did you do? Which ones were real hard or easy?") and gives the teacher the opportunity to reassure the child about the new program and the support the child will have in it. The child's earlier experiences of discipline, what control techniques do or do not work, and what the child expects about new program discipline may also be ascertained at this time ("What happened to you when you misbehaved in your last class? What did you do that got you in trouble? What is the best way to help you stop doing what gets you in trouble?") (Tompkins & Pace, 1991).

Entry time is the prime time, too, to check the child for possessions that are disallowed in the class, such as toys or potentially harmful objects such as penknives, projectiles, or weapons. Any prized possessions can be stored for later return so the child can take them home. Children really understand this, even with reservations, and they generally comply (Tompkins & Pace, 1991).

Children (as most people) tend to do better when they know what to expect. Interviews can be closed by describing the new program, the other kids, and rules and expectations, thus eliminating some anxiety about the unknown.

PLACEMENT, GROUPING, AND REGROUPING

As the student enters the program, the question arises concerning what type of group would best fit particular needs. Solutions have ranged from letting the youngsters form their own groups (Aichhorn, 1935, 149-151) to developing a list of criteria for group inclusion (Redl & Wineman, 1957, 32) to filling whatever space happens to be open at the time. However it is managed, the importance of grouping and the impact of the group on its members needs to be acknowledged.

The group serves as the basis for the youngster's continuing ego development. Social skills are best developed in the context of a peer group. A coherent group can go far to diffuse the anxiety caused by and inherent in pathological symptoms, thus allowing the child to gain control gradually. The group's role in providing safety becomes evident when a new child threatens the group or when one of its members experiments with different behaviors. However, the reverse is also true; problems that are too similar can aggravate and accentuate pathological reactions. It follows, then, that some care should be taken in the composition of the group in order to maximize its potential for the growth of its members.

Redl and Wineman (1957, 45-49, 311) suggested that the following characteristics of children be considered in grouping and in determining the type of group leadership required: physical and social/emotional development, preferred appropriate activities, relationships with adults, sex and language sophistication, organizational maturity (i.e., understanding the nature and structure of rules and regulations), and position on a toughness-shyness continuum. Other criteria that also might be used are age, sex, self-care skills, academic level, interests, and pathology. It is impossible to match group members on all these criteria, nor should they be matched too closely, but small groups matched on several of these as well as other criteria afford the maximum control and therapeutic benefits.

Teachers usually have no control over class size. Many teachers form sub-groups within larger classes, using clinical and group psychological criteria in grouping decisions. Most teachers are aware that very often a change in the group psychological constellation does away with problem behavior. The therapeutic environment must have the possibility of keeping the basic units very small, and regrouping is, ideally, entirely dependent on clinical consideration and free from other pressures (Redl & Wineman, 1957, 423). When teachers have the flexibility for regrouping on this basis, they can use the following guidelines, adapted from Redl and Wineman (1957, 423-424).

In the first level of regrouping, the child is excluded totally from the classroom because of serious conflicts between group and individual needs. Suspension or expulsion from public school could mean placement in a residential program for some children.

In the second level of regrouping, a shift in group composition occurs within the school's and classroom's limits. One teacher provided the following example of such a shift.

> Mike's behavior problems in Resource Room A continued to escalate. He refused to work, he cussed the teacher, mocked her, as well as instigating problems among the other kids. Finally, he totally refused to go into Mrs. X's Resource Room. So opposed to her was he that he took his complaints to the principal. The principal called in the other Resource teacher to ask if she would take Mike into her class. She readily agreed, as did Mike. The next day he went to Resource Room B but he refused to work out of his folder until his new teacher personally filled his work folder that had been sent over from the first resource room. Mike finished out the year without incident in a new resource room.

A third level of regrouping is making changes within a given group. One teacher illustrated this technique:

> Our four-year-olds have assigned seats in our large group activity area. As friendships developed and behavior problems arose, we found it necessary to change the arrangement. This in itself eliminated a lot of talking and off-task behavior.

Adolescents and Groups

Among adolescents, it is not uncommon for youngsters, particularly when they first come into a group setting, to remain isolated and seemingly indifferent or oblivious to the presence and activities of others. As one teacher reported:

> John, new to the class, refused to participate with the group, even in a school-wide event that he enjoyed--the sack races. A day or so after John's decision not to help the class with the sack races, I announced that I would be the needed player. The children groaned and foretold of their defeat with me being so very "old." But, I told them, I would need a coach to work with me because I knew absolutely nothing about Sack Racing. The atmosphere of the group was one of gloom. In one of John's quiet moments of isolation, I approached him and very sincerely asked if he knew anything at all about Sack Racing. I assured him that any help he could give me would be greatly appreciated. "Yeah, I know a little . . . but I ain't done it in a long time," he answered. "Great! Will you coach me?", I pleaded. Never looking at me, John answered, "I don't care."
>
> We worked together, just the two of us, and during those precious hours we began to talk to each other for the first time. There was even a slight trace of a smile on his face when I pretended to faint when he uttered his first complete sentence in my presence. During the following days, I discussed my family. I told of disappointments, events that I thought were unfair in my family, and good times with my friends. When John realized that I had problems with my family as a teen, he became eager to listen and I saw a look of despairing agreement in his eyes, though he didn't share his own family experiences with me.
>
> May Day came. I was prepared to stand in with my group as the eighth team member. I was feeling crushed that my original plan (to involve John) had backfired. I was not supposed to be in the sack race--John was. How did everything go so badly and how had I mishandled things so awkwardly? I was a failure.
>
> It was our turn to compete. I handled myself awkwardly and could not get inside the sack. On my third try in preparing to sack myself, I fell down. A shaky hand helped me get up and out of the sack. The sack was then filled with the legs of the

owner of the shaky hands--John. Well, we lost the sack race competitions, but John and I had won.

GROUP PSYCHOLOGICAL HYGIENE

The term *group psychological hygiene* refers to the therapeutic and antiseptic management of groups. Some activities or phases of the program may be perfectly all right for most children. At a certain stage of group development, however, a specific group may not at all be able to tolerate what another group would visibly thrive on and, when presented with an otherwise desirable activity, may become acutely disorganized (Redl & Wineman, 1957, 343). One teacher described such a situation.

> During my student teaching our school had a Fall Festival Carnival to raise money for the PTA. Each homeroom was to build a booth and operate it. My four boys quickly informed me that this year they too would have a booth (previously the special education classes had been excluded). After considerable thought between them and consultation with me, it was decided that, for 15 cents a throw, persons could throw a "pie" in my face. We waited until no one was in the gym to begin construction on our booth. Their initial enthusiasm died after 15 minutes of work. As their excitement level grew, so did their aggressiveness. They began bullying each other, fighting, throwing materials, and finally attempted to demolish another class' booth. I immediately escorted them back to the classroom. They were still wild, though one might say we were somewhat "saved by the bell." The booth was finished with the help of the Educable Mentally Retarded teacher. The night of the carnival, not one of my boys threw a pie--in fact, they all actively resisted throwing pies.

This teacher reported that this was a situation every other class, kindergarten through sixth grade, dealt with fairly effectively. Her boys had felt so sure they could manage a booth that she had been willing to take the risk, yet they failed in their attempt; it was simply too much to expect them to handle the planning, teamwork, delayed gratification, and stirring up of aggressive impulses that goes into such an event.

Group psychological hygiene may work in a more positive manner, however.

Richard was without question the class scapegoat. Being two years younger than Mark, Scott, and Darren, he somewhat inherited this position rather than truly deserving it. Seemingly the older boys never took Richard or his feelings into account. However, the Christmas season brought about one change. Mark, Scott, and Darren took up a collection among themselves to buy Richard a Christmas present. The reason, they stated, was "poor little kids like Richard--even if he is a jerk--deserve a Christmas present. The kid's not old enough to know the truth about Christmas--he expects Santa to come." None of them told Richard "the truth about Santa" nor did they laugh at him. In fact, they even helped him compose a letter to Santa. Is this a miracle of Christmas?

Principles of individual antisepsis (see chapter 4) may also be applied to groups for effective group management (Redl & Wineman, 1957, 343).

GROUP DYNAMICS AND GROUP PROCESS

Groups are a reality in life and people are influenced by groups. Social productivity, so essential to cultural survival, is increased through informed group processes. Group interaction not only channels individual effort but also, through full personal commitment to a shared project, becomes in itself a dynamic experience. Group experiences can help individuals develop cooperation and self-reliance, greatly aiding in the development of socialized personalities. Groups afford opportunities for release, sublimation, the use of the self through creative experiences, and the defining of ego-strengthening goals. Situations in groups also may be structured for moderate or graduated frustration, reality testing, and the promotion of self-awareness, both through the interaction of the members and by the leader's interpretation of the behavior displayed. Children as young as five or six years have been able to verbalize the meaning of acted-out behavior and to assimilate this experience (Hamilton, 1961, 19-20; Dupont, 1989, 6-7).

Groups definitely influence their individual members. It is by group experience that individuals become socialized, take on norms and values, and learn behaviors and life-styles. Groups affect one's identity and self-concept and one's attitudes and beliefs. In groups one learns not only facts but empathy, sympathy, and support for problem-solving approaches. Behavioral change also may come about as a result of participation in a group.

Each individual interacts with other individuals and groups through various cultural influences as well as within physical and economic conditions, so that learning to function in groups becomes a primary learning experience for children. The first group of influence for a person is the family, and each family is a group with particular qualities, producing expectations in children that carry over into the classroom group (Luft, 1970, 81). Schools often contain the next primary group experience for children.

Group Dynamics

Group dynamics is the study of behavior in groups (Luft, 1970, 1); it does not tell us what a group should or should not do, nor does it advocate doing things in groups. However, an understanding of group dynamics can aid teachers in answering questions such as: Are disciplinary actions related to group behavior? How can I communicate more effectively with my class? How can I get my students to learn more?

A group may be thought of as a developing system with its own unique structure, organization, and norms. Teachers can recognize group qualities that characterize the way pupils work and can speculate about and experiment with what it is that teachers do to enable the group to become more independent and more interdependent (Luft, 1970, 79-81).

Teachers, too, are influenced by groups. They should learn to recognize the development and power of group norms, the social and personal obstacles that groups might place in the way of learning, the teacher's power as a group leader, and the evolution of status and roles within a classroom group.

Developmental Process of Groups

It is useful for teachers to understand the process of how groups develop. Knowledge of the process is helpful not only in understanding what is at work in classrooms throughout the year, but in facilitating the positive influences of the group.

When a group first comes together, the most common interactions are social rituals and pastimes. This is a period of testing the expectations that individuals bring to the situation, and restlessness, tension, talkativeness, laughter, and withdrawal are common behaviors. Members are trying to find out where they fit in and are sizing up others. This phase may be shortened if the group leader mentions areas in which all present share concerns and focuses on the purpose for which the group is gathered. It may be helpful for the group to have some simple task requiring cooperation on which they can focus but which is only vaguely related to the purpose for which the group has gathered. Some tolerance during this phase is required, too, since efforts to move the individuals too soon to a more cohesive state may cause the group to lose motion and direction (Hartford, 1971, 74-77; Redl & Wineman, 1957).

Once the people who are in the group have begun to discern common purposes or goals, they begin to take on significance for each other and develop trust. At this stage, the group defines itself as an entity apart from other groups, with expectations, role systems, and patterns of behavior emerging. Now, the honeymoon is over and testing escalates. Negative social and emotional behavior, interpersonal conflicts, withdrawal, scapegoating of members (or even the leader), and expressed resistance to group influences and task requirements may occur. Defenses begin to be lowered and group members may become disenchanted with each other and with the amount of personal autonomy they will have to sacrifice in exchange for group membership. Members may have to focus on what is happening to their interpersonal relationships, their development as a group, and their capacity to work together before they can get on with the tasks of the group. Much time may be spent attempting to redefine tasks, establish rules, and redirect behavior. Redistributions of power, control, and competition for leadership may be issues. The Life Space Interview (see chapter 9), combined with an understanding of what is happening in the group, will be useful here. The leader (teacher) may confront group members with the nature of their conflicts or help them understand the naturalness of this phase so they can get back to work on tasks. If group leaders (teachers) are unaware of this natural phase in group development, they may become alarmed by it, but by bringing conflicts to the surface for resolution or finding small and attractive tasks that members can complete together, the leader may facilitate moving through this phase. It is helpful, too, if the leader can hold firmly to the stated purposes and help group members to work through or redefine tasks. The group then will move to a higher level of integration (Hartford, 1971, 77-84).

The next phase of group development is when the group settles in to accomplish its task. In this period, the group culture, style, way of doing things, and norms of the group are established and become observable. Members refer to the group as "we" and seek agreement from each other on issues and approval from each other in their activity. "The way we do things in this group" is clearly expressed in behavior.

Just when the group seems to be solidifying, a radical change may take place. There may be a strong forward thrust toward integration, or there may be conflict and disintegration, followed rapidly by reintegration or termination of the group. This "integration, disintegration, or reintegration" phase is often startling to those who do not know that this is a natural and expected phase of group development (Hartford, 1971, 84-87).

The final critical developmental phase for a group is termination of the group. There is a period of pretermination--when everyone knows the group will end (school will be out) and is preparing for it. Characteristics of this phase include group members trying to find ways to avoid or deny the reality of the ending, an upsurge of clinging together, working more enthusiastically on group tasks, rejecting the group or its leader, abdication of responsibility, excessive absenteeism, and regression to previous stages of group disorganization. The phenomenon of separation anxiety may appear in the group, with members blaming each other for bad behavior or lack of contribution (since it is so much easier, though not healthier, to leave a group when one is angry). The final separation may reactivate feelings of loss and abandonment from other life experiences and expectations that the leader will somehow hold the group together (Hartford, 1971, 87-93).

If the group leader emphasizes positive and negative summaries and evaluations of the group experience and helps its members deal with feelings--both good and bad--about the group, members often are better able to accept the separation and to resolve their relationships within the group, releasing control over each other and working on their relationships to each other rather than on group tasks or problems. Successful termination experiences in a group can help its members face endings appropriately, prepare them for the other inevitable terminations that may occur, and deal with feelings of grief and sadness upon future endings (Hartford, 1971, 92-93).

Personal Influence and Power in Groups

Personal influence is as powerful as the interpersonal relationships in any group. As people become involved in subgroups of two, three, or four, group members may acquiesce to the more dominant, influential, or aggressive members of the group. As groups form, group members may turn to each other for cues or approval, or be responsive to the "proverbial kick under the table from friend or colleague" (Hartford, 1971, 267). Interpersonal patterns emerge within groups, whether they are due to feelings of attraction or repulsion, interest alignments or antagonisms, and these patterns exert strong natural controls on individuals and subgroups and ultimately on the operation of the entire group (Hartford, 1971, 267-269).

Personal influence and power in groups are often reflected in behavioral contagion--the picking up of behavior from a person by others in the group. Group members of high status are more likely, intentionally or unintentionally, to cause others to imitate or "contage" their behavior: because people want to emulate those that they think have more prestige or power in the group than they have, they take on behavior, values, and life-styles of the status-holders. Persons thus influencing the behavior of others may not recognize the great amount of power they have. The stronger the group cohesion that has developed, the more the total group may be affected by the contagion factor of one or more members (Hartford, 1971, 267; Redl & Wineman, 1957).

Dealing with Groups

There are many different ways of reducing tension and resolving conflicts in groups, and a teacher may sense which method would be appropriate under which circumstances. One teacher might be able to change the group atmosphere by postponing lessons and asking the class to describe what happened in the group and what they feel about an incident so that everyone can share their reactions more openly and move toward alternative behaviors; (see chapter 9 about Group Life Space Interviews.) Another teacher might achieve equivalent results by suggesting that pupils join in smaller groups so that they can work and talk more informally and more freely. Children frequently work out their own problems of interpersonal relations and may be encouraged to do so within limits established by the teacher.

A class can participate with the teacher in setting goals and establishing structure, in developing its norms for behavior, and in finding its channels and means of communication. A group may need to build or reduce tension, which is related to strength of motivation. A group may need to test the limits governing its behavior, and to test its teachers and its other leaders before it trusts them. A class as a group may need to make its own mistakes--to learn by its own experience as well as by the experience of its teacher and the recorded experience of others (Luft, 1970, 85-86).

The teacher's task is to develop an atmosphere conducive to new group perceptions. Teachers who are sensitive to group cohesiveness will be able to balance the student's need to be accepted with the pressures on the student to conform to the prevailing code of the group.

CONCLUSION

A teacher's keen awareness about initial entry procedures and essential group issues increases the teacher's control of a classroom situation, allowing him or her to use to maximum benefit those common situations in classrooms. When teachers understand the states of mind with which most children enter schools, the anxiety accompanying the formation of a new group, and the predictable processes through which groups will move, they can better respond to these situations in a healthy and productive way, appropriate to the maintenance of a therapeutic milieu.

CHAPTER EIGHT

MILIEU INGREDIENTS OUTSIDE THE CLASSROOM

The classroom setting is but one of four primary milieu settings for a student. The others are family, neighborhood and community, and other school staff. Each has specific functions. The family's functions have traditionally involved socialization and caretaking of children, and decision-making. Child rearing, a major family function, consists of appropriate degrees of protection (but not overprotection) for children, consistent--firm but fair--discipline, and meeting children's physical and emotional needs. Other family functions include providing emotional and interpersonal gratification and basic security for family members, responding to crises threatening the family group, and interacting with the communities in which they live.

The stresses on today's family are monumental and well documented. Many families are failing in some of their basic functions. Unrealistic expectations and excessive dependency needs intensify parents' competitive strivings with their children to get needs met.

The neighborhood and community roles are broader and less personalized than the role of the family. Functions include maintaining a way of life or culture, satisfying common needs and goals, reflecting and instilling social consciousness, and meeting the environmental needs of the community. Families in trouble may perceive the community as a hostile force, thus failing to identify themselves as part of the community.

Inside school systems, the necessary ingredients for a wholesome school climate are numerous (Sullivan, 1987, 48; Essex, 1982, 22-31), extending far beyond the classroom. Principals and other staff can influence teachers' stress levels as well as the child's response to the classroom teacher's efforts, heavily influencing the total school environment.

While each of these primary environments is of critical importance to children, there are often conflicts between them. Families may hold values that clash with those of schools and communities. Schools may want communities to support them more than the communities are willing to do.

Schools may want families to do things outside their natural value systems. Not everyone involved with the child at school will understand all that operates in the therapeutic milieu and other staff at school may make this ideal hard to achieve. But, for maximum success, parents, teachers, and other adults in the child's life--both in and out of school--should be responsive to milieu enhancement techniques. Concerned teachers are caught in the dilemmas of these conflicts and in the stress of broadening their roles to meet children's needs when family or community functions fail.

FAMILIES

In spite of all the disruptions in modern society, "the major supporting [or diverting] agency in the child's life is still his family . . . . What should it provide? Love, security, concern, models, care, and systematic training" (Cheney & Morse, 1974, 307).

Children will respond to therapeutic attempts at school more readily if conditions at home permit. Maximum progress is made when parents agree with the program and support changes their children may make. If this is not the case, the growth that the school milieu can help to promote may be quite limited as children struggle to apply what they learn at school to their daily life at home.

In the past, without conclusive evidence about what caused mental disorders, there were many psychological theories concerning family causes of mental disorders. Freud developed the theory that neurosis was a result of early childhood experience and his followers had no hesitation in blaming early caregivers, chiefly the mother, for the child's problems (see, for instance, Fromm-Reichmann, 1948; Bateson, Jackson, Haley, and Weakland, 1956; and Wynne & Singer, 1965). Some proponents of Milieu Therapy in the 1950's saw the child's trouble as based in the way the parents had interacted with the child in early life and advocated that participation of parents should be limited in programming for disturbed children placed in residential settings (Bettelheim, 1950). But in recent years, much of the thinking toward families has changed. Families of mentally ill persons have come to be seen as involved, not as etiological agents, but as important factors in managing the lives of troubled persons (Tompkins, 1989, 18).

Troubled Families

If the child does respond to milieu efforts and begins to change, family reactions may be negative due to the unconscious needs of the family for the child to remain the same in order to maintain the status quo of family dynamics. Thus the child may find it difficult to continue responding to the school milieu without threatening his or her role in the family (Kemp, 1971, 229-235).

The aim of therapeutic milieu is reached when the child integrates new behaviors that are more acceptable than old ways, yet earlier patterns that were reflections of emotional and psychological upsets may be reinforced by the family. Patterns of behavior that the school expects may contrast drastically, even violently, with the family situation, putting the child in a vulnerable position at home.

As the child learns new ways of being and behaving but finds them not accepted in the family situation, confusion usually follows. Teachers and other school staff should be aware of the implications for the child of changes that are encouraged or demanded at school. Children's families are important to them, and to expect children to develop behaviors that defy family values may be asking too much. One teacher described the inherent difficulties.

> Within my range of home visitations (which were the only way I could personally meet with the parents after the initial meetings), I was dumbfounded at what I saw, heard, and felt. I witnessed physical brutality within the family; verbal abuse; support of stealing, lying and cheating; wit versus wit; infantile immaturity in parents, etc. All of these elements clearly stated to me that my children would probably be "eaten alive" if they reformed to the social or survival norms of the outside world.

Another teacher of children with serious disturbances said:

> In the case of my students, ten highly aggressive pre-adolescent children, many would have benefitted from a therapeutic milieu in a residential setting. They came from home surroundings that were undesirable and only added to their emotional problems. Those who were in the most need were from homes where parents had neither the desire nor the financial means to provide their child with a more effective or treatment-oriented environment. The overwhelming feeling of frustration I experienced after long efforts would be sabotaged by interference from parents . . . is hard to describe.
>
> For example, I had worked with one particular boy trying to establish rapport and trust, and did accomplish this. He needed extensive tutoring in science, was threatened and uncomfortable in any testing situation, and up until that time had not passed a single test in his class. He reached the point where he would avoid testing altogether by not coming to school at all. I somehow convinced him that if we studied

together, he would be assured of knowing the material and doing well. He agreed to this, and after two weeks of tutoring, he took the test and received a C. I was elated and he was very proud of himself. Our bubbles burst when his father's comment was "Why didn't you get an A?" This occurred after I had called the boy's parents to tell them before he arrived home and encouraged them to praise him for his achievement. I was back to step one again.

Scapegoating in Families

Some families are indeed difficult. While, on the one hand, families may have been scapegoated and blamed because of their children's difficulties, some families reflect what is truly a pathology in the family system through the scapegoating of a child. Family theorists have developed a considerable body of literature regarding families who label a member as the deviant one (Haley, 1971, 295-297). There is evidence that the processes that contribute to producing dysfunctional family structures are the same ones that produce important developmental deviations in children, giving rise to symptomatic adaptations in the children's behavior that allows the child to be labeled as "the sick one." When family problems are overlooked or ignored by mental health professionals who focus on the child and define the child as the problem, the dysfunction of the family is reinforced (Berman & Lief, 1975, 583-592; Barragan, 1976, 232-247).

One teacher described her observation of a teenager scapegoated in a chaotic family situation.

John's Individual Education Plan had to be signed so I took this opportunity to make a home visit and observe. When I arrived, John and his older brother were in the field walking. His younger sister rocked the baby under the carport. When I spoke, she got up, gripping the baby tightly, and went into the house, closing the door behind her. For a flashing moment, I resented her rudeness; then, I remembered John and all of his unsocial surface behaviors. Just as I walked to the door, it opened with great force. There stood John's mother apologizing for her daughter's behavior. In the very next second, John and his older brother were standing beneath the carport.

I directed my greeting to John. He spoke but only moved his lips without any sound. Without seeing John's lip movement, the brother immediately began verbally abusing him for not speaking. With a small audience and enormous embarrassment,

John physically struck his brother. The mother stood yelling for them to stop or she would "beat the hell" out of both of them. They ignored her. The sister then pushed the baby into the mother's arms and began scrambling between the two brothers. During this free-for-all, the mother proceeded to tell me how John is always getting into trouble and/or making trouble. She seemed to be oblivious to the fact that this altercation was initiated by her older son. I finally realized that for John to exist in his environment, he had been forced to some degree to arm himself with arrogance, hostility, untrustfulness, hate, and frustration.

The adaptive nature of children's deviant behavior is often not recognized. Children who are labeled as behaviorally deviant are usually involved in tensions in families, and the adult members of families, the parents, often project their conflicts onto the child (Haley, 1971, 296). This projection enables adults to maintain a relationship that outwardly appears reasonably harmonious, but the cost to the child's development is great.

The role of scapegoat increases the contrast between the child and everyone else in the family (Vogel & Bell, 1960, 382-397). Some chance characteristic of the child that differentiates him or her will cause the child to be singled out for this role, which may take many forms: "the mascot, the clown, the sad sack, the erratic genius, the black sheep, the wise guy, the saint, the idiot, the fool, the impostor, the malingerer, the boaster, the villain, and so forth. Literature and folklore abound with such figures" (Haley, 1971, 69).

The child who is the scapegoat may mediate conflict situations in a family through developing symptoms that flare up when there is a crucial family disagreement, particularly arguments between parents. Then the parents can divert themselves from a true but threatening conflict between them and unite around their common concern for the child (Haley, 1971, 298-299). Designating a scapegoat may keep a precarious family system from collapsing-- often, when a seriously disturbed or abused child is removed from a family heavily engaged in scapegoating, another "target" child will be chosen to be the one who is "sick or bad" so that others in the family may continue to feel that there is nothing wrong with them in contrast. This continued transference of group difficulties onto an individual is self-reinforcing, and the family never becomes aware of the true nature of its dysfunction.

Positive Family Involvement

Schools run the risk of subtly undermining parents by implying that their child-rearing practices and parental attitudes are inappropriate. While truly troubled families may not contribute to solutions to children's problems, it is also true that teachers are prone to identification with the children they teach, quick to judge values different from their own, and prone to assume that, with "better parents," children would be better off. This attitude denigrates the potential contributions of families and also denies the absolute importance of families to children.

Teachers are not trained to work with families nor to understand the complicated family dynamics, but they can be aware that even when the family situation is so bad that children must be removed, families of origin greatly influence the child's self-esteem, behavior patterns, and other deep and enduring factors. To identify families as "bad" and alternative situations as "better" tells children that a deep and irrevocable part of them is bad and that some of their deepest feelings toward their families of origin are "wrong." How much better to acknowledge all the feelings children have toward their families, including the good feelings, and to help children accept their parents' limitations and problems as well as strengths.

Many parents of troubled children have been unduly blamed, and some are understandably defensive. Schools must recognize that parents often know as much or more about their child as "the experts"; they are intimate with the details of the child's day-to-day life and may be much better attuned to what may be effective with a child than are people who have known the child for a shorter time. Frequently, when parents are involved as equal team members, they can contribute to the child's treatment, education, or both far more than might have been imagined (Vaughn & Leff, 1976, 125).

Most public school children live at home, and now, with P.L. 94-142, it is mandated that parents be included as part of the interdisciplinary team that plans programs for a child with handicaps. Many school personnel are finding that family members are not only benign, but can be extremely valuable members of such a team. Once communication lines are opened and barriers broken down, many parents who were previously seen as "hostile" or "bad for the kids" have contributed invaluably to solving problematic situations at school concerning their children.

Keeping parents involved can strengthen healthy ties within the family, provide schools with valuable information for planning children's programs, and help schools address some behaviors that the family finds distressing. By encouraging parents and other family members to visit classes and interact with staff, it is possible to clarify a family's misconceptions, fears, and tensions regarding both the child's progress and the program itself.

Kameya (1974, 159) is among those who have indicated that parents are potent agents in the maintenance of adaptive behaviors and the modification of maladaptive behaviors. Teachers should involve families in planning programs, especially for modification of a child's behavior, and there should be built-in generalization of the program to the home setting.

A teacher reported the following situation.

Mat was from a broken home. He would move back and forth between parents when he couldn't get his way. His mother was an alcoholic. She tried to initiate problems between Mat and his dad. Mat's father had custody of him. He appeared to be Mat's stability. He genuinely expressed his best interests for Mat. He cooperated with the school officials and followed any suggestions for treatment of Mat's problems. When Mat stayed with his mother, he was depressed, slept in class, argued with classmates, refused to work, cursed, and threatened suicide. When he stayed with his father, he completed his assignments in each class, came to school regularly, and kept a calm disposition. The mother had never met with the school; she had not received therapeutic counseling for her son. It made a big difference in Mat's behavior and performance when he lived with the cooperative, secure parent.

"Many disorganized children need to be structured and 'glued together' daily" (Crow, 1975, 513). One contributing teacher tells of such a child.

John was an abused child. He was not prepared to take his spelling test one day and was suffering severe anxiety over it. As my aide called the words out to him, he became more and more upset, almost to the point of tears. My aide stopped the testing and informed John that she would help him study and then he could take the test again later. I wrote a note explaining to the parents that time had not permitted John to take the test and that he could take it next week.

John had explained to my aide that his stepfather had told him he must make a hundred on the test. John was afraid that he would be beaten if he failed.

The parents sent me a note the following day requesting John's spelling grades. I replied that John was experiencing a lot of frustration with his spelling and I would like for them to come for a conference to discuss the issue. A regular sixth-grade teacher and I collaborated over the idea of placing John in a lower spelling book to reduce the difficulty level. John's parents had originally maintained that he must perform on grade level. The sixth-grade teacher had found a lower-achieving series that was on grade level. She and I met with the parents and presented the suggestion that John's vocabulary was more on that level and the words would be easier for him to understand.

The parents agreed that the words were becoming more difficult and somewhat nonfunctional for John in life. Since the book was on grade level, they agreed to the change.

John was an overly anxious child. He talked continuously in class. He cheated. He lied. He was overweight. He wasted time in class. He had to be coaxed continuously to complete his assignments. He had limited mental ability. He was extremely impatient when he needed assistance. He could not accept being asked to wait his turn. He was a difficult child to have to deal with on a day-to-day basis. Yet, he needed "tax-free love" and understanding. The day after the parent conference, John entered class smiling and hugged my neck. He said, "Thank you for putting me in that spelling book."

Strategies in Working with Families

The teachers cited above have given examples of ways they worked with difficult families by using their intuition and caring for their students. Home visits or other family outreach efforts, an integral part of early childhood education for children with handicaps or those at risk, have become a part of some schools' procedures with other students as well. The literature from social work and from early childhood education for children with disabilities, for example, will help with approaches to families for teachers of children with and those without disabilities.

Basic principles of interpersonal relationships are important in any attempt to involve either healthy or troubled families in the school lives of the children. In addition, such vehicles as parent discussion groups, parent counseling, conferences, parent-volunteer programs, informal parent gatherings sponsored and organized by the school (potlucks with food and social time seem particularly successful), "open houses," and parent training can minimize the distance between the child, the school, and the family. If teachers are not in a position to facilitate such groups, ancillary school personnel such as school social workers, can be called on to help. Training programs that offer alternatives to families for handling problem behaviors can go far toward correcting any family processes that might contribute to the dysfunction of the child.

Here are some questions that schools must ask in order to maintain good-faith efforts for positive family involvement. Are families included in meaningful ways in planning for their children? Do schools share with families strengths of the child as well as problems and consider the family as a prime leader of the interdisciplinary team seeking solutions? Are families' phone calls returned? Are their questions answered? Are they referred to resources outside the schools to help them solve other problems that are not directly school-related but may be affecting the student's school life as well as other aspects of his or her life? (adapted from Tompkins, 1989, 15-16).

Successful family involvement is a broad topic in itself, but the point to be made here is clear: families are a potent and important part of a child's environment, and successful inclusion of family members in therapeutic milieu programs will greatly increase the chances of the child's success in a program. Even when the therapeutic milieu is created in the public school classroom and the parents never set foot on the grounds during school time, the influence of the family must be recognized. In such a situation, engaging families as allies in understanding of and consistency in approaches to a child's problems will prove invaluable.

COMMUNITY INFLUENCES

Some children in schools come from families that are alienated or detached from community life or that are not sufficiently organized or purposeful to help the child develop a sense of identity with the neighborhood, the town or city. These children have little opportunity to discover that communities exist for people and, while the fit between the two may often leave much to be desired, an important part of education is for children to learn that community agencies and institutions exist for their welfare (Hobbs, 1966, 1105-1115).

The therapeutic milieu approach offers many possibilities for the educator. As the main "engineer" in the classroom, a teacher can develop a therapeutic milieu to help buffer outside influences. Contact with the child's larger environment--the community--can enrich the child's experience and help him or her learn to deal with the problems of reality that exist there.

There should be continuous collaboration between all concerned with children's welfare: schools, families, and those in the community. One teacher gave an example of this in an extremely serious case.

> Dan enrolled in my class upon release from a private psychiatric hospital. Personal contact with the staff of the hospital supplied information about behavioral progress, academic grades, and expectations of Dan's ability to cope in his natural environment. The local mental health center released information assessing the family's present status. His physician assured me of the correct dosage of medication he should be receiving at home and at school. Social Services released previous records of reports of physical abuse. Routine conversations with the parents provided insight into the current home situation. Involvement of all these people helped plan and regulate Dan's

therapeutic program and make it a success. Coordinating information between the hospital staff, parents, physician, social worker, and psychologist supported Dan in returning to his natural environment. He enjoyed school. He was able to achieve in the self-contained classroom. He functioned with compliance in his neighborhood.

PUBLIC SCHOOL STAFF AND THERAPEUTIC MILIEU

Even the best-planned program can fall on its face if the staff with responsibility for carrying it out is inadequate or inappropriate. Staff must be compatible with the basic philosophy of the program and with each other to facilitate communication and a sense of team effort. Their attitudes, personal warmth and maturity, the relationships they establish with the students and with other adults in the life space of the children, their gentle firmness in setting limits, and their ability and willingness to handle critical incidents that occur all contribute heavily to the making of a positive or negative experience.

While some teachers, by nature, possess the qualities needed to be a good, "natural" teacher (Hammer & Kaplan, 1967, 35-36), paper qualifications of personnel can belie their suitability for classroom duty in terms of personality, temperament, and basic philosophy. If principles of therapeutic milieu are to be adopted in the school setting, compatibility with this philosophy should be considered in hiring.

In a healthy environment, staff members show a sense of responsibility, an interest in children, spontaneity, a sense of humor and appreciation of the humor of others, and a desire to help children have fun. The best teachers are characterized as warm and concerned people who are able to relate in empathic and consistent ways to build students' trust and offer them acceptance and affection. Such teachers demonstrate, through their behavior, sensitivity to students' feelings and concerns. They are interested in what may be interfering with children's normal desires to learn and their healthy curiosity about the universe. They are in tune with individual relationships between members of the group, developmental issues, and the group processes of coming together in pairs or subgroups that occur in a child's life space on a day-to-day basis (Symonds, 1954; Brown, Yeomans, & Grizzard, 1975; Swift & Spivack, 1975; Morse, 1985; Long, 1986).

Good teachers are well trained and educated, able to be both firm and flexible. They nourish their own private resources for the refreshment of their own lives, have a sense of the value of today and the promise of tomorrow, and they are persons of hope and joy, committed to the belief that children with problems can be helped (Hobbs, 1966, 1106-1107). They are able to instill in others a feeling of comfort and security. They are self-assured and authentic--not mere role players--with clear identities. They understand confidentiality issues and adhere to them while maintaining the ability to interpret the program to the school at large and to the community. These qualities in teachers enhance children's security in learning new behaviors and attitudes (Hammer & Kaplan, 1967, 35-36).

Flexibility is a key criterion for staff. Regardless of what the planned program is, the staff must be ready for a change when the needs of the child or the clinical situation call for it (Redl & Wineman, 1957, 295; Grossman, 1990, 94-95). This characteristic of a therapeutic milieu is adaptable to the public schools, as earlier discussed. An extra person or community of people, willing to "pitch in" when needed, is very helpful, as one teacher pointed out.

> Having always been able to have an aide, a team teacher, or a student teacher, I have had little trouble in moving from a large group to a small group activity or vice versa. The extra set of hands is great in quickly setting up the next activity or in dealing with crises. Changes in routines outside of the classroom may be a bit more difficult to maneuver as there are other persons to consider. In emergency situations I have found that, in general, people are willing to help.

Children pick up on adults' sensitivities and biases and some will use this intuition to test teachers and their limits. It is important that staff be prepared to depersonalize taunting or acting out behaviors. The ability to maintain objectivity is also necessary in order to avoid overidentification among staff, and to allow for refueling and refreshing oneself when off duty. Self-aware teachers are reasonably free from the influence of personal needs and anxieties that distort perception. They have "emotional antennae" that are keenly sensitive to subtle cues conveyed through tone of voice and body language. They are in tune with verbal and nonverbal, cognitive and affective messages, opening possibilities of communication which otherwise would be closed. Such awareness enables the teacher to directly experience his students--to receive and transmit intuitively (Boy & Pine, 1971, 8).

Teamwork

Teamwork among staff can enhance the positive aspects of the school experience, but this is sometimes difficult in a school setting. Teachers sometimes feel they receive little help from their peers (Fimian, 1986, 49-53), as one teacher reports.

> How petty public school teachers can become. At our school, one teacher does not even talk to children in another's class.

Classroom doors stayed closed lest another teacher peek in and, heaven forbid, copy an idea. Some teachers would rather die than give another teacher credit on a job well done. I have found the special education teacher is often caught between a rock and a hard place on this issue. She breaks her neck to make the kids like the resource room and then must face the fact the other teacher resents that their kids "prefer" your class over the regular class. It's ironic that they usually do not like the special ed. kid to begin with, so why worry over where he's happiest?

A teacher of exceptional children relates how children with problems can be scapegoated by staff within a school setting.

In the public school, children in special education are the definite minority. The public school staff, in general, often seem to resent their presence. I found it very difficult to drum up much, if any, staff support in working with my kids. Everyone highly values kids who conform. If my kids could have conformed, they wouldn't have needed my special class. Obviously, the public school teacher has no control over the hiring of the rest of the faculty. For better or, usually, worse in terms of treatment, they are already there. Due to the nature of my kids' behavior, literally everyone at school could identify them. Consequently, much bias against my children existed.

Heavy doses of affection were generally a prescription only I would fill. The staff was not accepting of the children being served. They were equally unaccepting of my methods of treatment. During my first year of teaching, my children misread the faculty's reaction and turned the situation into a very positive experience.

My nine kids were very preoccupied by my "youth." Eddie and Gary never missed a chance to tell me, "You're too young to be a teacher." They were also embarrassed by my atypical ways of handling a class; my comments of "I really like you kids" and "No matter what you do, we're all here together-- no one is going to get thrown out"; my establishment of and consistent implementation of rules; and my rapidly growing conflict with the principal. Eddie was often heard to say, "Poor dumb teacher, all the teachers are laughin' at her." Then they'd laugh. But, almost before I realized it, they were going along with me. It was as if they were so ashamed to have a teacher this different that they were trying to save face by making me look o.k. Whatever their motives, we had quickly established ourselves as a group in the game of US v.s. THEM.--a confrontation in which no one wins.

Interdisciplinary and Transdisciplinary Approaches

A wide variety of services is necessary to help seriously troubled youngsters, leading to more specialized roles for school staff (Weintrob, 1974, 604-611; Bower, 1990, 15). School personnel working with children without such serious problems can learn something from the approaches taken in specialized programs. The people who take responsibility for the youngster must have well-defined roles in the program. Clear roles give the child a framework from which to develop expectations for each of these people and the staff a framework within which to operate. Frequently, teachers must play many necessary roles, such as child care expert, liaison between program and family or community, and others. However, there are always other people involved--perhaps a school social worker or other ancillary personnel such as psychologists, and speech, physical, or occupational therapists, aides, and others. An interdisciplinary or transdisciplinary approach, with family members and all relevant staff involved, is most successful and certainly most in keeping with the intent of P.L. 94-142 and other state-of-the-art legislation and thinking.

Teachers must feel that their work with children can be coordinated with that of practitioners of other disciplines and that it has the full support of the hierarchy from direct supervisors through principals, superintendents, and the school board. This approach requires certain qualities from all members of a staff. The principal or superintendent must set policies, rules and regulations that are consistent with a healthy philosophy and must have knowledge, imagination, and skill in dealing with adults as well as children. The therapist or school counselor must be able to communicate with other members of the staff as well as with their young patients. The teacher must be able to recognize the meaning of the child's behavior as well as attending to his or her intellectual development. The social worker interacting with the parents needs to understand the total educational plan in order to make possible the development of a healthier milieu for the child at home and also to help teachers and other staff in understanding the emotional and cultural environment of the home.

Not only every professional person but also every nonprofessional and support person should be involved in coordinated program efforts. Meaningful insights between colleagues are fostered and possibilities for program success are optimized when all the people involved are aware of the daily activities of and challenges to the students and when they share a general understanding of program techniques. One contributing teacher described such a program.

Nancy and I worked closely together on a daily basis. She was hired as my aide, and ideas and information were exchanged freely. John, a second-grader in our class, refused to follow class instructions. He was an abused and neglected child. His mother had arranged for him to take karate, which strengthened his violent behavior. John was on a behavior modification program to reinforce appropriate behavior and academic achievement. Daily progress cards were sent home for privilege restrictions. The cards were color coded, signifying what kind of day John had at school. Specified points were allotted for fairly good, excellent, and poor behavior. The program was explained to his mother and John prior to initiation. Privileges were allocated for fairly good and excellent days, and all privileges were denied on poor days.

Nancy and the psychologist spent periods of the day with John alone. Cooperation and collaboration between us was crucial for John's daily points. Regular consultation with the mother was necessary to make sure she was following through with privileges and restrictions. A progress chart was posted in the classroom to encourage peer support and develop intrinsic reinforcement. John's bar graph showed the need for assessment of his mother's duties or an upgrade in reinforcers. The program proved of value in John's behavioral and academic achievement.

Consistent response among staff is important in reinforcing appropriate behavior and discouraging inappropriate behavior. One teacher indicated the importance of such cooperation.

Ernestine and I worked closely together in a self-contained classroom for behaviorally handicapped boys. Ernestine was my aide. Rules, techniques, and teaching methods were practiced in unison to ensure treatment effectiveness and security for the students and to develop trusting relationships. Periodically, each student would try to manipulate us. The cohesion of our strategies prevented any divergence from the rules and instilled an overall acceptance from the boys. All of the boys made impressive behavioral and academic gains within the school year. The home base schools were impressed with the students' progress.

Another teacher also testified to the effectiveness of staff cooperation.

Mike was a self-destructive 14-year-old. He was explosive and irrational. He hung around an older crowd that was into a lot of drugs and alcohol. Mike was expelled from another school for possession of drugs on campus. His behavior got him into trouble constantly. The assistant principal, guidance counselor, in-school suspension teacher, and I all understood Mike's problems and worked toward minimizing attention toward his explosive acts. Our intent was to keep him in school, where he could receive therapeutic treatment, and off the streets, away from drugs. It required symptom tolerance of his behavior and antiseptic handling of unacceptable actions. Mike relied on all of us for help during these times when he would lose control. Mike continued to have good and bad days, but the bad days became fewer and far in between.

Stress and Staff Performance

Occupational stress has been implicated as a primary cause for burnout. Excessive demands on staff energy, strength, or resources can lead to loss of concern for the individuals under one's care and to distancing between oneself and those one is responsible for (e.g., less time is spent with individuals, there is insufficient eye contact during interaction, and an almost callous attitude toward the needs of individuals--sometimes including "blaming the victim"-- may develop).

Student-related factors such as high student to staff ratio; long hours of direct contact with the children, especially those with "behavior problems"; and lack of administrative support in dealing with difficult children have been related to job dissatisfactions (Tompkins, 1980; Weiskopf, 1980, 18-23; Fimian, 1986, 49-53). When hoped-for progress with children is not achieved, teachers feel stressed. Concentration on the child's problems and on unrealistic goals, rather than on progress or success within the relationship, causes feelings of failure and low self-esteem. Teachers also find that their role of providing a group of students with emotional support for five to six hours each day can be draining (Tompkins, 1980, 141-160).

On the other hand, Patricia Tompkins (1980, 141-160) found that factors not related to students caused the most stress among teachers of both handicapped and non-handicapped children. Such things as paperwork, meetings, poor facilities, conferences, counseling for parents, contact with other professionals, and teachers' feelings of inadequate training for the job were most often cited by teachers as stress producing. Teachers seem to go into the field because they want contact with children, and they can tolerate large amounts of stress during this contact.

Some measures can be taken to prevent or alleviate occupational stress among school personnel. After hiring, orientation is important for all new employees to familiarize them with the concepts through which the milieu will operate. Orientation may include a meeting with the principal or director of the program to describe the school's history and founding patterns; therapeutic and educational concepts and objectives; personnel policies, responsibilities, practices, and benefits; and inservice opportunities and communication channels. Facilities should provide a thorough and accurate job description and an opportunity to get to know the individual children and their degree and type of handicap.

Staff must learn to set realistic goals for themselves and the children in their charge. Staff/child ratios should be kept reasonable, and ancillary personnel, such as aides, paraprofessionals, and practicum students, can be assigned to some nonteaching tasks. Time spent in direct contact with the youngsters can be interspersed with other activities--while routine and repetition are essential for progress with children, there must also be room for creativity on the job (Weiskopf, 1980, 18-23; Fimian, 1986, 49-53).

Expanding the support base for teachers in public school need not be complex or extravagant. Some supportive strategies include: providing opportunities for support groups that accept feelings of colleagues; teaching stress reduction techniques; reinforcing realistic expectations among administrators; increasing knowledge and skill bases; giving teachers some degree of control in the school environment; and providing positive feedback (Tompkins, 1980, 141-160; Fimian, 1986, 49-53; Lauritzen & Friedman, 1991, 14).

Role of the Principal and Other Administrators and Supervisors

A school principal is in a key position to mobilize the school's resources and stimulate long-term planning (Morse, 1971, 6-7). Any program is heavily influenced by its director, whose personality, teachings, and philosophy will influence every aspect of it. In public schools, the principal functions as director and is critical to the achievement of a healthy environment, influencing the whole tone of the facility, including staff, programs, and the physical setting.

Effects on Staff

There is a relationship between the behavior of an administrator or supervisor and teachers' perceptions of stress and burnout. The principal controls potent reinforcers for school staff. Fatigue resulting from "hassles" with administrators can lead to teacher resignations. Simply acting as advocates for children places some teachers in danger of verbal reprimand or even being fired. Administrators' and supervisors' incompetence, lack of availability, lack of support in solving problems, or poor communication skills increases stress upon teachers (Fimian, 1986, 49-53).

There is evidence that stress levels among teachers are strongly related to the degree to which the teachers receive on-the-job administrative, supervisory, and peer support. Support from competent administrators can moderate teacher stress levels, enabling them to function better physically and mentally while reporting greater well-being and fewer stress symptoms (Fimian, 1986, 49-53; Algozzine, Ysseldyke, Kauffman, & Landrum, 1991, 7).

Teachers alone cannot be responsible for creating a wholesome environment within the school. Principals can play a supportive role by instituting some of the practices previously discussed and by initiating joint staff and parent planning for unified school policy, coordinating staff efforts to achieve better service delivery, and supporting viable and relevant curriculum. Carefully structured and high quality supervisory practices by the principal are essential to teachers, fostering a healthy climate.

A most critical function of the principal is as backstop to the teacher. Teachers have said if pupils know there is a principal who will really work problems through so teachers are not left alone to their own devices, that principal is less often needed. But if pupils know there is no one to do anything beyond the teachers, they test the system again and again. The principal should support staff while creating a fair, viable milieu for all children, including those who disturb the staff most intensively. This can be done by taking the role of mediator and problem-solver when staff difficulties in working with problematic pupils require highly specific or individual planning and school changes (Morse, 1971, 34-37).

Effects on Children

Troubled children frequently involve principals with them. Often a first response to an acting-out child is a trip to the principal's office. The processes and outcomes of such visits are as diverse as the principals who inhabit the offices. The principal can advance ideas of Milieu Therapy through carefully designed surroundings that contain mediating elements to help the student learn better methods of coping with internal and social problems (Morse, 1971, 5-6). In successful alternative school programs, many principals are able to recognize a child's anxiety and begin a helping process. But unacceptable behavior frequently results in corporal punishment or action to suspend or expel a student, and many students have learned to regard the principal as the school disciplinarian.

Successful principals are not biased--they believe that all students can learn and that improvement is possible. They provide rewards for individual achievement, knowing that when feelings of being valued prevail there is less likelihood of disruptive behavior (Harris, 1987, 46).

Flexibility, innovation, and a positive attitude toward change by the administration and staff facilitate program effectiveness and increase student satisfaction. Strong and supportive leadership by the principal in establishing a healthy climate influences the attitudes and behaviors of students as much as do attitudes and behaviors of teachers (Sarri, 1982, 5). It is essential that teachers and administrators be aware of their own perceptions and possible prejudices about children to ensure their effectiveness as positive role models (Riester & Bissette, 1986, 12-20).

The peer climate is an additional concern: the code for "what goes" in overt and covert social behavior is a principal's task to establish. An effective principal is one who sees the patterns of problems and ascertains which are those from within the pupils and which are produced or increased by the school (Morse, 1971, 19).

Conditions that look similar to the outsider may in reality be very different to the pupil. For example, children do not always behave in the same way in two different classrooms. The principal's contribution as an educational expert should be to provide a broad picture of both social and emotional problems that can come only as a result of seeing the whole school milieu. The principal has the skill and the authority to examine the psychological impact of the particular school environment for each child and to unmask ambiguous conditions so that appropriate changes can be made (Morse, 1971, 15). The goal is to reduce that portion of child disturbance produced by a negative school environment. This involves oversight of school personnel concerning their willingness to talk with youngsters, work out conflicts whenever possible, and recognize students' points of view even when their behavior cannot be accepted or their wishes honored. In creating a positive environment, it is also critical to have teachers who neither overtly nor covertly reject pupils; the principal is the one who has to set and clarify standards of child acceptance to protect students (Morse, 1971, 18).

Effects on Milieu

Some classrooms and schools have maximized their milieu to provide a rewarding, humanized school life, but the vast majority have a long way to go (Morse, 1971, 4; Paul & Epanchin, 1991, 232-233). How fast they move is a matter of the leadership of the principal (Morse, 1971, 4), Unfortunately, lack of responsible leadership, especially for chronically disruptive youth, is prevalent in public schools, and one cannot always count on sterling qualities in a principal or other supervisor. Some teachers have found ways to deal with this situation. One teacher described her approach.

> Within my classroom, the best I often could hope for was that every part of my classroom supported the treatment process. Direct teaching of alternate reaction patterns was utilized to negate damage from external influences upon the children.
>
> I had a principal who loved nothing better than to come in and remind my children how bad they were and how no one cared about them. He then would add, shaking his head, that Ms. X (I) was dumb enough to think she could help them--that I was their last resort. Needless to say, this increased the kids' level of agitation against the principal. Often they entered into name-calling, obscenities, physical aggression against each other, and mocking of the principal. After such an incident we would discuss their feelings and mine. I conveyed to them that I too detested this type of behavior from the principal; however, I was powerless in stopping it. I told them that as a group we would have to learn to ignore such comments.
>
> I expressed that this is often very difficult, even for me. I also reassured them that while not everybody cared, I did, and so did some of their parents, our student teachers, and their friends.

The school needs an authority who will commit time and energy to planning whatever is appropriate for integrated work of the specialists and regular personnel for the benefit of the students. Being "tough" or "soft" should not become a role function. Some problems require strong structure and stringent requirements; others do not (Morse, 1971, 6-7). Principals need to be environmental diagnosticians for determining influences on pupils. They serve as the interface between special services and regular education.

CONCLUSION

"The psychological mortality and limitations of school programs should be recognized as stemming from a complicated set of variables, only one of which is the teacher" (Morse, 1985, 315). Teachers cannot by themselves sustain a therapeutic environment, and children cannot bear the entire responsibility for changes in their behavior. Children's lives and experiences are profoundly affected by significant others in their overall life space, including parents, school staff, supervisors, principals, and those in the community.

At school, the major supporting agent in the child's program is the teacher, supported by the school principal and other staff. Organizational dynamics, including teachers, supervisors, and principals, must be considered, and the behavior of staff should be seen as an essential agent for change in children and the programs that staff institute as part of the overall plan for improvement (Thomas, 1982; Apter & Conoley, 1984; Wood, 1982; Nelson, 1983; Brown, Copeland & Hall, 1972; Copeland, Brown & Hall, 1974; Sullivan, 1987; Essex, 1982). At home, the major supporting agent in the child's life is still the family, supported by neighborhoods and communities. School leadership, teachers, community agents, and families are crucial to the changes and growth that we desire to facilitate in children (Morse, 1985, 180-181).

CHAPTER NINE

THE LIFE SPACE INTERVIEW

All children and youth, at some time, will feel overwhelmed by their feelings. All will need help with clarifying perceptions, connecting to feelings, with self-control, learning new skills, and protecting themselves from the manipulation of others (Wineman, 1959; Redl, 1959a; Fagen, 1981; Merritt, 1981; Apter, 1982; Brendtro & Ness, 1983). All can use assistance in more personally and socially desirable ways of dealing with problems (Reilly, Imber, & Kremmens, 1978; Bloom, 1981; Tompkins, 1981); in improving academic and social performance (DeMagistris & Imber, 1980); and in increasing problem solving abilities rather than acting on impulse alone (Naslund, 1987).

School personnel cannot afford to wait to learn about causes of disturbance before intervening in children's problems. When children are confused and overwhelmed, something must be done *now* (Redl, 1969b, 112-113)--at the time of the problem and in the immediate life space of the child. The Life Space Interview (LSI) was developed by Fritz Redl as a way of handling life conflicts of children constructively and close to the time and place that conflicts occur. This way of talking with children grew out of Redl and Wineman's work with seriously disturbed boys at Pioneer House and provided a supportive, therapeutic way of responding to the boys' problem behaviors throughout each day as they occurred (Reinert, 1980, 58; Kauffman, 1981, 138).

Students and teachers regularly encounter crises in schools. Crises are time-limited periods when usual coping capacities are weakened, anxiety is high, and the homeostasis (balance) of an individual or a situation is upset. During a crisis--a traumatic event, a new external situation, or stress occasioned by a developmental stage--adaptive capacities are overwhelmed.

A period of crisis is either an opportunity or a threat to the individuals involved. Crises are often the times when people are most open to learning (Wood & Long, 1991, 3) and ready to accept help. As crises are resolved, a person either develops more adaptive modes of life response or regresses into increased defensiveness. Crisis periods are not the time to study and explore underlying causes of problems; immediate help is called for to restore balance and to prevent further problems (Compton & Galaway, 1975, 95).

The Life Space Interview is a non-threatening means of verbally responding to actual or potential crises as well as a tool for providing children with self-awareness (Cullinan et al.,1983, 1-2; Paul & Epanchin, 1991, 437-439). The LSI is in keeping with the underlying assumption of Milieu Therapy that many important opportunities for therapeutic intervention occur at unscheduled moments (Westman, 1979).

Here is a summary of a Life Space Interview conducted by James Tompkins (1981, 26-28).

> Bill was in a rotten mood and his friend Joe came by and flipped him a "bird." Bill jumped up and punched Joe in the ribs. Suddenly the two were in a violent fight filled with screams and kicks. The teacher yelled for them to stop and grabbed Joe while another teacher held Bill. Ten minutes later they were in the conference room, controlled enough to talk about the incident. Bill's interpretation was that Joe was asking for a beating. He had taken Bill's prized pen, cheated in Monopoly, tripped him in the gym, and called his mother a name. He deserved to be punched out, and he was lucky the teachers broke it up or Joe would be a bloody stump by now. Joe's perceptions were entirely different. He had an explanation for each event. "It's true, I gave him the 'bird', but what's the big deal? We do it all the time. It's like saying hello. I don't know what got into Bill today. We usually get along, but today he acted like a crazy man." Bill's angry response was, "For a week you've been picking on me, and I should beat you up four times instead of one time!" After some review of the sequence of events, Joe seems to understand Bill's feelings, but Bill continues to stick to his story--"Joe got what he deserved!" The teacher sends Joe back to the room and begins LSI with Bill to confront his unacceptable behavior.

In the first chapter of this book we briefly defined the Life Space Interview and described its value in school settings. In this chapter, the Life Space Interview, its component parts and objectives, and their corresponding therapeutic values are described in depth. Examples are given for the various kinds of interviews that may be done in public schools. We also discuss here considerations and guidelines for conducting a LSI and important characteristics of the interviewer, and we summarize the appeal, advantages, and limitations of the technique.

WHAT IS THE LIFE SPACE INTERVIEW?

The Life Space Interview is a way of talking therapeutically with an individual child or with groups of children in times of crisis. It can be used to intervene in children's inappropriate behaviors or simply to deal with those behaviors that show, in one way or another, that a child is in pain. It helps students to understand and cope with conflicts that they cannot handle on their own (Wood & Long, 1991, 106). The LSI is conducted by an adult who is a part of children's natural environments and, if possible, by someone who has observed the event around which the interview occurs. If the adult has not been present, the crisis event can be reconstructed by the child or others so that the event is recreated. The LSI takes place as soon as possible after a behavioral crisis occurs, and, if possible, in the same location as that incident.

The LSI is designed to take care of an immediate behavioral incident or crisis and to gain what is possible in therapeutic communication with the child without waiting for the therapy hour. The interviewer acts as mediator between the child and the environment (Shea, 1978, 275). The interview conveys to a child that problems can be solved, that the interviewer is the child's advocate, that the child has the potential to develop the skills needed to solve problems and deal with crises, that the adult sees the good qualities in the child, and that though the student must exercise constraints in behavior, he or she is valued by the interviewer as an individual (Wood & Weller, 1981, 61; Wood & Long, 1991, 106). Because the LSI deals with both behavior and affect (i.e., the outward expression of feelings), it provides a means by which children can be helped to understand the results of their thinking, feelings, and actions. It can affirm their feelings, help them in understanding the inappropriateness of the action that followed the feeling, and finally, can move them to the consideration and adoption of more appropriate alternative behaviors (Gardner, 1978; Apter, 1982; Paul & Epanchin, 1991, 437-439).

A Life Space Interview can clear anxiety interfering with children's enjoyment of or participation in an activity, warn children of a possible outcome that they may not foresee, help them understand the reasons for their actions, or explain a piece of behavior in another person that they seem to have misunderstood. The LSI can also be used to help free children who are blocked to engage in important solitary activities or social interactions. It helps children toward more reality-correct activities and is also used to head off behavioral incidents by defusing situations before they escalate.

When a problem already exists, the content of a Life Space Interview involves identifying the specific problem as perceived by the child (what happened?), exploring why it happened, clarifying distortions to establish what really happened, and developing a plan for things that can be done to prevent further difficulties (Carek, 1972, 185; Morse & Wineman, 1957; Redl, 1959a; Morse, 1963, 1965; Long & Newman, 1965; Brendtro &

Ness, 1983, 177). The child's understanding of the event and his or her feelings that evoked the behavior are first explored. Then the reality of others' reactions to the behavior is pointed out. In the process, focus shifts from the incident itself to an understanding of more basic issues underlying the event that the student is not aware of or cannot easily express. Finally, problem exploration moves to problem solving, with the adult and child exploring ways to deal with both the immediate incident and the more basic problems relevant to the event. Specific behavioral steps are outlined that will allow more constructive responses to future stress (Wood & Long, 1991, 7-8).

USE OF THE LIFE SPACE INTERVIEW

The type of children around whose treatment Life Space Interviewing was first developed find it virtually impossible to manage themselves for long without the eruption of behavioral episodes that indicate their disturbance (Wineman, 1959, 3). However, the techniques can be applied to any child who needs assistance in everyday situations.

The idea that normal and healthy children don't need any therapy is basically correct. The further assumption that being normal and healthy also means freedom from the danger of being overwhelmed by the complexities of life is a naive illusion. Most healthy and normal kids are equipped with a considerable amount of resilience. They can handle many experiences that would send their more disturbed compatriots into psychotic blow-ups or neurotic convulsions. This, however, does not mean they can manage all of them. Take any child no matter how well endowed, how healthy, how wonderful, even in the best conceivable classroom. At some time during some phase of his life he will find himself in . . . predicaments in which he will need an adult to stand by. Indeed, during such a time it will make a lot of difference just how well this adult handles himself in this task. (Redl, 1963a, ix)

Redl (1963a, ix-x) elaborated that children will need assistance from the adults in their environment in two general circumstances--when they are overwhelmed by confusion or conflict from within and by experiences and events from without. All children, from time to time, find themselves overwhelmed by internal factors such as rage, fear, shame, fury, embarrassment, anger, or fear of consequences; or by life situations such as the birth of a sibling, loss of a friend, or death or divorce in the family. Even ordinary events such as that painful period before an exam, first disappointments (betrayal by a friend, ridicule from a hero), or a performance before an audience can bring on temporary problems for children during which they will need support. During the onslaught of such experiences, normal youngsters are much more similar to the legitimately disturbed ones than to their own normal selves. The same child who can listen respectfully under ordinary circumstances may be hard to reach while in tears, sulking, or overly excited. The same words, phrases, and looks that may ordinarily work well with a particular child will not do the trick in such crises.

Long (1963, 723-725) pointed out that adults living and working closely with children get to know them very well. Their characteristic pattern of avoiding pain becomes evident. Some children run away; others become ill, develop irrational fears, or experience profound guilt over imagined acts. Some children become aggressive, experience little guilt, and blame others for their troubles. Children are usually unaware of their own patterns in dealing with frustration and have little motivation to change. The LSI, however, can help make these patterns conscious and thus can help relieve the symptoms that the patterns produce.

Use of the Life Space Interview with Groups

Bloom (1981), Redl and Wineman (1957), Morse and Small (1959), Paul and Epanchin (1991), and Wood and Long (1991) are among those who have suggested that LSI techniques can be used to help solve group issues as well as individual problem behaviors. Examples of issues for group discussion include social realities that prohibit group desires, methods by which members can admit mistakes and misdeeds, and ways of identifying common problems and reaching mutually acceptable solutions. Wood and Long (1991, 106) used the LSI process frequently with two or more students when they had been involved in the incident precipitating the intervention or when one student had played a central role in a crisis but the group had been involved.

Use of the LSI with a group emphasizes both group and individual responsibility in maintaining an effective group (Wood & Long, 1991, 106) and is useful in organizing group functions, solving group problems, reinforcing group values and expectations, setting up and maintaining a healthy group perspective, and creating awareness of group progress (Morgan, 1981, 37). Group LSI helps children participate in group discussion and problem solving, interact appropriately with peers, respond positively to group leadership, express feelings in a group, respond to group suggestions, respect others' opinions and values, and understand interactional nuances of group situations (Wood, 1979, 1982).

Since group relationships are typically tentative, volatile, and potentially destructive to individuals if psychological hygiene in the milieu is not maintained, the use of the LSI with a group mandates that the adult take and maintain the controlling role. Behavior from group members such as face-saving and posturing for peers is characteristic (Wood & Long, 1991, 106).

Group LSI may occur after individual LSI, or the interviewer may choose to begin with group LSI and follow up with one or more individual LSIs, depending on the circumstances involved. If it is unclear who the instigator, perpetrator, or victim of a situation is, beginning with group LSI may help to clarify the situation and to identify those in need of individual LSIs (Wood & Long, 1991, 106).

With certain groups, however, complexities of group dynamics (see chapter 7) such as group contagion and anti-adult pressures make application of the LSI very difficult or at times impossible.

Considerations Before Conducting a Life Space Interview

The following factors should be considered before initiating a Life Space Interview.

(1) Is there sufficient time? LSI can take 30 seconds, 30 minutes, or more, depending on the goal of the interview. It need not interfere with group or individual activities. The interviewer should be able to make an educated guess about the depth of the interview needed and whether a one-minute intervention will be effective or a more extensive time period may be needed. Thirty minutes to an hour may be needed for in-depth Clinical Exploitation of Life Events.

(2) Is the child in the right frame of mind? The child must be psychologically ready to enter the discussion--neither too upset nor having put the problems out of his or her mind. Do not begin a full-fledged LSI (Clinical Exploitation) if a student is out of control, but instead use behavioral controls or Emotional First Aid.

(3) Is the interviewer in the right frame of mind? The interviewer must be in control, not overwhelmed by the situation or his or her own feelings, to conduct an effective interview.

(4) Is the setting appropriate? Private matters should not be discussed in public, and confidentiality should be protected. Too stimulating an environment may prove distracting.

(5) Is the issue closely related to other issues the child is presently working on? Targeting too many issues at once may dilute the power of the interview.

(6) Is the issue one the child is prepared to understand? The issues and problems must be within the range of the child's conscious understanding and dealt with during "teachable moments," when the child is ready to understand (Redl, 1959a, 1-18; Wood & Long, 1991, 153-154).

Guidelines for Conducting a Life Space Interview

There are guidelines to follow in conducting a Life Space Interview.

1. Be polite. Offer the child a chair or tissue, if needed. Try to avoid interruptions and apologize if they occur. Don't interrupt the child. Don't answer your own questions.
2. Don't tower threateningly over a child; kneel or sit so that eye contact is established. Have child-sized furniture for small children.
3. Have reliable facts and information and tell the child what you know about the unacceptable behavioral incident. Ask about and listen to the child's impressions about the problems without demanding the child to know his or her motivations. Focus the interview only on the incident.
4. If the child is overwhelmed by guilt or anxiety, try to help him or her reduce these destructive feelings. Encourage him or her to verbalize the feelings; give sympathetic, supportive responses. Assure the child that the feelings are not unusual--that everyone has such feelings at times.
5. Help the child plan how to avoid or improve similar situations in the future. Find out (by asking) how you can help him or her with the plans.
6. Let the child ask you questions.
7. Do not use physical punishment, blame, disgust, or sarcasm. Be considerate, kind, and respectful. Be fair and impartial. Never twist or distort facts, even if it is painful for you to confront them head-on.
8. Weigh the significance of the truth from the child's point of view and the point of view of others involved in the problem. Explain or share these insights with the child (Bernstein, 1963, 41-43; Wood & Long, 1991, 158-191).

Finally, Wood and Long (1991, 186-187) summarized major principles in using LSI. These include: maintain a positive relationship and two-way communication with students; acknowledge the child's goodness and good intentions consistently; convey respect and unconditional acceptance through words and tone of voice, even if you can't approve of the behavior; stay calm and in control of the LSI and the situation; avoid unethical manipulation of students in order to get a confession; give solutions equal time to problems; help students to frame solutions in their own words and to describe, for themselves, the behaviors they will use to move toward solutions; visualize and communicate changes that will produce good results for the child; decode and push for greater insight, when appropriate; and, let the child know that, when the interview ends, that is not the end of communication--that the two of you will talk again.

The Interviewer

The purpose of a Life Space Interview is to teach, not to punish, the child. The role of the adult conducting such an interview is crucial. The interviewer decides the interview goal, based on an understanding of the child's recurring problems and assessment of needed behavioral change. Interview goals may range from keeping the program or classroom intact and maintaining the child in the group to using a situation for a clinical purpose for one child. The interviewer controls the pace of the interview and decides when it is over (Wood & Long, 1991, 153-154).

To talk with a child in moments of strain may require an approach more similar to the work of a clinician than to the usual task of the classroom teacher (Redl, 1963a, ix), but the LSI is most often conducted by a teacher, principal, counselor, parent or other adult who is on the scene and perceived by the child to be an important part of his or her life space (Redl & Wineman, 1957; Wineman, 1959; Heuchert & Long, 1981; Heuchert, 1983; Wood & Long, 1991). Crucial to successful interviewing is a positive relationship with the child. Successful interviewers have the capacity to relate to the pupil without becoming defensive or counteraggressive. The empathetic potential that the adult has in working with children--that subtle capacity to see through and relate to the deeper feeling, rather than reacting to the defensiveness of the child--is necessary to make the interview effective (Long & Morse, 1965; Bloom, 1981; Heuchert & Long, 1981).

Self awareness and self-control are essential to adults who will successfully use the Life Space Interview. In moments of strong emotion, the central goal of the adult must remain to help the student rather than to express personal reactions--to detach from one's own needs and channel energies into resolving the problem at hand (Wood & Long, 1991, 158). It is essential that adults stay in control while conveying objectivity and concern about the crisis and remaining sensitive to the emotions and personal issues of the child (Wood & Long, 1991, 14).

Successful interviewers adjust their language to a level that children can understand. They convey an empathy with children's need for protection (from embarrassment, ridicule, hurt by others, violation of privacy, or failure), and their requirement for gratification (the hope that things will get better and experiences will bring pleasure). Further, adults teach responsibility by considering the group as a whole and by restraining natural impulses to take over or tell students how to handle problems or solve crises (Naslund, 1987, 14; Wood & Long, 1991, 14).

Because there are many children whose difficulties surface only during crisis situations, an understanding of each child's view of the self and the world, coping behaviors, and defense mechanisms is important (Westman, 1979, 288-299; Morse, 1981, 67-70). It is expecting too much that the child would be aware of his or her own temptation to "buffalo" the interviewer; thus, the interviewer, through insight into the child's behavior, thwarts this temptation and avoids the trap (Morse, 1985, 213). An understanding of the child's history with other adults is also important, since children tend to respond in crises as they have learned to do in the past (Wood & Long, 1991, 73). Clues in decoding the child's behavior and comments may be gained from knowledge of the child's history and will help to direct the interview successfully, avoiding breakdowns in rapport and reinforcement of the child's manipulative tendencies. Issues of authority (who is in charge; adult or child?), responsibility (who must design a solution to the crisis?), and safety (assurance that the personal needs of the student will be considered) will all be apparent in both historical and current situations (Wood & Long, 1991, 73).

LIFE SPACE INTERVIEW TECHNIQUES

The Life Space Interview may be done for two basic reasons--either to provide the child with ego support in emotionally laden circumstances and episodes where children's control is precarious or to exploit the child's crisis-laden behavior for some educational or clinical insight. In keeping with this dual purpose, there are two major components of Life Space Interviewing: Emotional First Aid on the Spot and Clinical Exploitation of Life Events. These can and should be used flexibly, considering the child's needs and the interviewer's goals. These categories are not mutually exclusive, and the process for interviewing does not always occur in orderly steps. Interviewers may find themselves going back through earlier steps, combining therapeutic goals, or not completing all steps as they are described in theory. They may find good reason, even in the middle of an interview, to switch from the original intent of the interview to another focus (Redl, 1963b, 64; Long & Morse, 1965, 12-13; Wood & Long, 1991, 154).

The adult on the scene must decide whether Emotional First Aid or Clinical Exploitation is most appropriate in a given situation. It is difficult or impossible to know in advance which of these to use; frequently both objectives may be pursued in a single interview. The choice of which tools to use lies not so much in the nature of the event around which the need for the interview arose (i.e., "the issue"), but in the decision about what the adult wants to do with the issue and how he or she wants to use it. If the adult wants to help a child by disentangling a complicated web of emotions in which the child is caught and "get the child over it" so the child can continue with an activity, Emotional First Aid on the Spot is the technique of choice. No long-range goal is intended here; the purpose is to help the child over the rough spot so that he or she can go on. On the other hand, the interviewer may take the opportunity to help the child come to grips with an issue in his or her life that so far has not been brought to awareness (Redl, 1963b, 63-64;

Tompkins 1965, 24). Determination about whether to move into deeper clinical exploitation should be based on understanding of the child's patterns, time available, and receptivity of the immediate situation to such insight.

Teachers must decide quickly about how to react to children's difficulties and what interview strategy to use. For example, a group of children is about to go on an anticipated trip. Everyone is excited! There is a delay because of a futile last-minute search for a lost wallet. Group impatience and irritability surge and the children begin bickering, pushing, and hitting. One child curses the boy who is looking for his wallet, swearing he will never go on this trip or any other one in his whole life. Never! Now the child is screaming, nurturing his grudges about everything and tallying up new evidence that life is rotten and people are mean. He is nearly out of control. The teacher must decide, then and there, to repair the situation for the child to go on the trip with quick first-aid-on-the-spot, or attempt a much more complicated clinical exploitation Life Space Interview. The teacher may decide to use this opportunity to start an interpretational interview and relate this current event to many similar ones involving this child in the past, or to patch it up and get on with the trip (Redl, 1963b, 63-64).

Most teachers who do Life Space Interviewing will spend most of their time using Emotional First Aid techniques, which, when effectively used, can contribute to decreasing the need for Clinical Exploitation and the amount of time needed to solve serious problems.

Emotional First Aid on the Spot

Students often need help and support when their defenses become ineffective and they are overwhelmed by feelings in a crisis. Flooding emotions distort perceptions of reality and dominate behavior--children who are overwhelmed in this way believe that the last emotion or perception experienced in a crisis is the correct one. At these times, children are not ready to think or talk rationally and are unprepared to explore underlying issues through "clinical exploitation" of the event (Wood & Long, 1991, 161). Techniques of Emotional First Aid provide needed direction to children at these times.

The aim of Emotional First Aid is to pull a child through a behavioral storm or emotional crisis by having the adult opt to "sit it out" with the child until the child is ready and able to go about his or her regular business. The techniques can help children over common rough spots of everyday life, allowing them to return to the activity at hand; can aid in reducing emotional intensity to the point that the child can participate in a Life Space Interview more fully; and can defuse potential escalation of a conflict cycle by early intervention. Problems are prevented, potential crises are disarmed, and equilibrium is restored when Emotional First Aid techniques are used to drain off excess ill will, help children regain control of their upset feelings, find a positive perspective to a situation, or keep communication going to defer withdrawal (Wineman, 1959, 5; Fagen, 1981, 9-11; Wood & Long, 1991, 161).

Redl (1959a, 11-14) defined five categories of specific techniques for Emotional First Aid on the Spot. These are drain-off of frustration acidity; support for the management of panic, fury, and guilt; communication maintenance in moments of relationship decay; regulation of behavioral and social traffic; and umpire services. These categories, with examples, are further described below.

Drain-off of Frustration Acidity

This technique, also described as draining off emotional intensity, helps children through times of frustration by sympathetic listening and decoding feelings and behavior. Frequently, explosive behavior follows children's disappointments and frustrations. Many children become infuriated when they are interrupted during pleasurable activities. Sympathetic communication with them about their anger or sadness at having been interrupted; warning of changes in routine in advance; helping prepare children for the grades they are going to receive; helping organize homework assignments; and allowing them to practice test-taking to avoid potential anxiety and frustration are all ways in which constructive drain-off can be accomplished. Such techniques assure students that their feelings are normal and temporary and that others have the same feelings. Examples of use of the technique include such messages as "I know you're upset. Most people would be right now. But things will get better and I'll help you 'till they do" (Newman, 1963; Redl, 1963b, 67-68; Merritt, 1981, 16-19; Wood & Long, 1991, 162-163).

Support for the Management of Panic, Fury, and Guilt

Most children--especially those who harbor excessive guilt, hate, anxiety, or anger--are vulnerable to being overwhelmed by their feelings. This technique supports a student engulfed in intense emotion (Wood & Long, 1991, 163), protecting both the student and others from the rage, confusion, and other intense reactions of the situation. Firm but supportive structure and guidance, sometimes to the point of physical intervention (or holding a student), will let a student know that the adult is going to be in charge until the situation restabilizes (Wood & Long, 1991, 164). This technique gives the message "I will be your control until your control takes over" (Merritt, 1981, 16). During and after episodes in which the children have been unable to cope effectively with their feelings, such support can help put these problems and feelings into perspective.

Support can be given in several ways, the most basic of which is staying with children, no matter how severe their tantrums or anxiety attacks may be, to let them know that we will help protect them and keep them safe from their own impulses and others' reactions to their behavior. Being with children right after stressful incidents can help them put things back into focus again and also can ease their return to the common course of activities or social life without the aftertaste of unresolved hurt (Redl, 1963b, 68). Phrases such as "I will protect you until you can help yourself," or "It's safer for everyone if we follow the rules, and I'm going to see that we all stay safe" are helpful as part of this technique.

Communication Maintenance in Moments of Relationship Decay

At times of intense emotions, some students withdraw, sulk, and become uncommunicative. If this shield proceeds uninterrupted, the fantasy world into which children retreat can become more destructive to them than the world of reality. This technique maintains communication when relationships break down and aims at preserving the relationship with a child during a crisis to prevent withdrawal. The positive communication link between the student and teacher is especially vulnerable to decay when the teacher is intervening in behavior problems.   Maintaining a communication link helps keep the child "here" and may prevent him or her from moving away into self-pity and noncommunication, or into more out-of-touch states through out-of-control behaviors. The link is maintained by engaging the children in any kind of conversation until they feel less anxious about their thoughts and feelings. Gadgets, food, or humor also are effective ways of maintaining this link. To maintain communications, face-saving alternatives for the child, such as a quick change of subject or task, can be built into the interview process (Wood & Long, 1991, 165).

Tompkins-McGill gives the following example of a use of this technique.

> Laura was sullen and quiet after being given a time out for inappropriate behavior. She kept her head in her book, refused to make eye-contact, and did not budge when the rest of the class went out to recess, nor did she respond to verbal overtures. I put on a record I knew she would like and started straightening my desk. After a brief time, she looked at me and asked what the music was. From there, we were able to talk, first about the music, then about the time out and her feelings: the link was maintained.

Regulation of Behavioral and Social Traffic

In regulating social behavior, the goal is to remind children about rules and policies without moralizing or lecturing. During moments of impulsivity and emotional upset, some children may have difficulty in understanding appropriate roles and consequences. For children who lack adequate controls, benign authority figures may provide support through these critical times with reminders of the rules, warnings about potential consequences if present behavior continues, and indications about where deviations are potentially dangerous, even though the child was lucky this time (Redl, 1963b, 69-70; Wood & Long, 1991, 166). Tompkins-McGill gives a brief example.

> When Barbara began to whine toward the end of a quiet period, I only had to remind her that it was quiet period, but almost time for active games, for her (and the rest of the group) to settle back into their rests.

Umpire Services

The interviewer may act as umpire in order to help children in decision making about choices of right and wrong and to arbitrate interpersonal disputes, such as common but complicated arrangements about swapping, borrowing, or trading. Students often try to cast adults in this role, and much can be gained when the adult acts as an impartial mediator. Relying on the child's sense of fairness, an adult acting as an umpire may intercede in conflicts to help the child decide between their better or worse sides (Redl, 1959a; Redl, 1963b, 70; Wood & Long, 1991, 166-167). The assumption is that appeals to values or a code of fairness will be more readily accepted than a demand for conformity. Tompkins-McGill suggests an example.

> Harry and Sam approached me with whines threatening to escalate to shouts. They had agreed to trade five of Sam's baseball cards for three of Harry's miniature cars, but when the goods were actually exchanged, Sam was upset because the cars were scratched and missing wheels--now he wanted five cars for five cards. As we talked, they both conceded that the original agreement was five for three; nevertheless, Harry agreed to give up one more car. I helped them write a "contract" that clarified the agreement (five for four) and suggested that, in future trades, they each examine the goods before concluding negotiations. I also congratulated them on seeking adult assistance when they reached an impasse at resolving the problem on their own.

Clinical Exploitation of Life Events

Clinical Exploitation of Life Events uses an immediate incident or crisis event as an opportunity to explore habitual behavioral characteristics and the child's perceptions of those characteristics in order to attain a long range clinical or therapeutic goal (Redl, 1959a, 8; Wineman, 1959, 5-6). "A therapeutic goal differs from behavioral, academic, or developmental goals in that it is concerned with helping students gain some new insights about their behavior" (Wood & Long, 1991, 189) in order to help a child make basic changes in his or her interpersonal style or life theme and work through problems that are typical of the child's difficulties.

The use of Clinical Exploitation of Life Events occurs in several phases. The interviewer hopes to help the child reconstruct what has just occurred, perceive cause-effect relationships, and bring distorted perceptions, hidden values, reactions to group pressures, and undesirable behavioral responses to conscious awareness. An implicit goal is to expand children's psychological boundaries to include adults and to encourage self-acceptance. Better ways of dealing with problems are explored with the child as perceptions are clarified, feelings are connected to behavior, the child's self-control system is strengthened, new skills are taught, and the child is protected from the manipulation of others (Redl, 1959a; Morse, 1963, 1976a; Shea, 1978; Bloom, 1981; Fagen, 1981; Brendtro & Ness, 1983; Clarizio & McCoy, 1983).

Each therapeutic goal is selected specifically for each individual student. To make this approach worthwhile, something must happen that is important enough to explore. An isolated one-time event probably will not merit much attention; certain incidents may be ignored until one worthy of in-depth exploration occurs. The interviewer, having recognized an appropriate event, seeks to understand the student's perception, however distorted, of the crisis incident. The tactic at this point of the LSI is not the gathering of "facts" but assessing the child's values, perceptions, and interpretations to gain insight into the child's behavior. The depth and breadth of the crisis issue is measured by noting the child's reaction to the reconstruction of the event and his or her feelings about the incident. It is here that both expression and release may occur for the child as his or her perceptions of the event become clearer.

Problem-solving then begins, with focus shifting to "what should be done about this?" Alternative solutions to the problem when it is again encountered are sought and compared to the reality factors now perceived in the milieu (e.g., the alternative of not fighting and the necessity of getting along). A plan for behavior change is then developed, including how the child might be supported or assisted in carrying out the plan, and both child and interviewer commit to the plan. The plan also should include alternatives for the child to pursue if the agreed upon resolution to the problem turns out to be inadequate (Morse, 1976a, 267).

There are five categories of techniques in Clinical Exploitation of Life Events: reality rub-in, symptom estrangement, massaging numb value areas, new tool salesmanship, and manipulation of the boundaries of the self. These five techniques and the goals they incorporate are not discrete categories; rather, they often overlap and are meant simply to be illustrative (Redl, 1959a, 8-10). Below, we discuss each of the five categories.

Reality Rub-In

Children often need help interpreting even ordinary events in their lives. They are unaware of problems they themselves create and the social context of situations. They don't connect their own behavior to something bad that happens to them right after that. Some children, for example, may unfailingly think that the teacher is against them. Reality Rub-In, in the understanding spirit of "I accept you but not your acts," is designed to help a child organize reality when he or she does not see an event as others see it, to become aware of the actual event, to see his or her behavior accurately (including the inappropriateness of certain behaviors), and to interpret the situation correctly (Bloom, 1981, 22; Wood & Long, 1991, 191-192). It is important that intervention be as soon as possible; delay usually allows forgetting or rationalization of the problem.

Redl and Wineman (1957, 497-499) gave examples of helping youngsters at Pioneer House understand the consequences of their behavior-- e.g., swearing loudly in the yard may cause the neighbors to call the police and get the whole organization in trouble. Responses to children's unacceptable behavior in this case goes something like this: "I like you, and I know you're upset. But you may not yell in public. That is not acceptable behavior. And when you do that, other people get upset and we all get in trouble." The tone of voice and attitude used in this intervention are important: children will maintain their defenses and not see the connection between their behavior and more trouble (even if they stop yelling!) if they feel they are confronted by a disciplinarian.

Symptom Estrangement

This technique, a benign confrontation when a student doesn't want to change (Wood & Long, 1991, 205), is aimed at helping distance children from their inappropriate behavior. The purpose of this technique is twofold: to devalue negative behavior by demonstrating how the child pays too much through the creation of additional problems for limited secondary gains (e.g., the pleasure received in being aggressive); and to help the child begin to see that more appropriate behaviors with greater payoffs may be substituted (Tompkins, 1981, 26-28).

The assumption is not that one can simply argue children into letting go of their symptoms. Such letting go will require other means of help as well, including verbal and nonverbal feedback from the children's social environment about why their behavior is inappropriate. The interviewer can, however, provide children with insights that will encourage their desire to liberate themselves from the load of their unproductive behaviors (Redl, 1963b, 65).

Unlike other LSI techniques, this one deliberately increases students' anxiety by confronting what they are doing and saying in order to encourage owning of responsibility rather than blaming others to protect themselves. Such students are often masters at distracting, role reversals, excuses, and rationalizations. They often switch tactics to confuse and frustrate adults and use their verbal skills to avoid talking about an incident. "He started it," "It was an accident," "She asked for it," and other such diversions are common (Wood & Long, 1991, 205-206).

James Tompkins (1981, 26-28) has described how difficult this type of confrontation can be. The adult must maintain communication with the student while controlling his or her own reactions and emotions and staying focused on the behavior that is being confronted. When exposing students' defenses in this manner, there is always the risk that they will withdraw or rally more vigorous defenses. Patricia Tompkins-McGill offers the following example of such an interview.

> Jimmy and Billy have been acting up in class, "low-level," most of the morning--passing notes, throwing spitwads, giggling, etc. Reminders and admonitions have not worked to quell the behavior, which escalates to the point that Jim pushes Bill, who falls over in his chair (chair and all!) with a loud shriek, crash, and curses. The chair and Bill's head both hit the wall, and Bill receives quite a bump. Bill is sent to the school nurse (an LSI about his involvement in the incident will be conducted later, when we're sure he's o.k.). The teacher confronts Jim.
> T. "What happened, Jimmy?"
> J. "Nothin'" (looking down, refusing eye contact).
> T. "Yes, Jim, something did happen, because there is a chair on the floor, Bill has had to go to the nurse, and the rest of the class has gone to lunch, but you and I are here talking. What happened?"
> J. "Bill hit me."
> T. "Is that the first thing that happened?"
> J. "I dunno'."
> T. "Think about it, Jim. Have I spoken to you about your behavior this morning?"

J. "Bill was the one throwing spitwads! Not me!"

T. "I saw both you and Bill throwing spitwads. I'll talk to Bill about his behavior. Right now, you and I need to talk about yours."

(J. does not respond. After a silence, the teacher continues).

T. "Do you remember my asking you this morning not to throw spitwads?"

J. "Yeah," (he begins kicking one leg: he is getting more anxious).

T. "What other behavior did I ask you to stop?"

J. "I'm hungry. I want to go to lunch."

T. "You can have lunch after we finish talking. But there has been a problem and we have to get it straightened out now. What else did we talk about this morning?"

J. "Notes."

T. "Anything else?"

J. "I was asking about homework--I wasn't cutting up."

T. " What other behavior happened? (pause) Remember the giggling and noise?"

J. (looking down--now kicking both legs and squirming in his seat). "Yeah."

T. " Did you stop when I asked you to?"

J. (very softly) "No."

T. "And now what happened?"

J. "Bill got hurt. Is he going to be o.k.?"

T. "I don't think he's hurt real bad. The nurse will take care of him. What about your part in how Bill got hurt?"

J. "Well he started it. He hit me."

T. "What did you do when he hit you?"

J. "I just wanted to push his chair away from me. It was an accident!"

T. "You pushed Bill's chair?"

J. "Yeah."

T. "And it tipped over when you pushed it?"

J. "Yeah."

T. "And now you are in trouble?"

J. "Yeah."

T. "What can we do about this, Jim?"

J. "I want to eat lunch."

T. "Not yet, Jim. Let's talk about what you might have done different, so next time you'll have an alternative."

J. "I coulda' told you he hit me instead of pushing him."

T. "That might be a good alternative. But I know that's hard to
    do sometimes--rat on a friend. You like Bill, don't you?"

J. "Yeah, I guess so."

T. "Do you think the spitwads and notes and giggling had
    anything to do with Bill hitting you or you pushing Bill?"

J. "Bill got too excited."

T. "From the giggling and stuff that happened earlier?"

J. "Probably."

T. "Did you get too excited, too?"

J. "Maybe."

T. "So what's another alternative."

J. "Don't throw spitwads and giggle."

T. "That probably would help. But is it hard to stop that, even
    when I ask you?"

J. "Yeah! It's fun!"

T. "I know, but is it worth what's happened here? Bill is hurt
    and you are missing lunch and worried that you're in
    trouble. Maybe you can think about that next time and
    wait for recess to have giggling fun?"

J. "O.K. Can I go eat now?"

This teacher actually had a fairly tractable child who easily (compared
to many!) came around. Nonetheless, the child tried all the tricks and the
teacher did not buy it, sticking instead to the behavior of the child she was
talking to, and refusing to get ruffled or angry when the child did not respond
in what she might have considered an appropriately penitent way.

Massaging Numb Value Areas

Some children will be burdened with guilt and remorse after an
incident, to the point that they set themselves up to be caught and punished.
This technique is designed to take advantage of those times to awaken in the
child or the peer group appropriate values that strengthen self control and to
appeal to and strengthen positive value areas that are weak or lying dormant.
Because of the child's inner conflicts, these value areas are not prominent in
the child's consciousness and thus, are ineffective in helping the child control
his or her behavior under stress. Typically, children who react with remorse
to behaviors that are contrary to their own dormant values benefit from this
technique. In these cases, the interviewer works to increase children's potential
for stronger impulse control by magnifying the flickering signs of control and
reawakening positive value areas. (Werner, 1981, 29-31; Wood & Long, 1991,
221-223).

Acknowledging sensitivity to values feels to most youngsters like losing face, but some values are easier to acknowledge than others and can be framed so that face is saved. When children would rather be seen dead than conforming, the appeal to certain codes of fairness is acceptable to them. Hooking them into issues of fairness or other similar values may be quite successful. However, while children need to have their good points emphasized, they often cannot tolerate compliments in public (e.g., in front of the class) because they are then seen as "teachers' pets" or otherwise negatively labeled in their own or their peers' eyes. Value areas thus often need to be emphasized in private or in nonverbal ways (Redl, 1963b, 65; Wood & Long, 1991, 175).

Redl and Wineman (1957, 147) give an example of a verbal massage of numb value areas with a boy who stole a wallet from an adult he liked and whose fairness the boy recognized. This youngster was delinquent with a history of stealing, but his own value system would reject stealing from a nice adult, seeing that as unfair. The child admitted the theft and said he felt it was mean--he couldn't explain why he would do such a thing to such a nice guy. He said he just needed the money. The child was able to separate the issue of stealing from that of hurting a friendly adult. He really wanted to be punished for stealing so he wouldn't have to feel guilty about hurting his friend. After an in-depth clinical exploitation interview, the child was finally able to allow himself to feel the full impact of his love for the adult and of his guilt. Then he was helped to cope with the guilt that arose. This intervention will have a much longer lasting impact on the child's behavior than being punished for stealing.

New Tool Salesmanship

A major difficulty for many children, especially those who are troubled, is their behavioral inflexibility. They express affection or desires to be close by hitting, bragging, contradicting, disavowing interest, clowning, and other inappropriate behaviors (Wood & Long, 1991, 242). They have difficulty considering alternative behaviors to problem situations and finding acceptable ways of expressing desires, such as for friendship, help, achievement, or acceptance. Some children may not learn these alternatives simply through experience (Bower & Lambert, 1976; Sanders, 1981).

The aim of New Tool Salesmanship is to teach new social skills and to encourage the adoption of a larger, more appropriate repertoire of behavioral reactions. This technique helps the child develop plans for substituting new and more satisfying socially acceptable behaviors for old and less satisfying maladaptive ones. These plans cannot be imposed, however, but must be the product of a joint effort between interviewer and child, with the child emerging as the final "owner" of the plan (Brendtro & Ness, 1983). The plan should be very specific, be able to be stated clearly by the child, and include provisions for follow-up evaluation (Fagen, 1981; Wood & Long, 1991, 241).

This technique is rarely used early in a relationship or program, since a trusting relationship with an adult is essential to it's effective use. The most difficult phase of this technique is to identify the genuine feelings being inappropriately expressed and to see through the behavior to the child's desire for positive results (Wood & Long, 1991, 242-243). Tompkins-McGill gives the following example of the use of this technique.

Peter was constantly teasing Peg--pulling her hair, tripping her as she passed his chair, calling her names, and throwing spitwads or even larger objects at her. She was in tears almost constantly as a result of his harassment. I finally decided that I had to intervene.

I asked Peter to spend a few minutes with me when the other children went out to play. We spent some time clarifying what his behavior actually was and talking about Peg's reaction. Than I asked Peter if he wanted to make an enemy of Peg and her other friends, or if he liked her and wanted to be her friend. He admitted that he really liked Peg and wanted to be her friend, but that he was also embarrassed about this because he thought the other boys would make fun of him. I told him that I understood that fear, but that the way he was behaving toward Peg was not making her feel friendly toward him, and it was also getting him in trouble. Then we brainstormed about other things he might do to let Peg know he wanted to be her friend in a more clear way without leaving himself liable to being teased by the other boys. He decided he would apologize to Peg in private for past behavior and tell her that, even though he hadn't acted like it, he liked her. He vowed not to repeat his teasing in class and to try to interact with her in more positive ways, perhaps away from the classroom where he wouldn't be in such a "fishbowl" with the other boys. I offered to support him in this plan, and he said that he wanted to try this for three days. I told him that sounded great, and that after those three days, we would find a time to talk again to see how it was going and maybe come up with some other ideas to make the situation more comfortable for him.

Manipulation of the Boundaries of the Self

Some children feel that it is important to have friends, even if their friends get them in trouble. Because of their desire for social acceptance, they have a strong tendency to become victims of individual or group contagion, getting sucked in to inappropriate behaviors and made the culprit. This technique exposes students who abuse, isolate, or exploit others (Wood & Long, 1991, 261). The goals are to foster feelings of self-worth, facilitate healthier peer relationships, and help the vulnerable child recognize the boundaries of personal desires and actions. It is hoped that through LSI support (i.e., discussion on how the student in question is being exploited), desensitization to "contagion" and redirection of behavior will result (Long, 1981, 34-35).

Redl (1963b, 66-67) gives an example about group contagion. It was time to intervene in the "group psychological suction" one boy was involved in. The Life Space Interview was used to help him see that he was being exploited by other members of the group, who got him to "act up" for them. One day two boys in the group tried it again, but this time, the youngster didn't get involved and the instigators themselves got out of hand, having to be removed from the group. When they were out of the room, the boy turned and said to the teacher "Gee, am I glad I didn't get sucked into this one."

ADVANTAGES AND LIMITATIONS
OF THE LIFE SPACE INTERVIEW

Advantages

Many advantages of the Life Space Interview have been reported in the literature. These include that it is insight producing, it focuses on behavior and/or attitude change, it has promise of long-term behavior gain, it yields a plan for constructive future action, and it helps the child become responsible for his or her behavior without focusing blame on the student (Sabatino & Mauser, 1978, 137).

With the LSI, problems are presented in an open, nonjudgmental manner and students can identify feelings that cause inappropriate behaviors and express themselves in an environment that does not judge them. Issues are clarified while they are "hot," preventing blaming, forgetting, or the use of defense mechanisms. The professional at hand is enabled to help children with problems at the time they occur. LSI techniques can be used in most crisis situations. Crises are used toward productive ends, when the child's defenses are down and new information may be assimilated more readily, resulting in more openness to change and constructive activity. Students learn skills to solve problems and teachers are more comfortable dealing with behaviors when the Life Space Interview is one of the tools at their disposal (Caplan, 1961; Kitchner, 1963, 720-722; Tompkins, 1965; Trieschman, Whittaker, & Brendtro, 1969; Clarizo & McCoy, 1983, 490; Gardner, 1990, 111).

The LSI is compatible with behavior modification and social learning theory as part of a tool bag for behavior management. Used to interfere with inappropriate behavior and to encourage more acceptable actions, it can be used *with* rather than *instead of* other techniques, broadening approaches to increase effectiveness. Behaviorism has been criticized because it does not respect the meaning of symptoms (Day, 1978, 194-196) and does not produce long-term change (Meichenbaum, 1980, 83). But even for professionals whose approach to teaching students is behavior modification, crises must be handled skillfully and healthily (Wood & Long, 1991, 6). The Life Space Interview is a good way to do that.

Limitations

The literature discusses several limitations of the Life Space Interview. These include that it is not useful with some children; it needs to be used consistently by all staff but is not easy to learn; teachers lack time to conduct LSIs and when they do, time is taken away from academic work; it's use may be reinforcing behaviors that we want to change; and there is a lack of empirical knowledge about it's effectiveness.

There are several authors who feel that not every child can be helped by some of the techniques of the LSI, specifically the more in-depth Clinical Exploitation of Life Events. The young or nonverbal child who lacks verbal concepts may find difficulty with the traditional verbal approaches to the LSI (Morse, 1985). James Tompkins (Krupicka, 1988) felt that very young children up to the age of six would be unable to engage in the Clinical Exploitation of Life Events. Lack of maturity and cognitive development and inability to use abstract thinking or to disclose their feelings and connect feelings with behavior are some of the characteristics of this age level that contraindicate use of in-depth Life Space Interviewing. One exception to the chronological age guideline, Tompkins said, might be the highly intelligent or gifted young child. Wood and Weller (1981, 61-66) found the LSI to be most effective with children who had typical socioemotional skills of those beyond the age of eight. Wood and Long (1991, 11, 280) feel that children need the following prerequisites before Clinical Exploitation can take place: adequate attention span, ability to listen to and retain what has been said, minimal verbal skills for spontaneous language and understanding the meaning of words, some reasoning ability to understand the "essence of the incident and the problem it produced," remembering and understanding of sequences of events, ability to relate pieces of an incident to a central incident, ability to connect feelings to behavior, and trust in the adult.

Some children, regardless of chronological age, may be developmentally unprepared to benefit from the LSI. Tompkins (Krupicka, 1988) felt that lower-functioning mentally retarded children could not be successfully engaged in a LSI, because the interview requires not only that children understand and verbalize about complex social circumstances and their involvement in the group but also that they have the potential for insight about their feelings and behavior. He felt that these children would have great difficulty engaging in a demanding interview that involved analysis of group social dynamics, their role in contributing to crisis events, and how their feelings and behaviors related to the other children and their behavior. While these limitations must be considered, Patricia Tompkins-McGill has found LSI, particularly Emotional First Aid, useful, with modifications, with children and adults with developmental disabilities.

Tompkins indicated that another group of children who could be predicted to have difficulty in responding to the LSI are brain-injured, neurologically impaired children, because, in the traditional understanding of neurological impairment, many unacceptable behaviors, such as hyperactivity, may simply be out of the child's control and thus could not be considered as a basis for interviewing (Krupicka, 1988).

Wood and Weller (1981, 61-66) have suggested modifications to the LSI to accommodate children who lack prerequisite skills, and Wood and Long (1991, 277-301) describe an "abbreviated LSI" as appropriate intervention for very young children or those who are developmentally delayed, noting that young children must "struggle through a series of difficult understandings that are the same essential ones included in a full LSI with older students, but in embryonic form." Abbreviated practices may include "talking about the incident and the issue, developing a solution by selecting new behavior, and enhancing self-esteem " (Wood & Long, 1991, 278).

Tompkins (Krupicka, 1988) saw children who demonstrated well-crystallized, well-established symptoms associated with psychopathic reactions to life as notably resistant to the Life Space Interview. The LSI, he said, depends not only on the reconstruction of a recent crisis event or troublesome circumstances, but also requires children's understanding and confirmation of their contribution to the trouble as well as access to their feelings, especially of anxiety or remorse, surrounding an incident. The Interview also formulates a commitment and a plan to modify subsequent inappropriate behavior. Individuals with psychopathy have immense and virulent incapacities and resistances about guilt and remorse feelings and generally are not committed to developing appropriate alternative behavioral responses. However, it is just this type of child that the LSI process was designed for, and although these children may be more resistant to the process, it is useful with them (Redl & Wineman, 1957).

In order to be most successful, the LSI should be used consistently by all staff and personnel (Shea, 1978, 276). Unless cooperation is attained among all members of the school staff (especially between the teacher and the principal), those unsympathetic to the technique are likely to discourage its use and undermine its effects (Long, 1963, 723). But some LSI techniques (Clinical Exploitation) are not easy to learn (Wood & Long, 1991, xii), and teaching effective use of LSI to school personnel may be difficult (Gardner, 1990), although it has been done successfully (see, for instance, P.Tompkins, R. Newman, B. Morse, and N. Long).

Because the use of the LSI requires a recognition of action overtones as well as deeper dynamics, some feel that it is a relatively complex clinical technique that can be as complicated to use as traditional therapy, and thus, that it is best used with training and follow-up. Many teachers and school systems are unable or unwilling to commit to this training. "To read about LSI does not provide the reader with the necessary training to develop this skill" (Heuchert & Long, 1981, 5) and effective use of the full LSI "goes well beyond the intellectual knowledge of the five clinical interviews" (Long, 1990b, 124). While minimal training and experience is required for application of Emotional First Aid, (indeed, these techniques have been successfully employed for years), Clinical Exploitation of Life Events should, in the opinion of some practitioners, be conducted only by those who possess appropriate training and experience (Shea, 1978, 275). A major obstacle in bringing the complete LSI procedure to fruition among practitioners has been and continues to be the unavailability of training in the more in-depth Clinical Exploitation techniques. If training teachers to use these techniques is a barrier to its full use in public schools, it is even more difficult to obtain philosophical consistency and train *all* adults who will interact with children in a school setting.

On the other hand, when Krupicka (1988) asked James Tompkins if potential practitioners of the LSI needed a psychiatric or a formal clinical background or training to use the LSI, Tompkins' reply was "no." To illustrate his point, he described the University of Michigan Fresh Air Camp, where students with a variety of backgrounds learned and used the Life Space Interview.

> During the 1950's to approximately 1968, The University of Michigan developed a highly recognized summer short term therapeutic camping program called the University of Michigan Fresh Air Camp. The camp was for approximately 99 seriously disturbed and aggressive children. It was an eight to nine week experience, as well, in the training of matriculated upper level

undergraduate and graduate students. This program was administered and staffed with such notable personalities as Dr. William Morse, Mr. David Wineman, Dr. Elton McNeil, Dr. Nicholas Long, Dr. Richard Cutler--to name only a few. Dr. Fritz Redl usually visited the camp for several days every summer. Ms. Eve Citrin and Ms. Mary Lee Nicholson worked there--they were also on the Pioneer House Staff with Redl and Wineman. The thrusts of the program were to train entry level professionals in the understanding and use of therapeutic milieu principles and practices and in the understanding and use of the Life Space Interview, as well as to provide intensive treatment for seriously emotionally handicapped aggressive children.

The University of Michigan Fresh Air Camp trained students in regular and special education, social case work, nursing, psychology, and other related fields. They had the widest possible scope of clinical backgrounds, from none to extensive. Of course, the more extensive the clinical background the person has, the more likely that person could call upon related learning and experience to facilitate their use of the LSI. (Krupicka, 1988)

Tompkins also recalled that, at Hillcrest Children's Center, he and Nick Long trained staff in using the LSI who had not completed their undergraduate work (Krupicka, 1988).

A further disadvantage cited is that a one-to-one interview is difficult or impossible for many teachers to manage in a classroom full of students. In most school situations, the LSI process may be seen as taking up too much academic time (Gardner, 1990) and the classroom teacher has limited opportunity to conduct a Life Space interview. Rarely is the teacher free to conduct such an interview at the moment of trouble. Often the best the teacher can do is to take the child out of the room and talk with him or her for a few moments in the hall. If the teacher cannot leave the class, the teacher must be able to find help elsewhere. Fritz Redl suggested that all schools should have a person to assist at the moment of flare-up (Bernstein, 1963, 36). Often that person will be the school principal or counselor. In some situations, a crisis teacher or extra staff person who is trained in these methods of interacting with children is utilized during crisis situations. The crisis teacher may supervise the class while the teacher conducts the LSI, or the child can be sent to the crisis teacher for the interview (Morse, 1976b, 249-302). Even so, with LSI techniques, teachers "on the spot" can more skillfully handle what they, because of their positions and proximity, must handle anyway.

Some professionals working with troubled children, after having heard about the LSI for the first time, say they have used the LSI with their children all along (Krupicka, 1988). Tompkins responded by saying that if one doesn't have a structured, planned interview with a specific goal, a predictable clinical outcome revolving around a single issue or incident, and if the interview is not conducted in or near the time and place of the child's difficulty, one is probably not using in-depth Clinical Exploitation Life Space Interviewing techniques, though they may be using Emotional First Aid or counseling techniques. But if teachers learn the major elements of what constitutes the LSI, they themselves can answer the question of whether or not their intervention is really an LSI (Krupicka, 1988).

Many experts have spoken to the criticism that Life Space Interviewing takes time away from the academic work which children are in school to accomplish. LSI advocates point out that if a child's behavior is so out of control that he or she cannot attend to the academic work, they are not learning anyway, and time is taken to deal with the behavior regardless of the approach used. Why not use an effective means of dealing with that behavior? Also, as discussed in earlier chapters, the notion that the school's only purpose is to teach academics is rapidly expanding, whether because of changes in philosophy or out of the necessity produced by schools under stress, to include behavior and attitude change and social skills enhancement in schools' goals for students.

Reinforcement of undesired behaviors has been cited as another problem with the LSI. Reinert (1980, 60-61) noted that some children may learn to manipulate the teacher into Life Space Interviewing through inappropriate behavior because they get secondary gains, such as the teacher's attention or one-to-one time. Hammill and Bartel (1982, 6) and Gardner (1990) similarly noted that, in removing a child from a classroom situation to a one-to-one personal interaction, there is a risk of reinforcing rather than changing negative behavior. Krupicka (1988) asked Tompkins about the one-to-one attention being highly reinforcing and sustaining the child's unacceptable behavior. Tompkins responded:

> That sort of reaction is based on simple misunderstanding of Redl and Wineman's position. What does any professional do when any intervention seems to be reinforcing the target behavior? The question raised about using the LSI with the child reinforcing inappropriate behavior needs to be addressed by clinicians or teachers using any intervention. If you use a particular technique or intervention to redirect children's unacceptable behavior and there is some evidence that the approach is reinforcing the target behavior, one must deal with the subsequent behavior and revise or modify the approach

used. In the contingency management approach, for example, the experts suggest the implementation of a reversal design to ascertain the effectiveness of the technique or discover the other variables reinforcing the behavior in using that technique. The same issues are at stake in using the LSI or accompanying a child in Time Out procedures.

Let me give an example. I remember a little boy, Marty, from Hillcrest Children's Center. At one time, and after Marty developed an important relationship with me, he began to act out in the classroom simply to visit and be with me. Marty liked me. Did I abandon the LSI with Marty when I realized I was in the bind of supporting his acting out behavior via his experiences with me and our interviewing approaches? Of course not! This issue, that is, Marty's behavior to be with me, became the focus of a Life Space Interview. When we both realized what was happening, I arranged to see Marty periodically on a legitimate one-to-one basis. Marty and I were together. It wasn't the LSI that was reinforcing; it was me and my premium for time with Marty.

The prime time for scheduling crisis interventions is during crisis times to maximize the therapeutic influence. If the crisis intervention supports or reinforces behavior, you deal with it; but don't chuck the crisis (LSI) intervention.

Gardner (1990) is among those who criticize the lack of empirical research about LSI. Long (1990b, 122) acknowledges that "the literature does not reflect current practices of LSI by special educators with emotionally disturbed students," but Wood and Long (1991, 303-311) trace the history of the field validation of LSI for the past 40 years, noting it's successful use in numerous situations during that time, including public school classrooms. Little controlled or experimentally oriented research has been conducted on the effectiveness of the LSI. Studies that have been conducted, however, have supported the efficacy of the procedure in improving academic and social performance (DeMagistris & Imber, 1980, 12-15); in reducing inappropriate target behaviors (Reilly et al., 1978, 2); and in improving the child's ability to apply logic to problem-solving situations rather than acting on impulse alone (Naslund, 1987, 12-20).

CONCLUSION

The Life Space Interview is not meant to be a substitute for any other form of support or intervention nor is it purported to be better or worse than anything else. It is an *additional* resource for ego support for disturbed and also healthy children. Thus, the LSI increases the management resources or "tool bag" from which teachers and others can draw. It can be combined with effective individual and group techniques to enable teachers to act more purposefully and feel more secure as they find they can recognize and deal with predictable phenomena as well as crises in the classroom.

For personnel who feel uncomfortable using only behavioral or other particular techniques, the Life Space Interview process holds another possibility for intervention into disturbing behaviors. It is grounded in reality and at the same time aimed at producing insights. The LSI supports an emergent insight for both the child and the staff and provides adults with tools for more constructive handling of both the illness and the health of the child (Vernick, 1963, 466-467). The interview can be used to highlight the child's behavior in such vivid detail that the child is brought face-to-face with the implications of what he or she is doing and what it means in terms of reality consequences (Redl & Wineman, 1957, 488). Because it is not necessarily tied to a single mode of treatment and because it stands on its own as a valuable tool in dealing with day-to-day and moment-to-moment events, LSI can thus enrich techniques and methods that teachers are already using. The methodology can be learned and taught and thus can become an important adjunct to other forms of therapy and an important preventive ingredient in moments of stressful living.

The Life Space Interview, then, is an intervention that fits naturally in the child's life space, as adults who are seen by the child as a natural part of their school-life experience engage in the LSI. It affords a comfortable opportunity for school personnel to talk with youngsters about specific target behaviors and associated difficulty-filled circumstances that derail children into potentially traumatizing experiences. Finally, the LSI dramatizes the value of assisting children to verbalize about themselves and how they see life, how they view their troubles in the context of program and school demands, and how they perceive other children and adults around them. The LSI supports a significant management approach by singling out the child's difficulty for instant, unmuddled, and undisguised therapeutic handling--at the time and place that the difficulty occurs.

CHAPTER TEN

THE THERAPEUTIC RELATIONSHIP AND THE EDUCATION OF CHILDREN

Interpersonal relationships are essential for children's healthy emotional development. People grow and thrive in supportive, responsive relationships that satisfy basic and legitimate needs. Relationships that teachers provide in school can have a tremendously positive impact on children, as one teacher reported.

Leon had been taken from his parents and placed in a foster home at a very young age because of physical abuse. He had been bound to a chair and had repeatedly been locked in a small dark closet for hours at a time. This was in addition to being beaten.

Leon would not express his frustrations or anger with aggression. He had the tendency to withdraw completely from a situation. Leon would sit or stand completely still--not making a sound or moving a single muscle. One day, Leon became upset with one of the other students and went into his catatonic-like state at his desk. I sat in a chair beside Leon and began talking softly and as reassuringly to him as possible.

I seemed to be getting nowhere fast with Leon, and I felt tears rolling down my cheeks. I moved my hand to brush the tears away. Evidently this movement caught Leon's attention and he turned his gaze toward me with a look of bewilderment. I told him that I cared about him and wanted to help him and to be his friend. At the same time, I placed my hand on top of his. For the first time he didn't jerk away, but gave me one of his "rare but beautiful" smiles.

The process of change begins with someone who cares. Relationships act as catalysts, challenging people to change. As children begin to identify with those who are most important to them, their personalities may begin to reorganize. Such relationships certainly enhance growth, often spurring the child to further development of talents, interests, and desires (Hizer, 1972, 11-15; Arent, 1992, xi, xiv-xvi).

The professional literature consistently emphasizes the necessity of a positive therapeutic relationship in the milieu treatment and education of seriously socioemotionally impaired students. In the archipelago of various intervention ingredients, the relationship between the teacher and child is the most dominant issue. Changes in children's attitudes, behavior styles, and self-images are created through the development of trust in a school facility, its program, and its staff. A relationship is sought that leads the child to feeling valued and competent. The establishment of such a relationship can influence certain kinds of behavior. Of the many programmatic dimensions involved in the education and treatment of *all* children, therapeutic relationship may well be the most important aspect (Trieschman et al., 1969, 51-56).

This chapter discusses the nature of therapeutic relationship and the relevance of its use in educational settings with children and adolescents. There are, of course, a wide variety of notions about therapeutic relationship and its definition, its characterization, and its worth in Milieu Therapy and education. Through a review of literature on the subject, several of these are explored and examples of relationships in public school classrooms are given.

THERAPEUTIC RELATIONSHIP DEFINED

Therapeutic relationships are responsive to needs. In a therapeutic relationship, people can reveal themselves without fear of criticism or condemnation, and growth of self is an important value (Moustakas, 1966). Caring and love foster identification that springs from an affective bond between children and adults. Children try to become like the people they love as they incorporate elements of the loved ones' nature, behavior, values, and styles of coping (Morse, 1985, 151-152). When one is loved, one experiences an unconditional regard for one's self from the loving one, though this does not necessarily include approval of given behavior. One is loved and accepted, not because of good deeds, but in spite of undesirable behavior. When this occurs, pretense and defensive behavior are unnecessary. One feels secure and of value to another human being, is listened to, responded to. This is essential in both parenting and the surrogate parenting that is teaching. Through the process of being so accepted, one comes to care about and love one's self (Morse, 1985, 141-152).

Redl and Wineman (1957, 303) advocated "tax-free love" for children. Love, affection, and gratifying experiences should occur without needing to be earned. These should never be made bargaining tools; they are basic minimum requirements in the lives of children.

Qualities of therapeutic relationships such as realness, genuiness, and authenticity are critical in establishing an effective relationship in which children can learn to trust teachers. Prizing, accepting, and trusting even troubled children can convey to each child that he or she is a person of worth and dignity. The adult response of unconditional positive regard is as essential in all classrooms as it is in therapy and remedial special education (Knoblock, 1983, 148).

Within a good relationship, children's activities are organized so they can master more difficult tasks and gain experience (Bettelheim, 1950, 45). Spontaneity and flexibility--not to be misconstrued as license or chaos--make questions of schedule or routine subservient to the relevance of interpersonal relationships. The place where therapeutic relationships occur is a therapeutic milieu, characterized by an inner cohesiveness that permits children to develop a consistent frame of reference as they become part of meaningful interpersonal relationships. Such conditions permit psychological insights and internalization of controls and support the child's personality development (Bettelheim & Sylvester, 1948, 192).

> The desire and the ability to live an orderly life becomes part of one's personality only when this has been internalized by being exposed to an orderly life situation that is much more attractive than all countervailing tendencies. But even all the advantages of a well-organized existence in and by themselves are not sufficient for internalization; they have to be mediated through a personal relationship with somebody one loves and admires. The wish to become more like this cherished person, and to gain his affection more securely by living in accordance with his values, underlies the process of identification, and with it internalization of behavior and values. (Bettelheim, 1974, 10)

Bettelheim's Sonia Shankman Orthogenic School designed the treatment milieu for autistic children to be reliable and consistent; the children could depend on its response. Trust in adults was developed as each child was accepted for what he or she was. Psychic order was fostered by the experience of living in an orderly world. Living day in and day out among nurturing adults helped provide the children with images of reasonable and orderly living after which they could pattern, first in external and then in internal life. At the Orthogenic School, one adult became the primary care provider for the child, making possible the opportunity to develop a continuous relationship. This person saw that the child's dependency needs were gratified, permitted the child's defensive behavior, and mediated between the child and the environment whenever such help was needed. A primary goal was to support the child's ego in control of behavior by organizing and explaining the child's world so that everyday tasks could be done with confidence. Each time and setting of the routine day, whether it was eating, bathing, playing, going to bed, or waking up, was viewed as having particular therapeutic possibilities through the use of relationship (Bettelheim, 1950, 82, 152).

When young babies encounter attachment, bonding, and fulfillment of dependency needs with significant adults in their lives, a viable relationship emerges. As children grow in awareness of themselves as separate from their caregivers, their own personalities develop. For this to occur, relationships must be loving, reliable, and supportive, bestowing self-esteem. A build-up of memories of experiences, good or bad, within significant relationships becomes a part of children's self-image. "A child who feels depleted and devalued as a person does not conceptualize himself worth much" (Malmquist, 1976, 174).

Adults are models for children and the child should see mature, reasonable, and useful behavior from adults. The entire educational process rests upon certain attitudinal qualities existing in the personal relationship between the facilitator and the learner. The role of the teacher is that of a facilitator of learning, not that of a director. The most successful teacher is one who has qualities of basic realness or genuineness, of prizing learners for their feelings and opinions, and who is seen by students as a person who is fundamentally trustworthy and capable of empathic understanding. If teachers try to make only *one* non-evaluative, accepting, and empathic response per day to a student's demonstrated or verbalized feelings, they will discover the potency of this kind of understanding. This involves risk-taking, but when the constructive tendencies of the individual and the group are trusted, the teacher discovers that he or she has initiated an educational revolution (Rogers, 1969, 3) and that each student tends to feel liked by all the others, and to have more positive attitudes toward themselves and toward school. The empathic relationship that the teacher generates underlies any techniques and is more important in its impact than is the method per se (Morse, Ardizzone, MacDonald, & Paick, 1980, 90).

Acceptance

Any ability to help others effectively rests on a basic respect for the human personality, a belief in the intrinsic value and dignity of each person, and a deep conviction that the individual has the right to self-direction and self-determination. Every true relationship between two persons begins with acceptance--a sincere belief in people and a recognition that they have capacities for working out their difficulties.

All people wish to be confirmed as what they are, what they can become. Acceptance is the innate capacity to confirm others in this way. Confirming means first accepting the whole potentiality and reality of the other. The person is respected not only when good will, gentleness, and politeness are expressed, but also when fears, hatreds, resentments, and destructive behaviors surface (Moustakas, 1959, 90; Berkowitz & Rothman, 1960, 117-118; Buber, 1965, 36-37).

Good therapy is merely an extension of one's right to be oneself. Karl Menninger calls for "love unsolicited" for the patient. This is another way of affirming the human dignity of the patient's own personality. The main guideline should be the unconditional acceptance of patients, if not necessarily their behavior (Devereaux, 1949, 494-500; Reinert & Huang, 1987, 55-56).

An accepting person encourages others to state their perceptions and sees their views as valid and important. Expressions of feelings are supported without threats or unclarified misunderstandings. Behavior is observed without condemnation or hostility, regardless of how it may differ from one's own values. There is a genuine and deep acceptance for people as they are at each moment.

Acceptance is important if students are to find support in their relationships with teachers. Interpersonal warmth, a gift for intimacy, respect for differences, and acceptance of each individual at each moment are critical attributes for teachers. In believing that they are accepted by school personnel, children will have less need to defend themselves. The teacher must maintain an unyielding trust in the value of the child as a person with capacities and talents that, when free to be expressed, will result in positive experiences. The teacher must support children as they develop their own potential, creating opportunities for them to choose their own ways of learning. The child's feelings and thoughts are valued as teachers facilitate expression, convey understanding of the child's perceptions, and accept the child's tempo and pace and the child's way of relating to the life of the classroom (Moustakas, 1966; Arent, 1992, 95).

Acceptance does not mean that we do not hope to effect a change in the child. It is important to see the child's positive and negative attributes. The teacher must maintain a reality orientation, respecting children while not approving or concurring with deviant behaviors, helping them have a realistic view of their situation while avoiding a sense of resignation about the "problems" (Erickson, 1992, 113).

As students face reality, they must face problems as their own. While this is often difficult, youngsters can more easily "own" their behavior when their feelings are accepted and they can express themselves in a relationship of security and trust. Such acceptance can reduce or compensate for anxiety-related problems and permit self-revelations about limitations and mistakes without detriment to the children's inner sense of dignity.

Empathy

To help people in a therapeutic relationship, it is necessary to have at least a kernel of positive feelings for them. When the goal is mental health and social adjustment, an intimate relationship in which feelings, thoughts, and motives are readily comprehended is not just desirable but necessary for maximum success. Empathic understanding draws on one's own inner experiences for discerning another's behaviors and feelings from their perspective. When communicated, understanding develops that not only supports an intervention design but also fosters a relationship that can maximize the success of that design (Peck, 1983, 64). Such understanding comes about more easily when the helping person can relate in a live experience, from the immediacy of that experience, rather than from later reflection.

Sympathy, too, is a mutual understanding or affection arising from relationship, but sympathy may involve pity, compassion, or other such strong emotional reactions that impede healthy relationships. Sympathy may come from projection or the unconscious attribution of one's own attitudes, desires, and feelings onto another. For these reasons, it is important to differentiate between sympathy and empathy.

People who are successful in work with children are empathic regarding children's deprivations and suffering without being overly affected. When adults react in strongly emotional ways, children become frightened because they feel that they have caused the adult to be unhappy, that they are very bad for having done so, and that they must avoid expressing their discomfort to this adult in the future. Children may also feel that adults are not strong enough to act as protectors, since they cannot even protect themselves from upsets. In this case, children may assume the protective role, reporting only things that will not cause the adult distress. This places much too much responsibility on children and often recreates problems they are already struggling with which they learned in their families of origin (Hammer & Kaplan, 1967).

Empathy, or a teacher's ability to experience accurately a child's private world and inner feelings without reacting strongly, is important in all areas of teaching; it is especially critical in the teaching of seriously troubled children who persistently experience both academic and emotional problems. Although many socioemotionally impaired children have been severely damaged by the nature of their past "caring" relationships, most children will eventually respond with trust when the new relationship is positive, supportive, and trustworthy (Morse, 1985, 151-152). Teachers must be on the alert for negative forces, both in the children and in themselves, in order to maintain high quality interpersonal relationships. Growing self-awareness helps teachers avoid relationship pitfalls such as projection and over-identification. Research has shown that, for emotionally disturbed children, relationships with teachers are more important than other factors in fostering adequate adjustment. The teacher should represent a prototype of adult models to children, and disturbed children pay more attention to the affective skills of teachers than to skills in teaching, curriculum development, or any other area (Morgan, 1979, 446).

Teachers should not minimize the role of empathy in the therapeutic relationship. Empathic communication may be the basis for children's receptivity to what it is we would like to accomplish with them. The importance of the child's receptivity, without which no change is possible, is all too often overlooked as a crucial aspect of children's permitting themselves to grow in any area. As a result of the capacity to relate warmly and genuinely to the child, the teacher helps to achieve this state of receptivity in the child.

RELATIONSHIP GOALS

While the conventional role for the teacher is that of judging performance, the teacher's function as helper is to increase children's awareness of their strengths and capabilities (Brown et al., 1975, 103). Such teachers interact from their values, ethics, and convictions, thus freeing children to explore their own uniqueness. For the teacher, such a relationship makes work personally satisfying; for the child, life in school becomes a real experience. In spite of pressures, frustrations and anxieties, when teachers and children can be honest and authentic persons, there is always hope that difficulties will be resolved and meaningful living experienced.

LaVietes (1962, 854) suggests a variety of goals in teacher/pupil relationships that will assist teachers in responding to children's feelings in a way that supports learning and achievement and favors social and personal development. These goals include helping the child feel adequate, hopeful, and unafraid in the group teaching experience; undoing distortions in interpersonal relationships through teachers' behavior toward the child; reducing anxiety in the child through appropriate and realistic expectations; presenting benign social reality to a child who has experienced distortions in reality perceptions in the past and who has withdrawn from adapting to reality; overcoming resistance to learning through nonpainful, nondangerous, pleasurable, ego-building learning experiences; and substituting mutual aid (cooperation, sharing, awareness of others' needs) for competition and suspicion.

Troubled Children

The psychic evolution of a child is achieved largely through objective interpersonal relations with the outer world. A central aspect of disturbed children is their isolation and abject friendlessness as they participate in a conspiracy of social quarantine. Having experienced more hurt and rejection than children enduring merely the usual knocks of life, they are slower to form relationships. Their experience has taught them to "expect" to be rejected; thus, their behavior "asks for" rejection and negative judgement from the adults in their environments. Feeling "no good," they act "no good," and adults react to their behavior as if the child himself were "no good."

Troubled children, those with emaciated ego strength, have had difficulties in their ability to form and gain gratification from their involvement with others and thus are particularly unlikely to have developed rewarding and satisfying interpersonal relationships. Some theorists hold that mental illness or psychopathology in children and adults is readily traced to their early, catastrophically devastated relationships with parents or other significant adults; the child was unable to receive love in those early life circumstances, the relationship was severed too early, or the required skills to relate were not reinforced (Bettelheim, 1974; Rogers, 1967).

"Psychopathology in the individual is a product of the way he deals with his intimate relations, the way they deal with him, and the way other family members involve him in their relations with each other" (Haley, 1962, 69). It is hoped that corrective experiences can occur through relationships with therapists, teachers, and others, but being successful in this regard "cannot be imagined if a meaningful relationship has not been accomplished between therapist and patient" (Gardner, 1975, 24). Even with all ingredients necessary for the development of a therapeutic relationship, the child still must be motivated for change. The forced association existing in most settings for emotionally disturbed children sets up more than the normal resistance in the child against the helper. Generally, children do not want to be in these settings. It is a "no choice" situation for them, so motivation to change is generally not present at first.

Socioemotionally impaired children have received so much rejection from peers, adults, and family because of their inappropriate behavior that a therapeutically corrective experience for them *must* include adult love and seeing adults as basically accepting even when limits are imposed. Instead, children who have distorted interpersonal relationships with adults are apt to see even minor limit setting as a deep, serious adult rejection. These children are conspicuously impaired in their ability to learn from adults, whom they perceive as deceptive and an unpredictable source of hurt and help. Such a child faces each adult with a predominant anticipation of punishment, rejection, derision, or withdrawal of love (Redl & Wineman, 1957, 266; Hobbs, 1966, 1105-1115).

Because the development of a personality is achieved through interaction of the child with the environment, it is important to offer a satisfactory life situation in which the child may ease his conflict and acquire awareness of self and environment (Osorio, 1970, 121-129). Milieu Therapy seeks to provide the child with dynamic possibilities for objective relations that will help the reconstruction of the child's inner world. The Kanner Institute in Brazil, for instance, focused on activities aimed at creating environmental conditions so that new patterns of identification could be established and more adequate standards of interaction could exist. A better sociofamilial integration of the child was attempted and a better use of the potentialities of each individual.

Teachers will need to be aware, to some extent, of circumstances that may be detrimental to the child. For instance, teachers are both legally and ethically bound to report suspected abuse of children. However, tracking causes for behavior can be time-consuming and unproductive if carried to an extreme, while behavior and emotional problems that present themselves in classrooms can be dealt with effectively on the spot. Hammer and Kaplan (1967, 37), in treating schizophrenic children, note that therapists need not trace the origin and causal factors of disturbance, any more than an orthopedic surgeon finds it necessary in treating a leg fracture to wonder what sort of truck hit the patient. Rather, the therapist must recognize that the pathology amounts to an inability in the schizophrenic child to establish stable interpersonal relationships and experience those realities that can truly gratify his or her needs.

Facilitating change with the emotionally disturbed child is a difficult task. Children's reputations precede them, and teachers' expectations of them may become self-fulfilling prophecies to many children (Rosenthal & Jacobson, 1968, 139). For change to occur, the child must have the capacity to perceive the overall good qualities that make up the relationship with the adult. The role of the teacher is to provide the conditions that are the basis for relationship development.

To build and maintain a relationship with a child whose trust has been shattered is not easy.

> If the child has experienced significant past disappointment in relationships, he may desperately test our ability to withstand his hate with worrisome attempts to dissolve the treatment relationships. In this case, the treatment is simply to manage to hold the child and the treatment setting together. In practice, this cannot be productively accomplished without love for the

child, which enables us to see the valuable part of himself he
reveals by his apparently negative behavior. (Weiner, 1970, 13)

INTERPERSONAL ENCOUNTERS

There seem to be some commonalties among the various
conceptualizations of what constitutes a desirable relationship between
children and adults. Those consistent themes focus on adults' roles as parents,
therapists, or teachers. The parental role is critical, but focus in this chapter
is on the roles of educators. In the literature, most references are to the value
of relationships between therapists and (children) patients. We have adapted
those ideas for their usefulness to educators.

Positive Relationship with Teacher or Therapist

A good relationship is the focal point around which various positive or
corrective experiences occur. It is essential that adults be able to relate well,
in a warm but not contrived way. The optimum experience that children can
have at school is to see school personnel as people who like them and as
adults who use their negative reactions to children's inappropriate behavior in
the service of helping children (Hammer & Kaplan, 1967, 38; Gardner, 1975,
18).

Adults, not children, are responsible for developing and sustaining
positive relationships. The contributions of the adult and the child to the
relationship will be quite different. With many children, adults must nurture
the relationship patiently for a long time before the child considers, at first
tentatively and with many reservations, the possibility of trusting enough to
relate. Initially, reticent or troubled children may struggle and resist the
relationship, seeming frustrated and disturbed (Moustakas, 1966, 259). But
gradually the child comes to be more present. Though adults may have a goal
in mind and proceed with it intentionally, the relationship must be meaningful
to both partners, each important to the other (Bettelheim, 1974, 10).

Children may view a therapeutic relationship as quite different from
any other they have known. They express and explore underlying attitudes that
in the past have seemed too threatening to reveal. They express themselves
fully without feeling ashamed and guilty. They project feelings and attitudes
through media such as paints, clay, sand, and water, using these materials
symbolically, giving them personal meaning. In the process, the children learn
to make decisions and to act spontaneously and confidently. Their experience
in therapy involves gradual attempts to grow within themselves to self-
awareness and a realistic understanding of their life (Moustakas, 1959, 90;
Daivte, 1992, 34).

The affection which adults have for children can serve to compensate for some of the deprivations children may have experienced in their relationships with others. The younger the child the greater the likelihood of behavior change to please the adult. One teacher of older students noted:

> Initially, I had a difficult time establishing a solid foundation for trust with my adolescent students. My background prior to teaching high school was with small children. It had been easy to gain their trust; after all, I was the teacher. My high school students did not give trust so easily; I had to work at it.

Children are constantly being told about whether what they do and say is good or bad, right or wrong. The teacher is another authority from whom children wish to gain acceptance. Adults can manipulate this phenomenon to healthy ends when they lavish praise on children for newly gained, healthier modes of behavior. Children can then engage in healthier adaptations, both in response to adult approval and from the experience that their life is much more gratifying when they do so (Gardner, 1975, 18-19; Arent, 1992, 93-96).

Interpersonal relationships also can help children correct distorted self-images.

> Intimately associated with the affection the therapist has for the child are the feelings of pleasure that the therapist experiences with the child. The child's appreciation, at some level, that he is capable of providing another individual with pleasure on a continual (but not necessarily uninterrupted) basis is gratifying and ego-enhancing. And this is yet another element in the therapist-patient relationships that can be therapeutic. (Gardner, 1975, 19)

Relationships are enhanced and maintained when child/adult communication, the child's responsiveness to social reinforcement, and the child's potential to model or identify with the behavior of the adult are increased. When the adult is significant to the child and can easily communicate, the child tends to imitate this adult and discovers pleasure in this context. The adult helps the child learn new ways of behaving. One major goal in establishing a therapeutic relationship is to facilitate this learning (Trieschman et al., 1969, 51-56).

> In order to be like the therapist, [the child] will do as the therapist does. The therapist, demonstrating his mature ego to the child through his own frustration tolerance and ability to accede to reality demands without temper outbursts or undue

> hardship, gives the child a model for maturity that the therapist
> would like the child to identify with and emulate . . . . The
> emotionally disturbed child will relinquish his need for
> immediate pleasure to emulate and please the therapist and so
> receive approval from him. By doing so, the child's ego grows
> and matures. (Hammer & Kaplan, 1967, 35-36)

In building a relationship with disturbed adolescents, the therapeutic impact of the relationship will usually depend on how well the therapist/teacher can maintain the flow of conversation with the youths, to foster the adolescents' positive identification with the therapist/teacher, and to regulate the youths' inevitable concern about the implications of that relationship for their independence. Building the relationship also will involve dealing with matters of comfort, engagement, and motivation. This constitutes the foundation for an effective relationship. Treatment procedures encourage adolescents to assess critically current behavior patterns and to recognize their unrealistic, self-defeating characteristics. These youths also need to learn to look at their behaviors in terms of the present (Weiner, 1970, 13).

Often, what we *do* has more impact on children than what we *say*. "It is only our actions and attitudes that count. The less we talk, the more we allow the child to watch us without having to listen to our words, the more he will trust" (Bettelheim, 1950, 16). With this in mind, one teacher of adolescents said:

> I decided my best investment that December would be a
> Christmas party in my home for all the students. They were
> enthusiastic about the idea (they were typically hard to enthuse)
> and wanted to know what food they would have to bring. I told
> them that I was giving the party and they wouldn't need to
> bring anything except hearty appetites and their "jamming"
> shoes. I also provided transportation to all who needed rides
> (which was almost everyone). My mother, father, and both
> brothers helped pick everyone up. About 35 students attended.
> One girl even brought her three-year-old daughter.
>   The party was a fantastic success. I served lots of food,
> as requested: ham, biscuits, fresh fruits, and vegetables, cookies,
> and a huge cake--everything I thought they might like. They
> brought their own records, and before the night was over they
> had organized a "Soul Train" line and everyone was "jamming."
> This helped greatly in establishing that I was a person who
> could be counted on and who enjoyed having fun.
>   I wish I could say that everyone was completely won
> over. However, a teacher with whom I worked laughingly

reported that everyone had a good time but they were certain that my mother and I had "combed" the house after they left to determine if anything had been stolen.

Another value in the relationship process is that of role modeling. Bandura (1969) described the process of learning by watching others. Modeling or displaying the desired behavior is planned by a role model so a child can actually see what is expected. This means that helping professionals --teachers, therapists, aides, or bus drivers--must be aware of their own behavior, how their behavior affects children, and how children perceive adult behaviors regarding their relationship. Some children may have never experienced such a positive model. Providing appropriate models can generate in children alternative expressions of feelings.

Gazda, Asbury, Balzer, Childers, and Walters (1977, 21-24) reviewed a model for human relations training that described the key concepts of a problem-solving relationship. The three-phase cycle involves self-exploration, better self-understanding, and a more appropriate action or direction. The first phase is based on establishing a good relationship with the helper. The therapeutic goal is, ultimately, self-actualization.

Adults' self-awareness is essential when dealing with emotionally disturbed children who do not accept themselves. These children's perceptions of reality are distorted. They are disturbed in their interpersonal relationships. They neither accept nor respect others, and they are unable to use their abilities in appropriate ways. The therapeutic process is one in which the adult's responses and behaviors act as reality checks for the child. In this relationship process, more systematic reinforcement occurs than would be provided ordinarily, making these facilitating conditions very powerful in terms of self-exploration.

Education and the Relationship Issue: Positive Pupil-Teacher Rapport

Carl Rogers (1969, 3) presented a strong commentary about the role of relationship in education.

The initiation of such learning rests not upon the teaching skills of the leader, not upon his scholarly knowledge of the field, not upon his use of audio-visual aids, not upon the programmed learning he utilizes, not upon his lectures and presentations, not upon an abundance of books . . . . No, the facilitation of significant learning rests upon certain attitudinal qualities that exist in the personal relationship between the facilitator and the learner.

Children learn best from those adults they respect and admire. If respected, the adult can teach children much that can be of therapeutic value (Gardner, 1975, 27). The most frequent issue in the education of emotionally disturbed children about which educators have generally agreed is the need for positive teacher-pupil rapport (Fiedler, 1950; Hirschberg, 1953; Liss, 1955; Devereaux, 1956; Berkowitz & Rothman, 1960; Soper & Combs, 1962; Morse et al., 1964; Morse, 1985; Erickson, 1992).

> School [personnel] and other pupils are the persons who are sensitive or insensitive to expressions of individuality . . . and can create a tolerant or a repressive mood in schools--not only in the way they deal with children but also in the way they deal with adults. Teachers are primarily responsible for the classroom emotional climate and for how restrictive or permissive, individualized or regimented the child's school day will be. . . . If the teacher delegates power to children and shows acceptance of all children in the class, there tends to be more pupil-to-pupil interaction, less interpersonal conflict and anxiety, and more autonomous work, independent thought, and moral responsibility. (Kauffman, 1981, 138)

Teacher-pupil relationship is a potential facilitator of change in children.

> Everything a teacher does can be viewed in the context of a relationship with pupils. Probably no teachers, however, face more constant or more various relationship issues than do teachers of emotionally disturbed children. . . . Teachers of the emotionally disturbed have no liberty to retreat from relationships with their pupils. . . . The psychoeducational teaching approach can help them to use the relationship to facilitate a child's growth. . . . The general aims are to present oneself as a complex, feeling person and to convey to the child (and group) that caring for each other not only feels good but also helps create an atmosphere that promotes skills development. (Knoblock, 1983, 120-121)

The complex nature of children's problems and their built-in distortions of adults' intentions and reliability make the forming of relationships a tremendous hurdle to overcome. In developing a personal relationship with a child, the teacher often maintains an attitude of unyielding patience. The feeling of not being understood or not understanding is a common experience among teachers. The teacher's interest and concern for the child can be projected, however. At times the child's behavior can become more destructive or withdrawn just when the teacher feels that important gains have been made. When the teacher maintains faith throughout the relationship, the definite though unpredictable growth strivings within the child begin to influence the child's behavior toward a more satisfying way of life in school (Moustakas, 1966, 201; Gursky, 1992, 19).

Davis (1966, 193) researched students' responses to teachers' attitudes and indicated that students' evaluations of their teachers' effectiveness are frequently as valid as educators' evaluations. For students, the effective teacher is not only a person who can teach but also one who maintains desirable personal relationships with them.

CONCLUSION

Educators have recognized that schools exert a mighty influence on the emotional and psychological development of children. Schools share in the responsibility for children's socialization. Schools can facilitate a child's capacity for mutually satisfying human relationships, can accept children's feelings and behavior, and can facilitate reciprocal acceptance in good, working teacher-pupil relationships. Schools and teachers can help children cope with reality, experience independence, and develop personal identity. The initial contact of the teacher with the child lays the foundation for future relations and may make the difference between a teaching failure and a teaching success.

Therapeutic relationships can be developed in schools. Because many troubled children have difficulty with positive interpersonal relationships, the personalization of school work involving people-to-people service is preferable (Nicolaou & Brendtro, 1983; Kauffman, 1977; Berkowitz & Rothman, 1960).

The effects of therapeutic relationships are powerful and numerous. Therapeutic relationships "assist the [troubled] child to achieve inner freedom in order to learn and to resume normal development" (Paul & Epanchin, 1982, 303). The child begins to grow emotionally, fostering more appropriate behavioral responses. In the interpersonal relationship with the therapist or teacher or both, the child develops respect for the role model the adult represents and cultivates the desire to take on the admirable qualities of that adult. Through this process children also develop the idea that they are acceptable and likable people. As children's self-esteem is heightened, they become more receptive to academic, social, and other developmental processes in themselves.

No research tells us whether the interpersonal relationship initiated in the classroom has lasting value. However, we know from reports in later life that many individuals have singled out the experience with a teacher as the turning point toward an increased sense of self-esteem, creative accomplishment, originality, and effective living. We also know that the impact of relationships in early life is lasting. It is reasonable to assume that a meaningful relationship in school leaves strong traces of permanent value (Moustakas, 1966, 259-260).

Pervasive and lasting personality changes may occur through relationships, as long-term, intensive psychotherapy has shown us. How much more significant, then, is the relationship developed in the classroom life-space of a child?

CHAPTER ELEVEN

THE THERAPEUTIC INFLUENCE OF STRUCTURE

Structure in the school milieu both sustains children and enhances other program elements in the classroom. This chapter establishes structure as a powerful influence in education. We discuss rationale and definitions for structure and present characteristics and elements of well-structured programs. Examples of implementation of therapeutic structure in various settings are given. Information about how structuring theory can be applied in programs and classrooms is grouped by topics that include the establishment of program goals; the arrangement of the learning environment; the grouping of students; the establishment of routines, rules, and limits; the curricula and activities; and the structuring of adult roles. While some of these aspects of therapeutic milieu have been discussed in earlier chapters in this book, they are here summarized in relation to structure theory. In addition, we discuss uncontrollable variables as complications in the positive influence of structuring.

Though important for all children, structure is critical for those who are troubled. There are many environmental influences and other elements that are essential in effective education and treatment programs for children with socioemotional impairments. These depend on and interact with each other and are given coherence by the introduction of well-designed structure into the school lives of these children. Special educators and clinicians find practices and strategies to fit these elements together into a program providing responsive services.

Structure theory and its application can be complicated because structure is interwoven with other physical, psychological, and programmatic aspects of the environment. The literature provides a variety of approaches in understanding structure and includes efficacy studies and cautions about structuring programs and experiences for students in schools.

While much of the literature on therapeutic structure describes programs for seriously troubled children, the concepts and practices of structure appear to be a *sine qua non* for the general welfare of children in schools. Thus, structural ideas are easily adapted from the socioemotionally impaired population to any classroom in which programming of fine quality is sought.

RATIONALE FOR STRUCTURE

We all need structure in our lives. Children attain their best overall behavior, development, and functioning when requirements and freedoms are defined in an ordered, predictable environment that is managed in a firm, consistent manner. It is essential to learn the reality of structure in living in order for development to proceed normally.

A self-demand educational program in which the child makes all the decisions regarding "what, when, where, how, and how well" is not likely to teach anything efficiently or well. A program pattern with implicit limits is necessary for the security of normal children, and even more so for troubled youngsters (Long et al., 1971, 443).

Most children are oriented to the here and now; they must learn to give up, postpone, deal with frustration, and limit immediate desires and gratifications (Morse & Coopchick, 1979, 74). Especially for children whose lives have been lacking structure and full of failure, externally imposed boundaries that reflect children's learning and emotional needs can sustain them and help them bring order into their lives. The milieu, with all its influences, serves for an otherwise bankrupt child as an "ego bank" upon which he or she now can begin to draw for his or her total life structure (Cruickshank, 1967, 61).

Structure provides a means by which children can learn and integrate self-control in a gradual, increasingly independent manner. Children learn to produce and practice approved behavior in parallel with other learning experiences. The structured atmosphere promotes recall and transfer of learning and enables students to accept responsibility for their actions as well as allowing an atmosphere that helps to solve many discipline problems immediately (Long et al., 1971, 443).

Structure enables the development of children's social skills; by restricting children's ability to communicate with one another and interact with their environment, classroom teachers deny them a powerful opportunity to learn.

At school, the realities of coming to class on time and conforming to classroom behavior standards are important. "The child who comes to class late and knows he is late must have many negative reactions when the teacher does not bring this to his attention. Am I so sick? Am I so different that my teacher does not apply this rule to me?" (Cohen, 1967, 72).

Rules and other structuring strategies that rest upon basic human rights are essential school requirements (Morse, 1985) and are supportive rather than restrictive. If adults fail to provide structure, children may remedy the situation by creating and formulating their own rules for guiding their interactions.

> The teacher's primary task is to structure or order the environment for the child in such a way that work is accomplished, play is learned, love is felt, and fun is enjoyed--by the child and the teacher. Structure and order cannot be provided by allowing the child complete freedom to choose for herself/himself what she/he will do. It must be recognized that disturbed children are in difficulty because they have made and continue to make, if unguided, very bad choices about how to conduct themselves. . . .
>
> Work, play, love, and fun are not learned by failure but by success and mastery. Pride, dignity, self-worth and other attributes associated with mental health are not learned by having wishes immediately gratified, but by struggling to overcome difficulties, meeting requirements, and finding that one's own efforts will achieve desired goals. . . . The teacher must have confidence in her own judgment . . . else there can be no effective structuring of the child's environment. (Kauffman, 1977, 264-265)

The structured approach is summarized by naming three primary components: clear directions; firm expectations that the child will do as directed; and consistent follow-through in applying consequences for behavior. Teachers need to be organized, emphatic, and consistent while still being flexible and reflecting individualized expectations for each child (Ross & Ross, 1976, 199; Paul & Epanchin, 1991, 40, 260).

Structure increases a teacher's ability to intervene early in or prevent inappropriate behavior (Haring & Phillips, 1962, 52; Hewett, 1968, 62; Apter & Conoley, 1984, 188). By providing children with a framework for self-control, the teacher can allow more classroom freedom.

Research about effective schools has pinpointed school milieu and climate as an essential variable. The characteristics of effective schools, classrooms, and instructional processes included, among other variables, orderly school climate, discipline, commitment to achievement expectations, and systematic monitoring of student performance (Goodman, 1985, 104).

A directive, structured approach based on a variety of practices will result in better learning and behavior in both normal and emotionally disturbed children than a less structured, more permissive approach.

Furthermore, on-task behaviors will improve over time in structured classroom systems that emphasize rule review (Kauffman, 1977; Riester, 1984; Ruhl, 1985; Rosenberg, 1986). Structured external control methods for seriously troubled children have produced significantly superior results in students' achievement of cognitive goals such as attending, retaining knowledge, and comprehension (Wright & Nuthall, 1970; Salomon & Achenbach, 1974; Rich, 1978).

Other studies show the benefits of structure on emotionally disturbed children. Morse et al. (1964, 57) established that desirable changes occurred in emotionally disturbed children who attended programs with a psycho-educational design characterized by "firm control in an accepting context." Schopler, Brehm, Kinsbourne, and Reichler (1971, 415) found that five autistic children, ages 4 to 8 years, reacted favorably to relative structure and that autistic children functioning on a lower developmental level had more difficulty utilizing relative unstructure than those functioning on a higher developmental level. Hewett et al. (1967, 31-32) demonstrated that children in classrooms using a systematic checkmark system showed more improvement in arithmetic fundamentals and a higher level of task attention than children in control classrooms not using this highly structured, engineered approach.

Haring and Phillips (1962, 59) compared three types of classrooms for emotionally disturbed children: a structured class, a typical class, and a permissive class. Results indicated that the children who were placed in the structured class "showed improvement in that they were: a) more constructive and tractable in the classroom and the home; b) eager to learn and accomplish academic tasks; c) significantly higher in school progress as a whole; and d) able to complete assigned chores in the home. In general their system of behavior became better organized."

There can be complications in the positive use of structure, however. Brophy and Good (1970), Garfunkel (1976), and others caution that the influences of a highly structured program may be complicated by uncontrollable variables that reduce the positive influence of structuring as a central tool. For example, there is evidence that classroom teachers hold different performance expectations for individual children in their classes and observably communicate these expectations to the children. Because children respond to such expectations, teachers may unknowingly be "pegging" children with ceiling limits. Some research has shown that students do better with high but realistic expectations and praise from their teachers and less well with lower expectations and less reinforcement (Morse & Coopchick, 1979). Teachers' recognition of success is a powerful reinforcer.

Happenings outside the classroom--for instance at home or recess--can affect a child's response to structure, too. It is important to identify such variables and recognize their potential impact as structure is planned.

Given this rationale, what, then, are the components that comprise the mosaic of "structure?"

CHARACTERISTICS OF STRUCTURE

Structure is neither good or bad in itself. The value of structure is determined in terms of purpose and outcomes. The purpose of structure is to address the specific needs and problems of the child and the subsequent goals of the teacher. Structure involves putting things in meaningful order; planning and organizing all tasks, assignments, daily activities, and learning experiences; and setting up realistic educational goals and behavioral objectives for each child.

A good program needs to be structured around and in a comfortable, nonthreatening atmosphere (Bettelheim & Sylvester, 1948; Redl & Wineman, 1957; Long et al., 1971). Basic conditions facilitating enhancement of self-esteem and learning in the classroom include acceptance of children as they present themselves; clearly understood and relatively demanding standards, expectations, and limits; and consequences for broken rules that are understood ahead of time (Hewett, 1968, 123; Schopler et al., 1971, 416; Coopersmith, 1975). Structure does not mean rigidity, however, and a good, structured program gives leeway for children's individuality, needs of autonomy, and expressions of these aspects of personality (Coopersmith, 1975). Such a program admits a variety of freedoms, activities, and experiences within clearly defined boundaries.

APPLICATION OF STRUCTURE THEORY

Opinions vary about the degree and kind of structure to employ and how to implement structure strategies effectively. The degree of structure ordinarily needed by a play therapist, for example, is notably less than that of a behavior therapist who subscribes to operant theory. A play therapy session is structured in terms of the place of therapy, the time of therapy, the length of the session, and the limits set on aggression and destructiveness. Structure in operant conditioning focuses around a specific target behavior to be modified and the reinforcement contingencies to be used (Schopler et al., 1971, 418).

There are various issues in the application of structure in programs. The level of functioning and chronological or developmental age of the child are primary factors in decisions about program structure. Applications of structure theory can be grouped topically according to (1) defining the goal of the program; (2) arrangement of the learning environment; (3) grouping of students; (4) rules, routines, and limits; (5) activities and curriculum; and (6) adult role structures. What follows is a discussion of these techniques and examples of various approaches to the therapeutic use of structure in the classroom.

Defining the Goal of the Program

The setting of goals enters into teachers' decision making as a powerful modulator of practice. "Without a general awareness among its members of the direction the group is to go, the group will at best probably fail in its purpose and may at worst be destructive" (Long et al., 1971, 442). Teachers define program goals and purposes, which then influence the structure, leadership, and methods they employ. These goals, varying from teacher to teacher, influence decisions about the size of the group, the time boundaries, and the kinds of behavioral limits set. The effectiveness of a program may be evaluated in terms of whether it accomplishes or approaches its aims or primary goals.

Studies of public school programs for the emotionally handicapped found that some of the general goals or aims of some of these remedial classrooms are to expedite change in pupils to enable them to return to regular class free of behavior problems; to promote normal educational achievement in emotionally disturbed pupils; to provide a useful, secure placement for disturbed pupils; to enable students to exist in the least extruded special environment; to foster social and emotional rehabilitation; to encourage students to conform to school and societal standards; to enhance students' internalized controls; to support growth of academic skills; to increase skills for future employment; to support students in surviving an adverse home or community environment; to maximize students' potentials; and to enhance self-esteem, adjustment and happiness (Morse et al., 1964; Morse, 1985, 3; Grosenick, George, & George, 1987, 1990).

Our goals imply our values. Individual Education Plans in special education are philosophical statements as well as educational and psychological ones (Morse, 1985, 3). Multiple goals, immediate and long term, overt and covert, direct classroom practice. We may have different--even conflicting--goals for different pupils. Indeed, goals for the same child are not always compatible, thus requiring prioritizing and sequencing. Not all goals can be worked on at the same time. It is important to be clear about what our aim is for each pupil and which are the most important and compatible goals to work on for a specific time period. For instance, the goals of learning to read and acquiring internal controls, adjustment, and happiness may require very different tactics to be reached.

In addition to the goals teachers set for individual students, there are the pupil's own goals, parents' goals for their child, and system goals that must be considered. For instance, the regular school may have keeping a frustrating pupil out of the mainstream as its goal, while a teacher's goal for a particular child may be to return him or her to a regular class. The parents' main goal for the child might be eventual employment, while the pupil's own goal is to be happy and less stressed. The same tactics will not suffice to meet all these goals; a melding of the most important and relevant goals from all concerned parties and an agreement on methods that will be used to meet them is essential.

Arranging the Learning Environment

As discussed in chapter 5, children are responsive to the atmosphere created by the physical design of the setting. Troubled children, who have low resistance to temptation and few controls, are easily swept away in moments of excitement. Structuring learning environments may involve control of extraneous stimuli to create a distraction-free environment and prevent overstimulation (Strauss & Lehtinen, 1947; Redl & Wineman, 1957, 287; Cruickshank, Bentzen, Ratzeburg, & Tannhauser, 1961; Haring & Phillips, 1962, 87; Hewett, Artuso, & Taylor, 1967; Gearheart, 1977, 119; Cheney, 1989, 1-3).

All space should be accounted for and used. Classrooms may be divided into areas designed for more demanding, difficult ("high strength") activities such as language, communication, or academic skills, which are located some distance from the "low strength" activity areas (Haring & Phillips, 1972, 59, 87). Hewett's "engineered classroom" is divided into three major working centers: the mastery and achievement center, which includes assignments in reading, written language, and arithmetic; the exploratory-social center, which involves science, art, and communication activities; and the attention-response-order center, which involves activities that require following directions. If a child fails to accomplish a given task successfully, he or she may be reassigned to another task center (Hewett et al., 1967, 59-61).

Stainback, Stainback, and Froyen (1987, 12-13) suggest effective ways to structure a classroom to prevent or at least to minimize the occurrence of discipline problems. Among their suggestions are arranging classrooms to permit visual monitoring of students; paying attention to how students will move around in the classroom; and reducing possibilities for bumping into things, shoving, and congestion.

Hewett et al. (1967, 59) are among those who see physical arrangements, including materials and furniture, as very important. They recommend that the engineered classroom "be set up in a large room which provides at least 100 sq. ft. per student." Indeed, the ideal floor plan may be one that includes 1200 to 1500 square feet.

Although some feel that a classroom for disturbed children need not be larger than or different from a regular classroom, unnecessary behavior problems may arise from either too much or too little space. Public school classes for disturbed children have often been located in regular-size classrooms that, although adequate, were far from luxurious. These classrooms were rarely specially designed, though sometimes they did have special equipment located in them. Desks, tables, comfortable chairs, learning cubicles, isolation booths, audio-visual equipment, and books and other instructional materials were common items found in these classrooms (Redl & Wineman, 1957; Haring & Phillips, 1962, 1972; Morse et al., 1964; Hewett et al., 1967; Gearheart, 1977).

Equally important is the arrangement of equipment, attitudes toward it, and its ability to withstand rough use by children. The way furniture is designed and how materials and books are kept can either invite creative use of them or indicate that they are to be protected and preserved. It is much better to have "old stuff" around, especially in the places in which rough behavior is to be expected. Having expendable materials "cuts down on unnecessary worry on the part of the adult, avoids embarrassment on the part of the shy child, [and] takes away the spice of triumphant rebellion from the otherwise harmless liveliness of the toughie" (Redl & Wineman, 1957, 286). Space for crisis management and private consultation with children is also important, especially to teachers of children with socioemotional problems (Morse et al., 1964, 47).

Grouping Students

Within a structured learning environment, paramount considerations are the size and composition of the group. With emotionally disturbed children, most professionals agree that group size should be kept small. In public school programs for emotionally disturbed pupils, the most common arrangement was a small core group of 7 to 10 pupils (Redl & Wineman, 1957; Haring and Phillips, 1962, 90; Morse et al., 1964, 28; Lansing, 1965, 423; Parrish & Foster, 1966, 5; Hewett et al., 1967, 63).

Whatever the size of the group, effective grouping demands that care be taken, whenever possible, in selecting the individual members. Students with poor impulse control who are grouped with well-behaved students display fewer disruptive behaviors and the group as a whole tends to remain well-behaved. This is also a more "normalized" approach than segregation of students into groups by level of behavior/impulse control. Because problems may arise out of the composition of the group in spite of the care taken in selecting individual members, grouping should remain flexible and, in some cases, one-to-one instead of group relationships will be needed (Bettelheim & Sylvester, 1948; Redl & Wineman, 1957; Haring & Phillips, 1962; Morse et al., 1964; Grossman, 1990). See chapter 7 for a more in-depth discussion of grouping.

Establishing Clear, Predictable Routines, Rules, and Limits

Classroom routines that are clear, predictable, and orderly--definite but flexible--are important structural ingredients (Strauss & Lehtinen, 1947; Cruickshank et al., 1961; Ross & Ross, 1976; Gardner, 1978; Paul & Epanchin, 1991). The structured approach to teaching establishes such routines and defines expectations regarding children's movement about the classroom. The teacher is directive, making decisions for the child until the child can wisely manage himself or herself. Consistent and reasonable consequences exist and are clearly stated. Scheduled routines should enhance the child's feeling of security and have a relaxing, quieting, and soothing effect.

Guiding principles for arranging the environment to teach effectively are to choose tasks that are appropriate for children and at which they can succeed, and to reinforce achievement and attempts to achieve (Kauffman, 1977, 265). Emphasis in the classroom is placed upon the structure necessary to help each pupil develop inner controls. Class routines provide limits, but freedom is allowed within these limits.

Clearly defined, consistent demands and consequences for behavior are important. Expectations and consequences that are specific and overt tend to reduce limit testing. Neither an overly permissive, inconsistent orientation nor an excessively authoritarian or rigid approach will meet the needs of children (Cruickshank et al., 1961; Strauss & Lehtinen, 1947). Sabatino and Mauser (1978, 137) summarize: "Establish a set of rules or standards governing appropriate behavior in the classroom or playground setting. Communicate those rules and standards directly. Inform pupils of what is expected of them in terms of acceptable classroom behavior in initial class periods. Identify and state the rules explicitly, then regularly rehearse and review the rules and the structure of the curriculum and classroom environment."

Virtually no one argues against the importance of setting consistent and firm limits for socioemotionally impaired children (Haring & Phillips, 1962; Parrish & Foster, 1966; Hewett, 1968; Long et al., 1971). Since these students have little inner control, structure for them must come from their external environment, both at school and at home (Camp & Lathen, 1967; Walker, 1980; Lloyd, Kauffman, & Hallahan, 1984; Strain & Sabatino, 1987). However, there is some disagreement about the number and kinds of limits to set. All programs seem to select aggression aimed at other people as the first item of prohibition. This is especially true of so-called permissive programs that usually designate only one limit or rule (Bettelheim & Sylvester, 1948, 196; Redl & Wineman, 1957, 302; Morse et al., 1964, 29; Reinert, 1980, 56). Morse (1957, 19) felt that limits should be set with scapegoating, gross misuse of food, gang campaigns against adults, and severely primitive behavior. Many teachers set limits about academic work. For example, students are required to start their work and follow through on their assignments (Hewett et al., 1967, 63), to work before they play, to finish each day's assignments, to exhibit good work habits, and to leave others alone who are working.

Some believe that rules should be kept to an absolute minimum to minimize disturbed children's tendencies to misinterpret adult motivation in limit-setting. Behavior that is symptomatic of the child's disturbance or that reflects a present developmental stage should be allowed, even if it is regressive. Adults must help children differentiate toleration of their symptoms from indifference to or even permissive enjoyment of their problems (Redl & Wineman, 1957, 117; Cheney, 1989).

Further, children need to learn that freedom does not mean license to do as one pleases; individuals are allowed to fulfill their needs as long as they do not deprive others of their rights in the process (Reinert, 1980, 122). Ideally, pupils can participate in the rule-making process once the basic boundaries are defined. A peer group management system, for instance, offers full participation by the children and a more informal classroom atmosphere (Virden, 1983, 71; Grossman, 1990, 57-61).

Once rules have been identified, each child's ability to discriminate his or her behavior in relation to the rules should be assessed. Stimulus conditions and situations that may prompt inappropriate behavior need to be identified and these precedents changed while children are learning more adaptive responses. Procedures that incorporate positive reinforcers for appropriate behavior and ignoring or mild negative reinforcers for incompatible, disruptive behaviors can then be started. Behavior change is best supported when contingencies are extended to all settings where behavior is problematic (Hewett, 1968; Schopler et al., 1971). Ideally, group contingencies are set up at school and individual contingencies at home.

It is important to structure the environment so that the limits set are not broken. Children need to know what they can do, and sanctions or consequences for breaking the rules need to be defined and enforced. This can be done by providing a good program and reasonable routines (Morse et al., 1964, 28; Long et al., 1971, 442); through grouping students, according to principles of democratic leadership, to share the responsibility of making rules (Morse et al., 1964; Dreikurs, 1979; Reinert, 1980); and by providing meaningful rewards (Morse et al., 1964; Parrish & Foster, 1966; Hewett et al., 1967; Haring and Phillips, 1972). Children are told that limits are for their protection and that they are accepted even though their inappropriate behavior is not condoned.

Discipline is more than a system of rewards and rules; it means channeling a child's energies and drives toward constructive goals, reducing the child's confusion through setting clear and reasonable limits, and letting the child know exactly what is expected. When limits are broken, the problem incident must be handled in the most constructive way possible, free of hostility or power issues in which the teacher attempts to dominate the child and make him docile and submissive (Fenichel, 1974, 179). The choice of intervention must be based on what will be most helpful to the child. This rules out verbal and physical punishment, which have been found to be of little value in dealing with most children, particularly those who are emotionally disturbed (Morse, 1957; Morse & Wineman, 1957; Redl & Wineman, 1957; Morse et al., 1964; Hewett, 1968).

Structuring Activities and Curriculum

Most children are uncomfortable with ambiguity and thus need to operate within a well-planned time structure that lets them know what they are doing, how long it will take, what they will do next, and how difficult the next task will be (Redl & Wineman, 1957, 292; Cheney, 1989, 3). Although in the therapeutic milieu children are not overwhelmed with too many activities, scheduled activities serve to structure the child's life experience. Pleasurable activities enhance interpersonal relationships as adults communicate acceptance and affection to children (Morse, 1957, 15).

In the curriculum, structure of materials presentation is essential. Teachers must organize what they expect to accomplish in the semester. Effective teachers employ a structuring phase in which they first explain the purposes and rules of the lesson and then proceed with consistent, logical, step-sequenced activities for both academic activities and behavior demands (Jones, 1991, 17-18; Paul & Epanchin, 1991, 352-353).

Some researchers endorse programmed instruction as one of the best methods for providing successful learning experiences for emotionally disturbed students (Rhodes, 1963; Morse et al., 1964; Lansing, 1965; Hewett, 1968; Long et al., 1971; Haring & Phillips, 1972). Planned instruction helps students arrive at short-term educational objectives leading to achievement of their long-term goals. Structured assignments are provided that are clear, relevant to the student's ability, meaningful to the student, and at which the student is likely to succeed. These criteria should be kept in mind whether the teacher is planning an individual lesson or an entire unit of lessons. Activities are planned sequentially, with feedback and reinforcement following every task. Student responses are observed so that the teacher can subsequently select appropriate materials, instruction, expectations, and reinforcement. Students' time on tasks is increased by starting with short periods of time that are gradually increased.

The creative teacher makes learning experiences meaningful for each individual child by selecting both procedures and materials suitable to the child's individual performance level, level of sophistication, and level of interest (Haring & Phillips, 1962; Rhodes, 1963; Morse et al., 1964; Long et al., 1971). Sequences of small steps lead the student toward an end goal. The first step is simple enough to assure success; each succeeding step offers both the challenge of continuing interest and the possibility for success at higher levels of achievements. The teacher, continually providing support to the child, is prepared to reduce the task's level of complexity and the criteria for success in order to maintain the child's feeling of security. Repetition of the material in new, pleasurable, and creative ways may be needed. Most teachers for the emotionally disturbed write daily individual plans for each student, provide concrete procedures and tasks (Haring & Phillips, 1962, 80; Morse et al., 1964, 124; Hewett, 1968, 67), require students to become actively involved with the materials (Rhodes, 1963, 61; Haring & Phillips, 1972, 59), present multisensory experiences (Rhodes, 1963, 63; Hewett, 1968, 115), and heighten the vividness and impact of stimuli (Hewett, 1968, 196).

When activities and routines of a classroom program are structured, the length of the daily schedule should be clarified (Lansing, 1965, 423). Most public school programs for emotionally disturbed children operate on a regular or slightly shortened school day; other programs have a different clientele in the morning and afternoon (Morse et al., 1964, 47). Hewett et al. (1967, 65) recommended a shortened school day running from 8:30 a.m. to 12:30 p.m.; such an arrangement has the advantage of providing sufficient activity for the students as well as providing planning time for the teachers (Haring & Phillips, 1962, 87).

Every meaningful learning experience is followed by an immediate consequence that serves to motivate the child to engage in future learning experiences (Rhodes, 1963, 61). Special educators differ on whether the consequences should be tangible (extrinsic) rewards (Hewett, 1968, 116) or whether they should be rewards that naturally occur in the classroom (intrinsic), such as praise or special privileges (Rhodes, 1963, 62). The engineered classroom systematically uses extrinsic (tangible) rewards such as check marks after each work period; these can be exchanged for such items as toys, candy, and trinkets (Hewett et al., 1967, 78).

Traditional curriculum for the disturbed child follows a well-planned educational program that includes the subject areas of reading, language, arithmetic, social studies, science, art, music, home economics, vocational education, and physical education. Some surveys have shown that academic subjects occupy more than 50 percent of the class time in 70 percent of the public school programs for the emotionally disturbed, while special activities such as music, art, and physical education are considered to be secondary in importance. Classes for the emotionally disturbed cover material on a more corrective teaching basis than do regular classes, with the rate, level, and particularly the expectation reduced. Few special classes include any type of planned group therapy or counseling sessions in their curriculum. Some researchers believe that the scheduled activities are therapeutic in themselves, with social learning taught through free and structured games and through reading about the problems of famous people (Morse et al., 1964; Long et al., 1971; Hammill & Bartel, 1982; Kauffman & Wong, 1991).

Rhodes (1967, 454) on the other hand felt structure should be in two major divisions, of equal importance. One division would carry on the present form of instruction with academic and social activities; the other would be the psychosocial division, whose purpose would be to educate the children toward a reasonable relationship between self and society. In this model, the life needs of each child determine scheduling into both divisions with the goal being to prepare the child to function effectively both as an individual and as a member of society. This approach relies more heavily on the resources of specialists in the fields of social work, psychology, counseling and guidance, special education, and child development.

In terms of content of instructional procedures, Rhodes (1963, 63) suggested five lesson forms for content: the unit, behavior training, skill training, discussion sessions, and group interaction. The more demanding academic-oriented subjects are undertaken in the morning when students are fresher, while non-academic subjects such as music and art are scheduled in the afternoon. Short periods of structured recreational activity may be used to break up the morning work periods (Haring & Phillips, 1962, 90).

Long et al. (1971, 442) recommended the unit, saying: "Within all of the confusion, the unit concept provides a start and a finish to an educational experience. From this the children get the much needed sense of accomplishment." The term "unit" refers to a single lesson cycle focusing on a discrete learning experience; for instance, learning to divide single digit numbers might compose a unit. The teacher explains the objective of the lesson and provides subsequent explanations, instruction, and structured procedures for practice and review.

In serving socioemotionally impaired children in public schools, some educators emphasize structuring content more than others. Perhaps the most structured curriculum is reflected in the engineered classroom (Hewett et al., 1967). In such a classroom, a developmental framework or hierarchy is used to describe the necessary competencies that each child must possess if he or she is to be successful in school. The seven stages or levels of learning that comprise the hierarchy are: the attention level, the response level, the order level, the exploratory level, the social level, the mastery level, and the achievement level.

> The "attention" and "response" levels are primarily concerned with establishing contact with the child, orienting him toward learning, and helping him to begin to participate in the learning process.
> At the "order" level, the goal for the child is learning to adapt to routines and structure.

The "exploratory" level goal for the child is to increase his multi-sensory involvement with the environment.

The "social" level confronts the child with the necessity of learning standards of social appropriateness.

The "mastery" and "achievement" goal levels complete the developmental sequence. Here the child acquires adaptive and intellectual skills and develops a self-motivation for learning. (Hewett et al., 1967, 2)

Each of these levels differs in terms of the learning tasks, the meaningful rewards, and the degree of structure necessary to ensure efficient learning. The teacher's job is to assess "the child's deficits according to the developmental sequence of educational goals and then 'engineer' a successful program of remediation through manipulation of the three sides of the learning triangle--task, reward, and structure" (Hewett et al., 1967, 4).

For O'Rourke (1977, 34-35), content for disturbed children is structured by pacing the program so that the schedule includes quiet times, active times, thoughtful-reflective times, and moving-action times, with seven different periods of time scheduled during a day. Most structured curriculum reflects basic, lower-level objectives that are concrete, specific, and more readily achieved in educational environments that are structured and behavioral in approach. Advanced, higher-level objectives requiring more elaborate cognitive and affective processing are achieved more readily by learners when the environment encourages interaction and social-emotional exploration (Rich, 1978). Examples of the latter type of environments are the psychoeducational and open education strategies.

Structuring Adult Roles

Structure involves patterns of relationship, including child to child, child to teacher, child to environment, or teacher to environment. Without the benefit of these relationships, a full and well-rounded structure cannot exist (Gardner, 1978, 99).

Adults in a program are part of a structured role distribution, and this hierarchy should be based on individual needs (Bettelheim & Sylvester, 1948, 194; Redl & Wineman, 1957, 312-313). Adult roles may vary from program to program. In most schools, teachers and counselors hold central roles, while some programs use parents, homemakers, retired teachers, or high school and college students in such auxiliary roles as aides, tutors, hall monitors, substitutes for the regular teacher, cooks, housemothers, and janitors (Redl & Wineman, 1957; Morse, 1965; Hewett et al., 1967).

Not all adult roles are the same. There is a definite difference between the role of a counselor or therapist and the role of a teacher. The therapist, whose goal is treatment and cure, will seek primarily to remove whatever is blocking the child or distorting his perception, motivation, or activity. The teacher, whose task is to help children learn, will attempt to engage their interest in the material so they will apply their abilities to making the materials their own (Long et al., 1971, 335-336). Regardless of who fills the roles, the adult protector provides gratification of the child's need for love, affection, and friendliness. The adult shields the child from negative handling and also from the child's own impulses (Redl & Wineman, 1957, 306).

The role of the teacher in the engineered classroom is a demanding one in which the adult constantly manipulates "the three essential ingredients in learning . . . the learning task, provision of meaningful rewards for learning and maintenance of a degree of structure . . . to ensure success for each student." In other words, "the teacher remains the manager rather than the managed, fostering pupil initiative and resourcefulness, yet limiting energy here and channeling it there" (Hewett et al., 1967, 59). In this role, the degree of adult control or structure changes from time to time and changes in relationship to the pupils (Long et al., 1971, 244).

CONCLUSION

Children need structure--some more than others--to feel comfortable and secure. Without it, some children act out. However, flexibility within structure is important, since a school program that is rigid and inflexible about procedures makes no allowances for fluctuations in behavior and resists modification for unusual events. Within the structure, tasks and responsibilities must be commensurate with the students' capabilities, changing as students change.

Structure is a characteristic of all programs for emotionally disturbed children, and some research shows its efficacy. Although there is diverse opinion on what constitutes structure and on the degree and kind of structure to use, structure is generally viewed as one of the main factors in successful programs with which participants are satisfied (Morse et al., 1964, 126).

Structure, which involves many areas of programming, can be pulled into a whole from many various pieces. As defined in this chapter, structure involves six basic areas: definition of the goal of the program; arrangement of the physical environment; grouping of students; clear, predictable routines and established rules and limits; structuring of activities and curriculum; and structuring of adult roles.

Perhaps, though, therapeutic structure is as much an attitude as a concrete application of theory. Rules are followed because we know from experience and through reason that they are practical and useful (Malinowski, 1932, 51). Thus we learn from our colleagues and predecessors the value of structure and how it can be applied in a therapeutic sense.

CHAPTER TWELVE

CONCLUSION

Two hundred years ago or more, compassionate and informed professionals and caretakers began milieu practices as they confronted institutional brutality. Programs of treatment began to emerge that used benign environmental influences to recast life experiences and mold therapeutic programs for the mentally ill. This rich heritage now gives us a means to develop more supportive, healing milieus in public schools.

Although therapeutic milieu concepts were hinted at as late as the end of the eighteenth century and have been actively and directly used since the late 1950s in the residential treatment of emotionally disturbed children, the ideas have seldom been applied methodically to public schools. Yet schools are likely to see most children at some time during their developmental period, and they are a critical climate for children and youth, guiding them toward healthier lifelong adjustments or adding to the difficulties they may already be experiencing.

As students come to school with problems, their emotions and behaviors, as much as their academic achievements, necessarily become the concern of schools. There are dozens of everyday opportunities to teach affective as well as behavioral lessons in the life-space of the classroom. Here, a child can receive affection and approval, and acceptance and positive self-regard can be nurtured. But affective education that is relegated to games and gimmickry to be used one hour a week will not work. Techniques which support healthy emotional development and positive behavioral adaptations must be integrated into the whole fabric of school life.

Special children need special consideration because they are so vulnerable. All educators, not just those in special education, need assistance in helping those youngsters, many of whom already are or will be in regular classes or less restrictive environments as the education scene changes.

In this book, we have described what therapeutic milieu practices consist of, what marks or features they exhibit, how they are related to everyday experiences in schools, and how it is possible to proceed to good program intervention in public schools. The therapeutic procedures we describe are much more than special amenities for troubled children--they are pragmatic, healthy practices useful for all children and youth. While these defined procedures are organized to respond to children's needs and to mitigate prior destructive experiences--to transform children in spite of past impediments--they are useful in a much broader sense.

ROLES AND RESPONSIBILITIES OF CHILDREN

We have discussed extensively the roles of adults and systems dedicated in a coalition toward the better adjustment of children. We have recognized children's resistances and adjustment difficulties as well as their developmental vulnerabilities. And we have discussed the expectation that children will initiate and sustain more acceptable behavior, that they will begin to want academic and social success, and that they will eventually engage in programs not because they are forced to, but because they want to. A major source of children's aggression is their frustration around unsatisfied desires to be better learners and better socialized.

Here we emphasize what has been scattered throughout our discussion: children, too, have responsibilities. In spite of defensive behavior, children know what they want. We expect that they want to be better. Wanting to be better, with milieu support, gives rise to actions to be better--something happens in the environment and in children that results in influences that work for children's betterment.

We expect children to become autonomous and responsible, active participants rather than passive spectators in their own programs. They have specific roles and responsibilities. These should be discussed frequently and even written contractually for some children. An understanding should be reached about this team effort early in the school experience.

A Word about Adolescents

Throughout the book, examples have been given about how to use Milieu Therapy techniques with children of all ages, including adolescents. Now we want to emphasize that working with adolescents requires an understanding of their special needs and, sometimes, an adaptation of techniques. Children change rapidly and dramatically when they become adolescents. To facilitate school success, it is critical to understand the nature of the academic environment in secondary school settings and to find effective ways to instruct and manage classroom behaviors.

The fundamental task of adolescents is the achievement of autonomy. They are struggling with simultaneous needs for independence and dependence. Before this dilemma is resolved, earlier developmental struggles may emerge. Family influences compete with increased peer pressure, and these forces both assist and inhibit adolescents' efforts to individuate and achieve a comfortable sense of self. Adolescents are both excited and anxious about these developments.

A central issue of adolescence is hormonally as well as socially induced: sexuality becomes a prominent theme. Exploring sexuality is a natural part of preadolescent and adolescent development. Secret conversations and profane and sexual language are common.

The problems of adolescents are more deeply ingrained than those of younger students, and they can be more difficult to manage in schools. Teachers are often not prepared to deal with these youngsters and find it hard to remain emotionally neutral or hopeful about these students' school success. Antisocial behaviors trigger management problems and exclusion from school. The reactions of school staff to these problems contribute to adolescents' dropping out of school (Huntze & Grosenick, 1980, 6-11; Shea & Bauer, 1987, 275-278). Well over half of children labeled as emotionally disturbed leave school before completing the 11th grade--they comprise the highest dropout rate in the United States in public schools (Nelson & Kauffman, 1978, 68; Halpern, 1979, 518; Safer, 1982, 21; U.S. Department of Education, 1987, 30-31). Few troubled adolescents who remain in school are in regular classes; only about a third are in resource rooms or partially mainstreamed (U. S. Department of Education, 1987, 30-31).

Adolescents present a special challenge, but the successes, when they come, are special too. Therapeutic milieu techniques can aid us on our path alongside these young people.

SCHOOL SYSTEMS

Schools, whose function it is to nurture children's minds, are under siege. As social crises in other institutions such as the family and the community accelerate, more and more children in schools are troubled. Schools' responsibilities have increased, but they are often not given the resources to meet these challenges, and students often do not receive what they need in schools. Teachers and others on the front lines in schools are on the spot. They are in systems that often choose to ignore children with handicaps, still embracing the discredited belief that these students are incapable of learning or behaving appropriately. School systems thus excuse children from academic, social, and behavioral standards; exclude and blame their parents; and excuse themselves from moral and legal mandates to support appropriate education for these children. Because many systems that should be supporting them are actually failing them, school personnel are not prepared to do all that is possible. Teachers are not trained in constructive use of the milieu. They are not supported to plan and structure the learning environment for children. They are often not aided in neutralizing derogatory attitudes and practiced prejudice toward troubled children.

Positive school climates include orderly atmospheres, strong administrative leadership, effective teacher involvement, emphasis on basic skills instruction, and ongoing assessment of pupil performance (Lipsky & Gartner, 1987, 70-71). Affective and social aspects of students' lives are given equal priority with their cognitive development. Students mature as they are accorded the rights and respect due them as individuals. Teachers can call upon and extend their treasury of strategies and can use them as they deem appropriate.

CONCLUSION

Adults and children are participants together in the environments of life. These can be a benevolent covenant with children in developing a commonwealth for them. In this book, we have re-established schools as environments where essential, important, normal desires, such as being pleased with oneself, having friends, and having basic physical and emotional needs met, are satisfied. Schools can affirm one's total life pattern, including future prospects, and can create joy through favorable turns of circumstances. They can provide respite from gloom, anxiety, restlessness, depression, discouragement, and shame.

The theme of our advocacy for children does not demean any approach or hold one as exclusive. In this book, we have noted the commonalties in interventions and applications, as well as the essence of thinking among various social science disciplines, including education, social work, and psychology. State-of-the-art thinking in most disciplines emphasizes interpersonal relationships, structuring, environmental manipulation, self-esteem, talking with (or "interviewing") children, social cognition procedures, contingent management principles, and individual psychology. These ideas are reflected in the theory and practice associated with Milieu Therapy.

Therapeutic milieu practices, properly used, reflect reasonable group and societal rules, norms, and values. Strategic management of school environments can help teachers and others do more than just survive times of escalating stress in the schools. With a well-managed environment, all who enter the school's life space can indeed thrive. We hope that educators and others who work with children, inside and outside the schools, have found here some ideas that will enhance their life spaces and those of children. We recognize that, as with friendships or therapy, a "fit" is important; not every tool is appropriate for every educator. And we know that techniques learned in the head but used from the heart are apt to be the ones that make real differences in the lives of those they touch.

BIBLIOGRAPHY

Abate, L. & Curtis, L. A. (1975). Teaching the exceptional child. Philadelphia: W. B. Saunders.

Aichhorn, A. (1935). Wayward youth. New York: Viking.

Algozzine, B., Ysseldyke, J., Kauffman, J., & Landrum, T. (1991). Implications of school reform in the 1990s for teachers of students with behavior problems. Preventing School Failure, 35(2), 7.

Alt, H. (1960). Residential treatment for the disturbed child. New York: International Press.

Apter, S. J. (1982). Troubled children/troubled systems. New York: Pergamon Press.

Apter, S. J., & Conoley, J. C. (1984). Childhood behavior disorders and emotional disturbance: An introduction to teaching troubled children. Englewood Cliffs, NJ: Prentice-Hall.

Arent, R. P. (1992). Trust building with children who hurt. Nyack, NY: The Center for Applied Research in Education.

Bandura, A. (1969). Principles of behavior modification. New York: Holt, Rinehart & Winston.

Bandura, A. (1982). Self-efficacy mechanism in human agency. American Psychologist, 37, 122-148.

Barragan, M. (1976). The child-centered family. In P. J. Guerin, Jr. (Ed.), Family therapy (pp. 232-247). New York: Gardner Press, for American Orthopsychiatric Association.

Bateson, G., Jackson, D. D., Haley, J., & Weakland, J. (1956). Toward a theory of schizophrenia. Behavioral Science, 1, 251-264.

Beare, P. L. (1991). Philosophy, instructional methodology, training and goals of teachers of the behaviorally disordered. Behavior Disorders, 16(3), 217.

Berkowitz, P. H., & Rothman, E. P. (1960). The disturbed child: Recognition and psychoeducational therapy in the classroom. New York: New York University Press.

Berman, E. M. & Lief, H. I. (1975). Marital therapy from a psychiatric perspective: An overview. American Journal of Psychiatry, 132, 583-592.

Bernstein, M. (1963). Life Space Interview in the school setting. In R. G. Newman & M. M. Keith (Eds.), The school-centered Life Space Interview (pp. 35-44). Washington, DC: Washington School of Psychiatry, School Research Program, P.H.S. Project OM 525.

Bettelheim, B. (1950). Love is not enough. Glencoe, IL: Free Press.

Bettelheim, B. (1974). A home for the heart. New York: Knopf.

Bettelheim, B.,& Sanders, J. (1979). Milieu therapy: The Orthogenic School model. In J. Noshpitz (Ed.), Basic handbook of child psychiatry (Vol. 3, pp. 216-230). New York: Basic Books.

Bettelheim, B., & Sylvester, E. (1948). A therapeutic milieu. American Journal of Orthopsychiatry, 18, 191-206.

Bettelheim, B., & Sylvester, E. (1949). Milieu therapy-indications and illustrations. Psychoanalytic Review, 36, 54-67.

Biber, B. (1961). Integration of mental health principles in the school setting. In G. Caplan (Ed.), Prevention of mental health disorders in children. New York: Basic Books.

Blackman, H. P. (1989). Special education placement: Is it what you know or where you live? Exceptional Children, 55(5), 459-462.

Bloom, R. B. (1981). The reality rub-in interview with emotionally disturbed adolescents. The Pointer, 25(2), 22-25.

Bower, E. M. (1990). A brief history of how we have helped emotionally disturbed children and other fairy tales. Preventing School Failure, 35(1), 11-16.

Bower, E., & Lambert, N. (1976). In-school screening of children with emotional handicaps. In N. Long, W. Morse, & R. Newman (Eds), Conflict in the classroom (3rd ed., pp. 128-133). Belmont, CA: Wadsworth.

Boy, A. V., & Pine, G. J. (1971). Expanding the self: Personal growth for teachers. Des Moines, IA: Wm. C. Brown.

Brendtro, L. K., & Ness, A. E. (1983). Re-educating troubled youth: Environments for teaching and treatment. New York: Aldine.

Bronfenbrenner, V. (1979). The ecology of human development: Experiments by nature and design. Cambridge: Harvard University Press.

Brophy, J., & Good, T. (1970). Teachers' communication of differential expectations for children's classroom performance: Some behavioral data. Journal of Educational Psychology, 61, 365-374.

Brown, G. B. (1981). Strong educational programs: Laying the foundations. In G. B. Brown, R. L. McDowell, & J. Smith (Eds.), Educating adolescents with behavior disorders (p. 10). Columbus, OH: Merrill.

Brown, G. I., Yeomans, T., & Grizzard, L. (1975). The live classroom: Innovation through confluent education and gestalt. New York: Viking Press.

Brown, R. E., Copeland, R. W., & Hall, R. V. (1972). The school principal as behavior modifier. Journal of Educational Research, 66, 175-180.

Buber, M. (1965). The knowledge of man. New York: Harper Torchbooks.

Calhoun, J., Acocella, J., & Goodstein, L. (1977). Abnormal psychology: Current perspectives (2nd ed.). New York: Random House.

Camp, W. L., & Lathen, L. (1967). A successful classroom program for emotionally disturbed children. Training School Bulletin, 64, 31-38.

Caplan, G. (1961). Prevention of mental disorders in children. New York: Basic Books.

Carek, D. J. (1972). Principles of child psychotherapy. Springfield, IL: Charles C. Thomas.

Cheney, C. O. (1989). Preventive discipline through effective classroom management (Report No. 572). San Francisco, CA: Council for Exceptional Children Preconvention Training. (ERIC Document Reproduction Service No. ED 304889), pp. 1-3.

Cheney, C., & Morse, W. (1974). Psychodynamic interventions in emotional disturbance. In W. Rhodes & S. Head (Eds.), A study of child variance (Vol. 2, pp. 253-396). Ann Arbor, MI: University of Michigan Press.

Cheney, C., & Morse, W. C. (1980). Psychodynamic intervention. In N. J. Long, W. C. Morse, & R. G. Newman (Eds.), Conflict in the classroom (4th ed.). Belmont, CA: Wadsworth.

Christof, K. J., & Kane, S. R. (1991). Relationship-building for students with autism. Teaching Exceptional Children, 23(2), 49-51.

Clarizio, H. F., & McCoy, G. F. (1983). Behavior disorders in children. New York: Harper & Row.

Cohen, S. (1967). Comments on "Hyperactive children: Their needs and curriculum". In P. Knoblock & J. L. Johnson (Eds.), The teaching-learning process in educating emotionally disturbed children (p. 72). Syracuse, NY: Syracuse University Press, Division of Special Education and Rehabilitation.

Colman, M.C. (1992). Behavior disorders: Theory and Practice (2nd ed.). Boston: Allyn & Bacon.

Compton, B. R., & Galaway, B. (1975). Social work processes. Homewood, IL: Dorsey Press

Cook, L., & Friend, M. (1991). Collaboration in special education: Coming of age in the 1990s. Preventing School Failure, 35(2), 24-27.

Coopersmith, S. (1975). Developing motivation in young children. San Francisco: Albion.

Copeland, R. E., Brown, R. E., & Hall, R. V. (1974). The effects of principal implemented techniques on the behavior of pupils. Journal of Applied Behavior Analysis, 7, 77-86.

Correa, V., & Tulbert, B. (1991). Teaching culturally diverse students. Preventing School Failure, 35(3), 20-25.

Crow, M. R. (1975). Quality control in child care staff selection. Child Welfare, 54, 513-519.

Cruickshank, W. M. (1967). Hyperactive children: Their needs and curriculum. In P. Knoblock & J. L. Johnson (Eds.), The teaching-learning process in educating emotionally disturbed children (p. 61). Syracuse, NY: Syracuse University Press, Division of Special Education and Rehabilitation.

Cruickshank, W. M., Bentzen, F., Ratzeburg, F., & Tannhauser, M. A. (1961). A teacher method for brain-injured and hyperactive children. Syracuse, NY: Syracuse University Press.

Cullinan, D., Epstein, M. H., & Lloyd, J. W. (1983). Behavior disorders of children and adolescents. Englewood Cliffs, NJ: Prentice-Hall.

Cullinan, D., Epstein, M., & Lloyd, W. (1991). Evaluation of conceptual models of behavior disorders. Behavior Disorders, 16(2), 148-151.

Cumming, J., & Cumming, E. (1966). Ego and milieu: Theory and practice of environmental therapy. New York: Atherton.

Cutler, R., & McNeil, E. (1962). Mental health consultation in schools: A research analysis (USPHS, Grant # MH 6706). Ann Arbor: University of Michigan, Department of Psychology, in cooperation with the Oak Park, Michigan Public Schools. Michigan Society for Mental Health.

Daivte, C. (1992, January). All work and no play. Teacher Magazine, 34-35.

D'Alonzo, B. J., & Boggs, E. T. (1990). A review of the regular education initiative. Preventing School Failure, 35(1), 18-23.

Danielson, L. C., & Bellamy, G. T. (1989). State variation in placement of children with handicaps in segregated environments. Exceptional Children 55(5), 448-455.

Davidson. G., & Neale, J. (1978). Abnormal psychology: An experimental and clinical approach (2nd ed.). New York: Wiley.

Davis, R. A. (1966). Learning in the schools. Belmont, CA: Wadsworth.

Davis, R., Myers, B., & Sarbo, P. (1989). Managing through change. In American Association of Residential Centers, Contributions to residential treatment (pp. 51-56). Washington, DC: Author.

Davis, W. E. (1989). The Regular Education Initiative debate: Its promises and problems. Exceptional Children, 55(5), 440-446.

Day, J. F. (1978). Behavioral technology: A negative stand. In H. Goldstein (Senior Author). Readings on emotional and behavioral disorders (pp. 194-196). Guilford, CT: Special Learning Corporation.

DeMagistris, R., & Imber, S. (1980). The effects of LSI on academic and social performance of behaviorally disordered children. Behavioral Disorders, 6(1), 12-15.

Devereaux, G. (1949). The social structure as a factor in total milieu therapy. American Journal of Orthopsychiatry, 19, 494-500.

Devereaux, G. (1956). Therapeutic education. New York: Harper & Row.

Dreikurs, R. (1979). Technology of conflict resolution. Journal of Individual Psychology, 28, 203-206.

Dupont, H. (1989). The emotional development of exceptional students. Focus on Exceptional Children, 21(9), 4-7.

Edgar, E. (1988, March). New directions for education as an intervention for quality of life. Paper presented at the International Conference of the Council for Exceptional Children, Washington, DC.

Endler, N. (1975). A person-situation interaction model for anxiety. In C. Spielberger & I. Sarason (Eds.), Stress and anxiety (Vol. 1). Washington, DC: Hemisphere.

Epanchin, B. C., & Paul, J. L. (1987). Emotional problems of childhood and adolescence: A multi-disciplinary perspective. Columbus, OH: Merrill.

Erickson, K. A. (1977). Disruptive youth and the rights of others. Today's Education, 66(1), 121-122.

Erickson, M.T. (1992). Behavior disorders of children and adolescents. Englewood Cliffs, NJ: Prentice Hall.

Essex, L. N. (1982, Summer). Supervision of teachers of students with behavioral problems in school settings: Special considerations. In R. B. Rutherford, Jr., A. G. Prieto, & J. E. McGlothin (Eds.), Monograph in behavioral disorders: Severe behavior disorders of children and youth (pp. 22-31). Tempe: Arizona State University, Teacher Educators for Children with Behavior Disorders and Council for Children with Behavior Disorders.

Fagen, S. A. (1981). Conducting an LSI: A process model. The Pointer, 25(2), 9-11.

Fagen, S. A., & Long, N. J. (1979). A psychoeducational curriculum approach to teaching self-control. Behavioral Disorders, 4, 68-82.

Fagen, S. A., Long, N. J., & Stevens, D. J. (1975). Teaching children self-control: Preventing emotional and learning problems in the elementary school. Columbus, OH: Merrill.

Farkas, G. M. (1980). An ontological analysis of behavior theory. American Psychologist, 35, 364-374.

Fenichel, C. (1966). Psychoeducational approaches for seriously disturbed children in the classroom. In P. Knoblock (Ed.), Intervention approaches in educating emotionally disturbed children. Syracuse, NY: Syracuse University Press.

Fenichel, C. (1974). Special education as the basic therapeutic tool in treatment of severely disturbed children. Journal of Autism and Childhood Schizophrenia, 4(2), 179.

Fiedler, F. E. (1950). The concept of an ideal therapeutic relationship. Journal of Consulting and Clinical Psychology, 14, 230-245.

Fimian, M. J. (1986). Social support, stress and special education teachers: Improving the work situation. The Pointer, 31(1), 49-53.

Fishman, K. D. (1991). Therapy for children. The Atlantic, 267(6), 55-56.

Fraser, M. (1974). The treatment of deviance by the mental health system: History. In W. Rhodes & S. Head (Eds.), A study of child variance. (Vol. 3). Franklin, TN: New Academic Press.

French, D. (1952, Winter). Science says: Studies of disturbed children throw light on normal behavior. Child Study, 53.

Fromm-Reichman, F. (1948). Notes on the development of treatment of schizophrenia by psychoanalytic psychotherapy. Psychiatry, 11, 263-273.

Gardner, R. A. (1975). Psychotherapeutic approaches to the resistant child. New York: Jason Aranson.

Gardner, R. (1990). Life space interviewing: It can be effective, but don't.... Behavioral Disorders, 15(2), 111-118.

Gardner, W. I. (1978). Children with learning and behavior problems: A behavior management approach (2nd ed.). Boston: Allyn & Bacon.

Garfunkel, F. (1976). Early childhood special education for children with social and emotional disturbances. In H. H. Spicker, N. J. Anastasio, & W. L. Hodges (Eds.), Children with special needs: Early development and education. Washington, DC: Leadership Training Institute. (Grant from Exceptional Children Program, Bureau of Adult and Occupational Education, U.S. Office of Education, HEW Grant OEG 0-9-336005-2452, 126-128).

Gazda, G. M., Asbury, F. R., Balzer, F. J., Childers, W. C., & Walters, R. P. (1977). Human relations development: A manual for educators (2nd ed., pp. 21-31). Boston: Allyn & Bacon.

Gearheart, B. R. (1977). Learning disabilities: Educational strategies (2nd ed.). St. Louis: C. V. Mosby.

Goodman, L. (1985). The effective school movement and special education. Teaching Exceptional Children, 17(2), 104.

Greer, J. V. (1989). Another perspective and some immoderate proposals on "teacher empowerment". Exceptional Children, 55(4), 294-297.

Grosenick, J. K., George, M. P., & George, N. L. (1987). A profile of school programs for the behaviorally disordered: Twenty years after Morse, Cutler, and Fink. Behavioral Disorders, 12(3), 159-168.

Grosenick, J. K., George, N. L., George, M. P., & Lewis, T. J. (1991). Public school services for behaviorally disordered students: Program practices in the 1980s. Behavioral Disorders, 16(2), 91.

Grossman, H. (1990). Trouble-free teaching: Solutions to behavior problems in the classroom. Mountain View, CA: Mayfield.

Gursky, D. (1992, February). Spare the child? Teacher Magazine, 17-19.

Haley, J. (1962). Whither family therapy? Family Process, 1, 69-120.

Haley, J. (1971). Changing families: A family therapy reader. New York: Grune and Stratton.

Halpern, A. S. (1979). Adolescents and young adults. Exceptional Children, 45(7), 518-523.

Halpern, A. S. (1992). Transition: Old wine in new bottles. Exceptional Children, 58(3), 209-211.

Hamilton, G. (1961). Theory and practice of social case work. New York: Columbia University Press.

Hammer, M., & Kaplan, A. M. (1967). The practice of psychotherapy with children. Springfield, IL: Dorsey Press.

Hammill, D. D., & Bartel, N. R. (1982). Teaching children with learning and behavior disorders (3rd ed.). Boston: Allyn & Bacon.

Haring, N. G., & Phillips, E. L. (1962). Educating emotionally disturbed children. New York: McGraw Hill.

Haring, N. G., & Phillips, E. L. (1972). Analysis and modification of classroom behavior. Englewood Cliffs, NJ: Prentice-Hall.

Harris, P. (1987). Characteristics of successful school principals. Teaching Exceptional Children, 19(4), 46.

Hartford, M. E. (1971). Groups in social work: Application of small group theory and research to social work practice. New York: Columbia University Press.

Heuchert, C. M. (1983). Can teachers change behaviors? Try interviews! Academic Therapy, 18(3), 321-328.

Heuchert, C., & Long, N. (1981). A brief history of Life Space Interviewing. The Pointer, 25(2), 5-8.

Hewett, F. M. (1968). The emotionally disturbed child in the classroom: A developmental strategy for educating children with maladaptive behavior. Boston: Allyn & Bacon.

Hewett, F. M. (1981, Summer). Behavior ecology: A unifying strategy for the 80's. In R. B. Rutherford, Jr., A. G. Prieto, & J. E. McGlothin (Eds.), Monograph in behavioral disorders: Severe behavior disorders of children and youth (p. 3). Tempe: Arizona State University, Teacher Educators for Children with Behavior Disorders and Council for Children with Behavioral Disorders.

Hewett, F. M. (1985, Summer). Person-environment fit: A unifying concept for special education. In R. B. Rutherford, Jr., A. G. Prieto, & J. E. McGlothin (Eds.), Monograph in behavioral disorders: Severe behavior disorders of children and youth (Vol. 8, pp. 1-17). Tempe: Arizona State University, Teacher Educators for Children with Behavior Disorders and Council for Children with Behavioral Disorders.

Hewett, F. M. (1987). The ecological view of disturbed children: Shadow versus substance. The Pointer, 31(3), 61-63.

Hewett, F. M., Artuso, A. A., & Taylor, F. D. (1967). The Santa Monica Project: Demonstration and evaluation of an engineered classroom design for emotionally disturbed children in the public school. Phase I-Elementary Level (Project No. 62893: Grant No., OEG 4-7-062893-0377). Los Angeles: University of California. (ERIC Document Reproduction Service).

Hirschberg, J. C. (1953). The role of education in the treatment of emotionally disturbed children through planned ego development. American Journal of Orthopsychiatry, 23, 684.

Hizer, D. (1972). The use of milieu rehabilitation in the adjustment training of socioculturally disadvantaged. Vocational Evaluation and Work Adjustment Bulletin, 5, 11-15.

Hobbs, N. (1966). Helping disturbed children: Psychological and ecological strategies. American Psychologist, 21, 1105-1115.

Hobbs, N. (1975). The futures of children. San Francisco: Jossey-Boss.

Huntze, S. L., & Grosenick, J. K. (1980). National needs analysis in behavior disorders: Human resources issues in behavior disorders (pp. 20-25). Columbia, MO: University of Missouri-Columbia.

James, W. (1899). Talks to teachers on psychology. Reissued 1946. New York: Henry Holt.

Jones, V. F. (1991). Responding to students' behavior problems. Beyond Behavior, 2(1), 17-19.

Jones, V. F., & Jones, L. S. (1986). Comprehensive classroom management: Creating positive learning environments (2nd ed). Boston, MA: Allyn & Bacon.

Kameya, L. I. (1974). Behavioral interventions in emotional disturbance. In W. C. Rhodes & M. L. Tracy (Eds), A study of child variance (Vol. 2, pp. 159-252). Ann Arbor, MI: University of Michigan Press.

Kauffman, J. M. (1977). Characteristics of children's behavior disorders. Columbus, OH: Merrill.

Kauffman, J. M. (1981). Characteristics of children's behavior disorders (2nd ed.). Columbus, OH: Merrill.

Kauffman, J.M., & Wong, K.L. (1991). Effective teachers of students with behavioral disorders: Are generic teaching skills enough? Behavioral Disorders, 16(3), 232-234.

Kemp, J. (1971). Family treatment within the milieu of a residential treatment center. Child Welfare, 50, 229-235.

Kipfer, J. F. (1961). Introduction to the action research project. American Journal of Orthopsychiatry, 32, 321.

Kitchner, H. L. (1963). The Life Space Interview in the differentiation of school in residential treatment. American Journal of Orthopsychiatry, 33(1), 720-722.

Knoblock, P. (1983). Teaching emotionally disturbed children. Boston: Houghton-Mifflin.

Kratochwill, T. R., & Morris, R. J. (1991). The practice of child therapy. Elmsford, NY: Pergamon Press.

Krupicka, W. M. (1988). An interview with Dr. James Tompkins about the Life Space Interview. Unpublished Interview, Appalachian State University, Boone, NC.

Lansing, M. D. (1965). Crafts for severely disturbed children. Exceptional Children, 31, 421-425.

Lauritzen, P., & Friedman, S. (1991). Teachers for children with emotional/behavioral disorders: Education's greatest challenge? Preventing School Failure, 35(2), 11-15.

Lawrence, P. A. (1988). Basic strategies for mainstream integration. Academic Therapy, 23(4), 349-355.

LaVietes, R. (1962). The teacher's role in the education of emotionally disturbed children. Exceptional Children, 32(3), 854-862.

Leone, P., Lutting, P., Zlotlow, S., & Trickett, E. (1990). Understanding the social ecology of classrooms for adolescents with behavioral disorders: A preliminary study of differences in perceived environments. Behavioral Disorders, 16(1), 55

Lewis, M., & Summerville, J. (1991). Residential treatment. In M. Lewis (Ed.), Child and adolescent psychiatry: A comprehensive textbook (p. 895). Baltimore: William and Wilkens.

Lipsky, D. K., & Gartner, A. (1987). Capable of achievement and worthy of respect: Education for handicapped students as if they were full-fledged human beings. Exceptional Children, 54(1), 69-74.

Liss, E. (1955). Motivations in learning. In A. Freud (Ed.), Psychoanalytic study of the child (Vol. 10, pp. 110-116). New York: International Universities Press.

Lloyd, J. W., Kauffman, J. M., & Hallahan, D. P. (Eds.). (1984). Effective teaching: New evidence for special educators. Special Education Today, 1(2). Charlottesville, VA: SET Press.

Long, N. J. (1963). Some problems in teaching Life-Space Interviewing techniques to graduate students in a large class at Indiana University. American Journal of Orthopsychiatry, 33(1), 723-725. Washington DC: Washington School of Psychiatry.

Long, N. J. (1969). Helping children cope with feelings. Childhood Education, 45, 367-372.

Long, N. J. (1986). The nine psychoeducational stages of helping emotionally disturbed students through the reeducation process. The Pointer, 30(3), 4-20.

Long, N. J. (1981). Manipulation of body boundaries. The Pointer, 25(2), 34-36.

Long, N. J. (1990a). Life space interviewing. Beyond Behavior, 2(1), 10-15.

Long, N. J. (1990b). Comments on Ralph Gardner's article "Life Space Interviewing: It can be effective but don't..." Behavioral Disorders, 15(2), 119-125.

Long, N. J., & Morse, W. (1965). Special classes for children with social and emotional problems in the public schools. In W. Wattenberg (Ed.), Sixty-fourth yearbook of the national society for the study of education (Part 1, Chapter 12). Chicago: University of Chicago Press.

Long, N. J., Morse, W., & Newman, R. (1971). Conflict in the classroom (2nd ed.). Belmont, CA: Wadsworth.

Long, N. J., Morse W., & Newman, R. (1980). Conflict in the classroom: The education of children with problems (4th ed.). Belmont, CA: Wadsworth.

Long, N. J., & Newman, R. (1965). Managing surface behavior of children in school. In N. J. Long, W. C. Morse, & R. G. Newman (Eds.), Conflict in the classroom. Belmont, CA: Wadsworth.

Lord, W. (1987). The night lives on. Reader's Digest Condensed Books (Vol. 3). Pleasantville, NY: The Reader's Digest Association.

Luft, J. (1970). Group process: An introduction to group dynamics. Palo Alto, CA: Mayfield.

Malinowski, B. (1932). Crime and custom in savage society. London: Collier MacMillan.

Malmquist, C. P. (1976). The theoretical status of depression in childhood. In E. J. Anthony & D. C. Gilpin (Eds.), Three clinical faces of childhood (pp. 173-204). New York: Spectrum.

McClellan, J. E., Jr. (1967). Philosophy of education: Influence of modern psychology. In P. Edwards (Ed.), The encyclopedia of philosophy (Vol. 6, pp. 243-247). New York: MacMillan & Free Press.

McDowell, R. L., Adamson, G. W., & Wood, F. H. (1982). Teaching emotionally disturbed children. Boston: Little, Brown.

Meichenbaum, D. (1980). Cognitive behavior modification with exceptional children: A promise yet unfulfilled. Exceptional Children Quarterly, 1(1), 83-88.

Merritt, C. A. (1981). Bandaid for the bumps: Emotional first aid. The Pointer, 25(2), 16-19.

Messer, S., & Winoker, M. (1980). Some limits to the integration of psychoanalytic and behavior therapy. American Psychologist, 35, 818-827.

Miller, N., & Dollard, J. (1941). Social learning and imitation. New Haven: Yale University Press.

Morgan, R. (1981). Group life space interviewing. The Pointer, 25, 37-41.

Morgan, S. R. (1979). A model of the empathic process for teachers of emotionally disturbed children. American Journal of Orthopsychiatry, 49(3), 446-453.

Morgan, S. R. (1985). Children in crisis: A team approach in the schools. San Diego, CA: College-Hill Press.

Morse, W. C. (1957). An interdisciplinary therapeutic camp. Journal of Social Issues, 13(1), 15-22.

Morse, W. (1961). The mental hygiene dilemma in public education. American Journal of Orthopsychiatry, 31, 331.

Morse, W. C. (1963). Training teachers in Life Space Interviewing. American Journal of Orthopsychiatry, 33, 727-730.

Morse, W. (1965). The mental hygiene viewpoint on school discipline. The High School Journal, 48, 396-401.

Morse, W. (1971). Classroom disturbance: The principal's dilemma. Arlington, VA: Council for Exceptional Children.

Morse, W. C. (1976a). Worksheet on Life Space Interviewing for teachers. In N. J. Long, W. C. Morse, & R. G. Newman (Eds.), Conflict in the classroom (3rd ed., pp. 267-270). Belmont, CA: Wadsworth.

Morse, W. C. (1976b). The crisis or helping teacher. In N. J. Long, W. C. Morse, & R. G. Newman (Eds.), Conflict in the classroom (3rd ed., pp. 249-302). Belmont, CA: Wadsworth.

Morse, W. C. (1981). LSI tomorrow. The Pointer, 25(2), 67-70.

Morse, W. (1985). The education and treatment of socio-emotionally impaired children and youth. Syracuse, NY: Syracuse University Press.

Morse, W. C., Ardizzone, J., MacDonald, C., & Paick, P. (1980). Affective education for special children and youth. Reston, VA: The Council for Exceptional Children.

Morse, W. C., & Coopchick, H. (1979). Socio-emotional impairment. In W. C. Morse (Ed.), Humanistic teaching for exceptional children: An introduction to special education (pp. 74-76). Syracuse, NY: Syracuse University Press.

Morse, W. C., Cutler, R. L., & Fink, A. H. (1964). Public school classes for the emotionally handicapped: A research analysis. Washington, DC: Council for Exceptional Children.

Morse, W. C., & Ravlin, M. M. (1979). Psychoeducation in the school setting. In J. D. Noshpitz & S. I. Harrison (Eds.), Basic handbook of child psychiatry: Vol. 3. Therapeutic interventions. New York: Basic Books.

Morse, W. C., & Small, E. R. (1959). Group Life Space Interviewing in a therapeutic camp. American Journal of Orthopsychiatry, 29, 27-44.

Morse, W. C., & Smith, J. C. (1983). Understanding child variance (Third Printing). Reston, VA: Council for Exceptional Children.

Morse, W. C., & Wineman, D. (1957). Group interviewing in a camp for disturbed boys. Journal of Social Issues, 13(1), 23-31.

Moustakas, C. E. (1959). Psychotherapy with children. New York: Harper & Row.

Moustakas, C. (1966). The authentic teacher: Sensitivity and awareness in the classroom. Cambridge, MA: Howard A. Doyle.

Mowrer, O. (1939). A stimulus-response analysis of anxiety and its role as a reinforcing agency. Psychological Review, 46, 553-565.

Myles, B. S., & Whelan, R. J. (1991). The regular education initiative without waivers. Focus on Exceptional Children, 23(7), 8-10.

Naslund, S. R. (1987). Life Space Interviewing: A psychoeducational intervention model for teaching pupil insights and measuring program effectiveness. The Pointer, 31(2), 12-20.

Nelson, C. M. (1983). Beyond the classroom: The teacher of behaviorally disordered pupils in a social system. In R. B. Rutherford, Jr., A. G. Prieto, & J. E. McGlothin (Eds.), Monograph in behavioral disorders: Severe behavior disorders of children and youth (pp. 1-12). Tempe: Arizona State University, Teacher Educators for Children with Behavior Disorders and Council for Children with Behavioral Disorders.

Nelson, C. M., & Kauffman, J. M. (1978). Educational programming for secondary school age delinquent and maladjusted pupils. In H. Goldstein (Ed.), Readings in emotional and behavioral disorders. Guilford, CT: Special Learning Corp.

Newcomer, P. L. (1980). Understanding and teaching emotionally disturbed children. Boston: Allyn & Bacon.

Newman, R. G. (1963). The school centered Life Space Interview as illustrated by extreme threat of school issues. American Journal of Orthopsychiatry, 33(4), 730-733.

Newman, R. G., & Keith, M. M. (1963). The school-centered Life Space Interview. School Research Program: P.H.S. Project OM 525. Washington, DC: Washington School of Psychiatry.

Nicolaou, A., & Brendtro, L. (1983). Curriculum for caring: Service learning with behaviorally disordered students. In R. B. Rutherford, Jr., A. G. Prieto, & J. E. McGlothin (Eds.), Monograph in behavioral disorders: Severe behavior disorders of children and youth (pp. 110-111). Tempe: Arizona State University, Teacher Educators for Children with Behavior Disorders and Council for Children with Behavior Disorders.

Noel, M. M. (1982). Public school programs for the emotionally disturbed: An overview. In H. G. Haring & M. M. Noel (Eds.), Progress or change: Issues in educating the emotionally disturbed: Vol. 2. Service delivery (pp. 1-28). Seattle: University of Washington Press.

Noshpitz, J. D. (1962). Notes on the theory of residential treatment. Journal of the American Academy of Child Psychiatry, 1, 284-296.

O'Rourke, R. D. (1977). Troubled children: A new design for learning. Teaching Exceptional Children, 9, 34-35.

Osorio, R. (1970). Milieu therapy for child psychosis. American Journal of Orthopsychiatry, 40, 121-129.

Ostrosky, M. M., & Kaiser, A. P. (1991). Preschool classroom environments that promote communication. Teaching Exceptional Children, 23(4), 6-10.

Parrish, A. K., & Foster, G. (1966). An approach to emotionally disturbed children: Re-education at Wright School. North Carolina Journal of Mental Health, 2(2), 5-20.

Paul, J. L., & Epanchin, B. C. (1982). Emotional disturbance in children. Columbus, OH: Merrill.

Paul, J. L., & Epanchin, B. C. (1991). Educating emotionally disturbed children and youth: Theories and practices for teachers (2nd ed.). New York: MacMillan.

Peck, M. S. (1983). People of the lie: The hope for healing human evil. New York: Simon and Schuster.

Pfister, O. (1949). Therapy and ethics in August Aichhorn's treatment of wayward youth. In K. Eissler (Ed.), Searchlights on delinquency. New York: International University Press.

Powers, D. (1980). Creating environments for troubled children. Chapel Hill: University of North Carolina Press.

Raiser, L., & Van Nagel, C. (1980). The loophole in Public Law 94-142. Exceptional Children, 46(7), 516-520.

Redl, F. (1959a). The concept of the Life Space Interview. American Journal of Orthopsychiatry, 29, 1-18.

Redl, F. (1959b). The concept of a therapeutic milieu. American Journal of Orthopsychiatry, 29, 721-736.

Redl, F. (1963a). Introduction: Why Life Space Interview? In R. Newman & M. Keith (Eds.), The school centered Life Space Interview. Washington, DC: Washington School of Psychiatry.

Redl, F. (1963b). Strategy and techniques of the Life Space Interview. In R. G. Newman & M. M. Keith (Eds.), The school-centered Life Space Interview (pp. 57-75). Washington, DC: Washington School of Psychiatry.

Redl, F. (1969a). Aggression in the classroom. Today's Education, 5, 29-32.

Redl, F. (1969b). Why Life Space Interview? In H. Du Pont (Ed.), Readings-Educating emotionally disturbed children. New York: Holt, Rinehart & Winston.

Redl, F. (1976). The oppositional child and the confronting adult: A mind to mind encounter. In E. J. Anthony (Ed.), Three clinical faces of childhood. New York: Spectrum Publications.

Redl, F., & Wineman, D. (1951). Children who hate. Glencoe, IL: Free Press.

Redl, F., & Wineman, D. (1957). The aggressive child . Glencoe, IL: Free Press.

Reilly, M., Imber, S., & Kremmens, J. (1978). The effects of Life Space Interviews on social behaviors of junior high school special needs children. Paper presented at the 56th International Conference for Exceptional Children, Kansas City, MO.

Reinert, H. R. (1980). Children in conflict: Educational strategies for the emotionally disturbed and behaviorally disordered. St. Louis: C. V. Mosby.

Reinert, H. R., & Huang, A. (1987). Children in conflict (3rd ed.). Columbus, OH: Merrill.

Reschly, D. J. (1988). Special education reform: School psychology revolution. School Psychology Review 17, 459-475.

Rhodes, W. C. (1963). Curriculum and disordered behavior. Exceptional Children, 30, 61-66.

Rhodes, W. C. (1967). The disturbing child: A problem of ecological management. Exceptional Children, 33, 449-455.

Rhodes, W. C. (1970). A community participation analysis of emotionally disturbed children. Exceptional Children , 37, 309-314.

Rhodes, W., & Head. S. (1974). A study of child variance: Vol. 3. Conceptual project in emotional disturbance. Ann Arbor: Institute for the Study of Mental Retardation and Related Disabilities, University of Michigan.

Rich, H. L. (1978). A matching model for educating the emotionally disturbed and behaviorally disordered. Focus on Exceptional Children, 10(3), 5.

Riester, A. E. (1984). Teaching the emotionally disturbed student. The Pointer, 28(3), 13-18.

Riester, A. E., & Bissette, K. M. (1986). Preparing the peer group for mainstreaming. The Pointer, 31(1), 12-20.

Rogers, C. R. (1967). The interpersonal relationship in the facilitation of learning. In R. R. Leeper (Ed.), Humanizing education: The person in the process. Washington, DC: Association for Supervision and Curriculum Development.

Rogers, C. R. (1969). Freedom to learn. Columbus, OH: Merrill.

Rosenberg, M. S. (1986). Maximizing the effectiveness of structured classroom management programs: Implementing rule-review procedures with disruptive and distractible students. Behavioral Disorders, 11(4), 239-248.

Rosenberg, M. S., Wilson, R., Maheady, L., & Sindelor, P.T. (1992). Educating students with behavior disorders. Boston: Allyn & Bacon.

Rosenthal, R., & Jacobson, L. (1968). Pygmalion in the classroom. New York: Holt, Rinehart & Winston.

Ross, D. M., & Ross, S. A. (1976). Hyperactivity: Research, theory and action. New York: Wiley.

Ruhl, K. L. (1985). Handling aggression: Fourteen methods teachers use. <u>The Pointer</u>, <u>29</u>(2), 30-32.

Sabatino, D. A., & Mauser, A. J. (1978). <u>Intervention strategies for specialized secondary education.</u> Boston: Allyn & Bacon.

Safer, D. J. (1982). <u>School programs for disruptive adolescents.</u> Baltimore: University Park Press.

Salomon, M. K., & Achenbach, T. M. (1974). The effects of four kinds of tutoring experience on associate responding. <u>American Educational Research Journal</u>, <u>11</u>, 394-504.

Sanders, L. S. (1981). New tool salesmanship. <u>The Pointer</u>, <u>25</u>(2), 32-36.

Sarason, I. (1966). <u>Personality: An objective approach.</u> New York: Wiley.

Sarri, R. C. (1982). Introduction for alternative programs for disruptive youth. In M. A. Thomas, D. A. Sabatino, & R. C. Sarri (Eds.), <u>Alternative programs for disruptive youth</u> (p. 5). Reston, VA: Council for Exceptional Children.

Schopler, E., Brehm, S. S., Kinsbourne, M., & Reichler, R. J. (1971). Effect of treatment structure on development in autistic children. <u>Archives of General Psychiatry</u>, <u>24</u>, 415-421.

Selye, H. (1974). <u>Stress without distress.</u> New York: Lippincott.

Shea, T. M. (1978). <u>Teaching children and youth with behavior disorders.</u> St. Louis: C. V. Mosby.

Shea, T. M., & Bauer, A. M. (1987). <u>Teaching children and youth with behavior disorders.</u> Englewood Cliffs, NJ: Prentice-Hall.

Simpson, R. L., & Myles, B. S. (1990). The general education collaboration model: A model for successful mainstreaming. <u>Focus on Exceptional Children</u>, <u>23</u>(4), 1-10.

Skrtic, T. M. (1987). An organizational analysis of special educational reform. <u>Counterpoint</u>, <u>8</u>(2), 15-19.

Soper, D. W., & Combs, A. W. (1962). The helping relationship as seen by teachers and therapists. <u>Journal of Consulting Psychology</u>, <u>26</u>(3), 288.

Stainback, W., Stainback, S., & Froyen, L. (1987). Structuring the classroom to prevent disruptive behaviors. <u>Teaching Exceptional Children</u>, <u>19</u>(4), 12-16.

Stainback, W., Stainback, S., & Wilkinson, A. (1992). Encouraging peer supports and friendships. <u>Teaching Exceptional Children</u>, <u>24</u>(2), 6-10.

Strain, P. S., & Sabatino, D. A. (1987). Preventive discipline as a practice in special education. <u>Teaching Exceptional Children</u>, <u>19</u>(4), 26-30.

Strauss, A. A., & Lehtinen, L. L. (1947). <u>Psychopathology and education of the brain-injured child.</u> New York: Grune & Stratton.

Sullivan, A. R. (1987). Develop a healthy school climate. <u>Teaching Exceptional Children</u>, <u>19</u>(4), 48.

Swap, S. M., Prieto, A. G., & Harth, R. (1982). Ecological perspectives of the emotionally disturbed child. In R. D. McDowell, G. W. Adamson, & F. H. Wood (Eds.), Teaching emotionally disturbed children (pp. 70-98). Boston: Little, Brown.

Swift, M. S., & Spivack, G. (1975). Alternative teaching strategies. Champaign, IL: Research Press.

Symonds, P. M. (1954). Characteristics of the effective teacher based on pupil evaluations. Journal of Experimental Education, 23, 289-310.

Teachers' Experiences. (1975-1985). Collection of term papers and oral reports from teachers. Appalachian State University: Boone, NC. Unpublished.

Thomas, M. A. (1982). Preface. In M. A. Thomas, D. A. Sabatino, & R. Sarri (Eds.), Alternative programs for disruptive youth (p. v). Reston, VA: Council for Exceptional Children.

Tompkins, J. R. (1981). Symptom estrangement interview. The Pointer, 25(2), 26-28.

Tompkins, J. R., & Allen, M. (1985). National needs analysis and related issues in behavior disorders. Lexington, MA: Ginn.

Tompkins, J. R., & McGill, P. L. (1988). Report: Needed educational and treatment services for children in trouble. Position paper: Boone, NC: Appalachian State University; and Espanola, NM: Las Cumbres Learning Services.

Tompkins, J. R., & McGill, P. L. (1989). Lack of educational and treatment services for students in trouble: A new proposal for help. The Pointer 33(3), 38-42.

Tompkins, J. R., & Pace, T. J. (1991). Therapeutic procedures for troubled children's entry into special education. Unpublished manuscript, Appalachian State University, Boone, NC.

Tompkins, P. L. (1965). An evaluation of the Life Space Interview in an experimental elementary school. Unpublished master's thesis, The Catholic University of America, National Catholic School of Social Services, Washington, DC.

Tompkins, P. L. (1980). An examination of stress and anxiety in teachers of handicapped and non-handicapped children. Unpublished doctoral dissertation, The University of Texas, Austin.

Tompkins, T. J. (1989). The role of the family in the treatment of mental illness: Changing attitudes and providing aid. Unpublished paper, Lyndon B. Johnson School of Public Affairs, The University of Texas, Austin.

Trieschman, A. E. (1970, April 12). Temper, temper, temper, temper, TEMPER! The New York Times Magazine. Reprint.

Trieschman, A. E., Whittaker, J. K., & Brendtro, L. K. (1969). The other twenty-three hours. Chicago: Aldine.

Tucker, J. A. (1989). Less required energy: A response to Danielson and Bellamy. Exceptional Children, 55(5), 456-458.

Uexküll, J. J. (1909). Umwelt und innerwelt der tiere (Berlin), summarized in P. Edwards (Ed.), Encyclopedia of philosophy (Vol. 7, 1972, p. 173). New York: MacMillan and the Free Press.

U.S. Department of Education, Office of Special Education Programs (OSERS). (1987). To assure the free appropriate public education of all handicapped children (pp. xv, xvi, xvii, 19, 29, 30-31 and 41-42). Ninth Annual Report to Congress on the Implementation of the Education of the Handicapped Act. Washington, DC.

Vaughn, C. E., & Leff, J. P. (1976). The influence of family and social factors on the course of psychiatric illness: A comparison of schizophrenia and depressed neurotic patients. British Journal of Psychiatry, 129, 125-137.

Vergason, G. A., & Anderegg, M. L. (1991). Beyond the regular education initiative and the resource room controversy. Focus on Exceptional Children, 23(7), 5-6.

Vernick, J. (1963). The use of the Life Space Interview on a medical ward. Social Casework, 44(8), 465-469.

Virden, T. (1983). Supportive peer groups: A behavior management program for children. In J. K. Grosenick, S. L. Huntze, E. McGinnis, & C. R. Smith (Eds.), L. Bartusek (Technical Ed.), Social/affective intervention in behavior disorders. Columbia, MO and Des Moines, IA: A cooperative Publication of the National Needs Analysis in Behavior Disorders Project, Department of Special Education, University of Missouri and Division of Special Education, Iowa Department of Public Instruction.

Vogel, E. F., & Bell, N. W. (1960). The emotionally disturbed child as the family scapegoat. In N. W. Bell & E. F. Vogel (Eds.), The family (pp. 382-397). New York: Free Press.

Walker, H. M. (1980). The SBS (Social Behavior Survival) inventory of teacher expectations and social behavior survival: Initial validation results. Eugene, OR: University of Oregon Press.

Weiner, I. B. (1970). Psychological disturbance in adolescence. New York: Wiley-Interscience.

Weintrob, A. (1974). Changing population in residential treatment: New problems for programs and staff. American Journal of Orthopsychiatry, 44, 604-611.

Weiskopf, P. (1980). Burnout among teachers of exceptional children. Exceptional Children, 47, 18-23.

Werner, A. (1981). Massaging numb values interview. The Pointer, 25(2), 29-31.

Westman, J. C. (1979). Psychiatric day treatment. In J. D. Noshpitz & S. Harrison (Eds.), Basic handbook of child psychiatry: Vol. 3 (pp. 288-299). New York: Basic Books.
Wicks-Nelson, R., & Israel, A. C. (1991). Behavior disorders of childhood. Englewood Cliffs, NJ: Prentice Hall.
Will, M. C. (1986). Educating children with learning problems: A shared responsibility. Exceptional Children, 52(5), 411-415.
Wineman, D. (1959). The Life Space Interview. Social Work, 4(1), 3-17.
Wood, F. H. (1979). Issues in training teachers for the seriously emotionally disturbed. In R. B. Rutherford, Jr. & A. G. Prieto (Eds.), Severe behavior disorders of children and youth (pp. 12-13). Reston, VA: Council for Exceptional Children.
Wood, F. H. (1982). Cooperative full service delivery to emotionally disturbed students. In M. M. Noel & N. G. Haring (Eds.), Progress or change: Issues in educating the emotionally disturbed: Vol. 1, Identification and programming (pp. 115-134). Seattle: University of Washington, Program Development Assistance System.
Wood, F. H. (1991). Cost/benefit considerations in managing the behavior of students with emotional/behavioral disorders. Preventing School Failure, 35(2), 18-19.
Wood, M. M. (Ed.). (1979). The developmental therapy objectives (3rd ed.). Austin, TX: PRO-ED.
Wood, M. M., & Long, N. J. (1991). Life space intervention: Talking with children and youth in crisis. Austin, TX: PRO-ED.
Wood, M. M., & Weller, D. (1981). How come it's different with some children? The Pointer, 25(2), 61-66.
Wooden, K. (1976). Weeping in the playtime of others. New York: McGraw Hill.
Wright, C. J., & Nuthall, G. (1970). Relationships between teacher behaviors and pupil achievement in three experimental elementary science lessons. American Educational Research Journal, 7, 477-491.
Wynne, L. C., & Singer, M. T. (1965). Thought disorder and family relations of schizophrenics: A research strategy. Archives of General Psychology, 9, 191-198.
York, J., Vandercook, T., MacDonald, C., Heise-Neff, C., & Caughey, E. (1992). Feedback about integrating middle school students with severe disabilities in general education classes. Exceptional Children, 58(3), 244-257.
Zabel, M. K. (1991). Teaching young children with behavior disorders. Reston, VA: The Council for Exceptional Children, ERIC Clearinghouse on Handicapped and Gifted Children mini-library, 11-14.

ADDITIONAL READINGS

Ahlstrom, W. M., & Havighurst, R. J. (1982). The Kansas City work/study experiment. In D. J. Safer (Ed.), School programs for disruptive adolescents (pp. 259-276). Baltimore: University Park Press.

Bandura, A. (1974). Behavior theory and the model of man. American Psychologist, 29, 859-869.

Bernstein, M. (1963). Life space interviewing in the school setting. American Journal of Orthopsychiatry, 33(1), 717-719.

Berry, K. (1972). Models for mainstreaming. San Rafael, CA: Dimension.

Bettelheim, B. (1967). The empty fortress. New York: Free Press.

Bettelheim, B. (1969). The children of the dream. New York: MacMillan.

Bickel, W. E., & Bickel, D. D. (1986). Effective schools, classroom and instruction: Implications for special education. Exceptional Children, 52(6), 489-500.

Bierman, K. L., & Schwartz, L. A. (1986). Selecting social intervention techniques for aggressive rejected children (Report No. CG019347: ERIC Document Reproduction Service No. ED 273883). New York: W. T. Grant Foundation.

Biestek, F. P. (1957). The casework relationship. Chicago: Loyola University Press.

Birch, J. W., & Reynolds, M. (1977). Exceptional children in America's regular schools: A first course for teachers and principals. Reston, VA: Council for Exceptional Children.

Braaten, S. A. (1985). Adolescent needs and behavior in the schools: Current and historical perspectives. In S. Braaten, R. Rutherford, & W. Evans (Eds.), Programming for adolescents with behavioral disorders, (Vol. 2, pp. 1-10). Reston, VA: Council for Children with Behavioral Disorders, Council for Exceptional Children.

Bricker, D. D. (1978). A rationale for the integration of handicapped and nonhandicapped preschool children. In M. J. Guralnick (Ed.), Early intervention and the integration of handicapped and nonhandicapped children. Baltimore: University Park Press.

Brown, V. (1984). Teaching independent student behaviors to behaviorally
    disordered youth. In J. K. Grosenick, S. L. Huntze, E. McGinnis, & C.
    R. Smith (Eds.), Social/affective interventions in behavioral disorders
    (pp. 121-149). Des Moines, IA: Dept. of Public Instruction.
Caplan, G. (1970). The theory and practice of mental health consultation.
    New York: Basic Books.
Carberry, H. (1976). How can this child be helped? Instructor, 85(5), 81-83.
Center, D. B. (1986). Educational programming for children and youth with
    behavioral disorders. Behavioral Disorders, 11(3), 208-211.
Clarke, R. V. G., & Cornish, D. B. (1978). The effectiveness of residential
    treatment for delinquents. In L. A. Hersov & D. Shaffer (Eds.),
    Aggression and anti-social behaviour in childhood and adolescence (pp.
    143-159). Oxford, England: Pergamon Press.
Conger, J. C., & Keane, S. P. (1981). Social skills intervention in the
    treatment of isolated or withdrawn children. Psychological Bulletin, 90,
    478-495.
Cruickshank, W. M. (1973). Straight is the bamboo tree. Journal of Learning
    Disabilities, 16, 191-197.
Cullinan, D., & Epstein, M. H. (1984). Research issues in behavior disorders:
    A national survey. Behavioral Disorders, 10(1), 56-59.
Cullinan, D., Epstein, M. H., & Kauffman, J. (1984). Teachers' ratings of
    students' behaviors: What constitutes behavior disorder in school?
    Behavioral Disorders, 10(1), 9-19.
Deshler, D., Rutnam, M., & Bulgren, J. (1985). Academic accommodations
    for adolescents with behavior and learning problems. In S. Braaten, R.
    Rutherford, & W. Evans (Eds.), Programming for adolescents with
    behavioral disorders: Vol. 2 (pp. 20-30). Reston, VA: Council for
    Exceptional Children, Council for Children with Behavioral Disorders.
Despert, L. (1965). The emotionally disturbed child: An inquiry into family
    patterns. Garden City, NY: Anchor Books, Doubleday.
Dinitz, S. (1982). A school-based prevention program to reduce delinquency
    vulnerability. In D. J. Safer (Ed.), School programs for disruptive
    adolescents (pp. 279-296). Baltimore: University Park Press.
Dittman, A., & Kitchner, H. (1959). Life space interviewing and individual
    play therapy: A comparison of techniques. American Journal of
    Orthopsychiatry, 29, 19-26.
D'Zurilla, T. J., & Goldfried, M. R. (1971). Problem-solving and behavior
    modification. Journal of Abnormal Child Psychology, 78, 197-228.
Eaton, L. F., & Menolascino, F. J. (1982). Psychiatric disorders in the
    mentally retarded. American Journal of Psychiatry, 13(10), 1297-1303.
Edgar, E. (1987). Secondary programs in special education: Are many of them
    justified? Exceptional Children, 53, 535-561.

Edwards, L., & O'Toole, B. (1985). Application of the self-control curriculum with behavior disordered students. Focus on Exceptional Children, 17(8), 1-8.

Epanchin, B. C., & Paul, J. L. (1982). Casebook for educating the emotionally disturbed. Columbus, OH: Merrill.

Epstein, M. H., Cullinan, D., & Rosemier, R. A. (1983). Behavior problems of behaviorally disordered and normal adolescents. Behavioral Disorders, 8(2), 171-175.

Eitzen, D. S. (1979). The effects of behavior modification on the attitudes of delinquents. In J. S. Stumphauzer (Ed.), Progress in behavior therapy with delinquents (pp. 295-299). Springfield, IL: Charles C. Thomas.

Emmer, E., Evertson, C., Sanford, J., Clements, B., & Worsham, M. (1984). Classroom management for secondary teachers. Englewood Cliffs, NJ: Prentice-Hall.

Fagen, S. A., Graves, D., Healy, S., & Tessier-Switlick, D. (1986). Reasonable mainstreaming accommodations for the classroom teacher. The Pointer, 31(1), 4-7.

Faulk, V., & Faulk, G. (1965). Use of social workers and the Life Space Interview with institutionalized children in the public school. Child Study Center Bulletin, 1(4), 27-31.

Filipzcak, J., & Wodarski, J. S. (1982). Behavioral intervention in public schools. In D. J. Safer (Ed.), School programs for disruptive adolescents. Baltimore: University Park Press.

Frith, G., & Armstrong, S. (1986). Self-monitoring for behavior disordered students. Teaching Exceptional Children, 18(2), 144-147.

Fritsch, R. E. (Ed.). (1985). The directory of public and private programs for emotionally disturbed children and youth. Phoenix, AZ: Onyx Press.

Gable, R. A., Hendrickson, J. M., & Young, C. C. (1985). Material selection and adaptation: Strategies for combating curriculum casualties among the behaviorally disordered. In R. B. Rutherford, Jr., A. G. Prieto, & J. E. McGlothin (Eds.), Monograph in behavioral disorders: Severe behavior disorders of children and youth (Vol. 8, pp. 70-85). Tempe: Arizona State University, Teacher Educators for Children with Behavior Disorders and Council for Children with Behavior Disorders.

Gable, R., & Kerr, M. (1980, Summer). Behaviorally disordered adolescents as academic change agents. In R. B. Rutherford, Jr., A. G. Prieto, & J. E. McGlothin (Eds.), Monograph in behavioral disorders: Severe behavior disorders of children and youth (pp. 117-124). Tempe: Arizona State University, Teacher Education for Children with Behavior Disorders and Council for Children with Behavior Disorders.

Gable, R. A., McConnell, S. R., & Nelson, C. M. (1985). The learning-to-fail phenomenon as an obstacle to mainstreaming children with behavioral disorders. In R. B. Rutherford, Jr., A. G. Prieto, & J. E. McGlothin (Eds.), Monograph in behavioral disorders: Severe behavior disorders of children and youth (Vol. 8, pp. 19-26). Tempe, AZ: Arizona State University, Teacher Educators for Children with Behavioral Disorders and Council for Children with Behavioral Disorders.

Gans, K. D. (1987). Willingness of regular and special education to teach students with handicaps. Exceptional Children, 54(1), 41-45.

Gardner, P. J. (1979). An overview of the Life Space Interview technique. Paper presented at the Annual International Convention, The Council for Exceptional Children (57th, Dallas, TX, April 22-27, 1979, Session W-67). ERIC Document ED 171 033.

Garner, H. (1982). Positive peer culture programs in schools. In D. J. Safer (Ed.), School programs for disruptive adolescents. Baltimore: University Park Press.

Gerber, M. M. (1988). Tolerance and technology of instruction: Implications for special education reform. Exceptional Children, 54, 309-314.

Gickling, E. E., & Thompson, V. P. (1985). A personal view of curriculum-based assessment. Exceptional Children, 52, 205-218.

Glasser, W. (1965). Reality therapy. New York: Harper & Row.

Glasser, W. (1969). Schools without failure. New York. Harper & Row.

Goffman, E. (1961). The mental hospital as a total institution. In D. R. Cressey (Ed.), The Prison. New York: Holt, Rinehart & Winston.

Gold, M., & Mann, D. W. (1984). Expelled to a friendlier place: A study of effective alternative schools. Ann Arbor: University of Michigan Press.

Goldstein, A. P. (1983). Structured learning: A psychoeducational approach for teaching social competencies. Behavioral Disorders, 8(3), 161-170.

Goldstein, A. P., Sprafkin, R. P., Gershaw, N. J., & Klein, P. (1980). Skillstreaming the adolescent. Champaign, IL: Research Press.

Graubard, P. S. (1969). Teaching strategies and techniques for the education of disruptive groups and individuals. In P. S. Graubard (Ed.), Children against schools. Chicago: Follett Educational Corp.

Grosenick, J. K., George, M. P., & George, N. L. (1990). A conceptual scheme for describing and evaluating programs in behavioral disorders. Behavioral Disorders, 16(1), 70-73.

Groves, D., Tessier-Switlick, D., & Hill, J. (1986). Reasonable accommodations for students with organizational problems. The Pointer, 31(1), 8-11.

Hallahan, D. P., Keller, C. E., McKinney, J. D., Lloyd, J. W., & Bryan, T. (1988). Examining the research base of the regular education initiative: Efficacy studies and the adaptive learning environment model. Journal of Learning Disabilities, 21(1), 29-35, 55.

Haring, N. G., & McCormick, L. (1986). Emotionally disturbed children and youth: An introduction to special education (2nd ed.). Columbus, OH: Merrill.

Heaton, R. C., Safer, D. J., & Allen, R. P. (1982). A contingency management program for disruptive junior high students. In D. J. Safer (Ed.), School programs for disruptive adolescents (pp. 217-240). Baltimore: University Park Press.

Hendrickson, J. M., Gable, R. A., & Shores, R. E. (1987). The ecological perspective: Setting events and behavior. The Pointer, 31(3), 43.

Hill, M. W. (1982, Summer). The acting out child: Research and strategies. In R. B. Rutherford, Jr., A. G. Prieto, & J. E. McGlothin (Eds.), Monograph in behavioral disorders: Severe behavior disorders of children and youth (pp. 4-5). Tempe: Arizona State University, Teacher Educators for Children with Behavior Disorders and Council for Children with Behavioral Disorders.

Hirshoren, A., & Heller, G. (1979). Programs for adolescents with behavior disorders: The state of the art. Journal of Special Education, 13(3), 275-282.

Hobbs, N. (1979). Helping disturbed children: Psychological and ecological strategies, II: Project Re-ED, twenty years later. Nashville, TN: Center for the Study of Families and Children, Vanderbilt Institute for Public Policy Studies, Vanderbilt University.

Hoffman, E. (1974). The treatment of deviance by the educational system: Structure. In W. Rhodes & S. Head (Eds.), A study of child variance: Vol. 3. Franklin, TN: New Academic Press.

Huneycutt, M. E. (1987). Teaching new behaviors. North Carolina Council for Children with Behavior Disorders Newsletter, 6(3), 6-13.

Irvin, E. C. (1986). Drama therapy in diagnosis and treatment. Child Welfare, 64(4), 347-357

Isaacs, S. (1930). Intellectual growth in young children. New York: Routledge.

Isaacs, S. (1933). Social development in young children. New York: Routledge.

Joint Commission on Mental Health of Children. (1972). Child mental health in international perspective. New York: Harper & Row.

Jones, R. L., Jamieson, J., Moulin, L., & Tower, A. G. (1981). Attitudes and mainstreaming: Theoretical perspectives. Mainstreaming: Our current knowledge. Minneapolis: University of Minnesota.

Jones, V. F. (1987). Major components in a comprehensive program for seriously emotionally disturbed children. In R. B. Rutherford, Jr., C. M. Nelson, & S. R. Forness (Eds.), Severe behavior disorders of children and youth. Boston: Little, Brown.

Kanner, L. (1943). Autistic disturbances of affective contact. Nerv. Child, 2, 217-250.

Kauffman, J. M. (1980). Where special education for disturbed children is going: A personal view. Exceptional Children, 46(7), 522-527.

Kauffman, J. M., Cullinan, D., & Epstein, M. H. (1987). Characteristics of students placed in special programs for the seriously emotionally disturbed. Behavioral Disorders, 12(3), 175-184

Kelly W. J., Salzberg, C. L., Levy, S. M., Warenteltz, R. B., Adams, T. W., Crouse, T. R., & Beegle, G. P. (1983). The effects of role-playing and self-monitoring on the generalization of vocational social skills by behaviorally disordered adolescents. Behavioral Disorders, 9(1), 27-35.

Kempe, R., & Kempe, C. (1980). Child abuse. Cambridge: Harvard University Press.

Keogh, B. K. (1988). Improving services for problem learners: Rethinking and restructuring. Journal of Learning Disabilities, 21(1), 19-22.

Kirigin, K. A., Wolf, M. M., Braukmann, C. J., Fixsen, D. D., & Phillips, E. L. (1979). Achievement Place: A preliminary outcome evaluation. In J. S. Stumphauzer (Ed.), Progress in behavior therapy with delinquents. Springfield, IL: Charles C. Thomas.

Knoff, H. (1983). Learning disabilities in the junior high school: Creating the six-hour emotionally disturbed adolescent? Adolescence, 18(71), 541-548.

Kohler, F. W., Richardson, T., Mina, C., Dinwiddie, G., & Greenwood, C. (1985). Establishing cooperative peer relations in the classroom. The Pointer, 29(4), 12-16.

Kratochwill, T., & French, D. (1984). Social skills training for withdrawn children. School Psychology Review, 13(3), 331-337.

Laneve, R. S. (1982). Pathways to success: Working with seriously emotionally disturbed students in a public school setting. In N. G. Haring & M. M. Noel (Eds.), Progress or change: Issues in educating the emotionally disturbed (Vol. 2, pp. 29-58). Seattle: Program Development Assistance, University of Washington.

Laneve, R. (1980). Mark Twain School: A special public school. In N. J. Long, W. C. Morse, & R. G. Newman (Eds.), Conflict in the classroom (4th ed.). Belmont, CA: Wadsworth.

Lawrence, C., Litynsky, M., & D'Lugoff, B. (1982). A day school intervention for truant and delinquent youth. In D. J. Safer (Ed.), School programs for disruptive adolescents (pp. 175-177). Baltimore: University Park Press.

Laycock, V. K., & Tonelson, S. W. (1985). Preparing emotionally disturbed adolescents for the mainstream: An analysis of current practices. Programming for Adolescents with Behavioral Disorders, 2, 63-73.

Lentz, F., & Shapiro, E. (1986). Functional assessment of the academic environment. School Psychology Review, 15(3), 346-357.

Lerner, M. C., & Goldenberg, D. (1987). Special education for the early childhood years. Englewood Cliffs, NJ: Prentice-Hall.

Levine, E., & Evans, M. (1983). The behaviorally disordered creative child: A challenge to our diagnostic and teaching procedures. Contemporary Education, 55(1), 28-32.

Levinson, E. (1985). Vocational and career-oriented school programs for the emotionally disturbed. The School Counselor, 33, 100-107.

Lewin, K. (1951). Psychological ecology. In D. Cartwright (Ed.), Field theory in social science: Selected theoretical papers by Kurt Lewin. New York: Harper & Row.

Lewis, R. B., & Doorlag, D. H. (1983). Teaching special students in the mainstream. Columbus, OH: Bell & Howell.

Lewis, W. W. (1965, May). Continuity and intervention in emotional disturbance: A review. Exceptional Children, 31, 465-475.

Lewis, W. (1967). Project ReED. Educational intervention in discordant child rearing systems. In E. Cown (Ed.), Emergent approaches to mental health problems. New York: Appleton-Century-Crofts.

Leyser, Y., & Abrams, P. D. (1984). Changing attitudes of classroom teachers toward mainstreaming through in-service training. The Clearing House, 57, 250-255.

Lieberman, L. M. (1985). Special education and regular education: A merger made in heaven? Exceptional Children, 51, 513-516.

Lipsitz, J. (1985). Programs for adolescents: What works and why? In S. Braaten, R. Rutherford, & W. Evans (Eds.), Programming for adolescents with behavioral disorders: Vol. 2. Reston, VA: Council for Exceptional Children, Council for Children with Behavioral Disorders.

Long, N. J. (1963). Some problems in teaching the Life Space Interviewing techniques to graduate students in education in a large class at Indiana University. In R. Newman & M. Keith (Eds.), The school centered Life Space Interview (pp. 51-56).

Long, N. J. (1965). Direct help to the classroom teacher. Washington, DC: Washington School of Psychiatry School Research Project, Chapter 5, Life Space Interviewing.

Long, N. J. (1979). The conflict cycle. The Pointer, 24(1), 6-11.

Long, N. (1984). Teaching self-control and pro-social behavior by using therapeutic signs and sayings in classrooms for emotionally disturbed pupils. The Pointer, 28(4), 36-39.

Long, N. J., Stoeffer, V., Krause, K., & Jung. C. (1961). Life space management of behavioral crisis. Social Work, 6(1), 38-45.

Lovaas, O. I., Schreibman, L., Koegel, R., & Rehm, R. (1971). Selective responding by autistic children to multiple sensory input. Journal of Abnormal Psychology, 77, 211-222.

Mahler, M. S., Pine, F., & Bergman, A. (1975). The psychological birth of the human infant. New York: Basic Books.

Mandlebaum, L. H., Russell, S. C., Krause, J., & Ganter, M. (1983). Assertive discipline: An effective class-wide behavior management program. Behavioral Disorders, 8(4), 258-264.

McGinnis, E. (1984). Teaching social skills to behaviorally disordered youth. In J. K. Grosenick, S. L. Huntze, E. McGinnis, & C. R. Smith (Eds.), Social/affective interventions in behavioral disorders (pp. 87-120). Des Moines, IA: State of Iowa, Department of Public Instruction.

McKinney, J. D., & Hocutt, A. M. (1988). The need for policy analysis in evaluating the regular education initiative. Journal of Learning Disabilities, 21(1), 12-18.

Mesinger, J. F. (1985). Commentary on "A rationale for the merger of special and regular education" or, is it now time for the lamb to lie down with the lion? Exceptional Children, 51, 510-512.

Mesinger, J. F. (1986). Alternative education for behaviorally disordered youths: A promise yet unfulfilled. Behavioral Disorders, 11(2), 98-108.

Michelson, L., & Wood. R. (1980). Behavioral assessment and training of children's social skills. In R. M. Mittersen & P. M. Miller (Eds.), Progress in behavior modification (Vol. 9). New York: Academic Press.

Morgan, S. R., & Reinhart, J. A. (1991). Interventions for students with emotional disorders. Austin, TX: PRO-ED.

Morse, W. C. (1953). The development of a mental hygiene milieu in a camp for disturbed boys. American Journal of Orthopsychiatry, 23, 826-833.

Morse, W. C. (1965). Intervention techniques for the classroom teacher. In P. K. Knoblock (Ed.), Educational programming for emotionally disturbed children: The decade ahead. Syracuse, NY: Syracuse University Press.

Morse, W. C., & Wineman, D. (1957). The therapeutic use of social isolation in a camp for ego-disturbed boys. Journal of Social Issues, 13(1), 32-39.

Myrick, R., & Dixon, R. (1985). Changing student attitudes and behavior through group counseling. The School Counselor, 3, 325-330.

Neel, R. S. (1984). Teaching social routines to behaviorally disordered youth. In J. K. Grosenick, S. L. Huntze, E. McGinnis, & C. R. Smith (Eds.), Social/affective interventions in behavioral disorders (pp. 151-181). Des Moines, IA: State of Iowa, Department of Public Instruction.

Nelson, C. M., & Kauffman, J. (1977). Educational programming for secondary school age delinquents and maladjusted pupils. Behavioral Disorders, 2(2), 102-113.

Nelson, C., & Polsgrove, L. (1984). Behavior analysis in special education: White rabbit or white elephant? Remedial and Special Education, 5(4), 7-14.

Nelson, C. M., Rutherford, R. B., Center, D. B., & Walker, H. M. (1991). Do public schools have an obligation to serve troubled children and youth? Exceptional Children, 57(5), 411-415.

Newman, R. G. (1967). Psychological consultation in the schools: A catalyst for learning. New York: Basic Books.

Paine, S. C., Radiccke, J. A., Rosellini, L. C., Deutchman, L., & Darch, C. B. (1983). Structuring your classroom for academic success. Champaign, IL: Research Press.

Pappanikou, A. J., & Paul, J. L. (Eds.). (1977). Mainstreaming emotionally disturbed children. Syracuse, NY: Syracuse University Press.

Parad, H. J. (Ed.). (1965). Crisis intervention: Selected readings. New York: Family Service Association of America.

Patterson, C. H. (1985). The therapeutic relationship: Foundations for an eclectic psychotherapy. Monterey, CA: Brooks/Cole.

Paul, J. L. (1985). Where are we in the education of emotionally disturbed children? Behavioral Disorders, 10(2), 145-151.

Polansky, N., Lippitt, R., & Redl, F. (1950). An investigation of behavioral contagion in groups. Human Relations, 3, 319-48.

Pollack, S. (1969). Theory and techniques for a therapeutic milieu. Journal of Individual Psychology, 25, 164-173.

Polsgrove, L., Rieth, H., Friend, M., & Cohan, R. (1980, Summer). An analysis of the effects of various instructional procedures on the oral reading performance of high school special education students. In R. B. Rutherford, Jr., A. G. Prieto, & J. E. McGlothin (Eds.), Monograph in behavioral disorders: Severe behavior disorders of children and youth (pp. 125-133). Tempe: Arizona State University, Teacher Educators for Children with Behavior Disorders and Council for Children with Behavior Disorders.

Powell, D. E. (1984). Teaching self-control to high-risk students in an urban environment. The Pointer, 28(4), 20-24.

Quay, H. C. (1972). Patterns of aggression, withdrawal and immaturity. In H. C. Quay & J. S. Werry (Eds.), Psychopathological disorders of childhood (2nd ed.). New York: Wiley.

Quay, H. C., Morse, W. C., & Cutler, R. L. (1966). Personality patterns of pupils in special classes for the emotionally disturbed. Exceptional Children, 32(5), 297-301.

Redl, F. (1949). The phenomenon of contagion and shock effect in group therapy. In W. Healy & A. Bronner (Eds.), Searchlights on delinquency. New York: International Universities Press.

Redl, F. (1959). Mental hygiene and teaching. New York: Holt, Rinehart & Winston.

Redl, F. (1963). The Life Space Interview in the school setting. American Journal of Orthopsychiatry, 33, 717-733.

Redl, F. (1966). Designing a therapeutic classroom environment for disturbed children: The milieu approach. In P. Knoblock (Ed.), Intervention approaches in educating emotionally disturbed children. Syracuse, NY: Syracuse University Press.

Redl, F. (1966). When we deal with children: Selected writings. New York: The Free Press.

Reinert, H. (1968). Decision making in the educationally handicapped and normal child: A comparative study. Unpublished doctoral dissertation, Colorado State College, Greely.

Reynolds, M. C., Wang, C., & Walberg, H. J. (1987). The necessary restructuring of special and regular education. Exceptional Children, 53, 391-398.

Rioch, D., & Stanton, A. (1953). Milieu therapy. Psychiatry, 16, 65-72.

Rothman, E. P. (1980). From the desk of the principal: Perspectives on a school based community treatment program for disruptive youth. In J. B. Jordan, D. A. Sabatino, & R. C. Sarri (Eds.), Disruptive youth in schools. Reston, VA: The Council for Exceptional Children.

Rogers, C. R. (1950). A current formulation of client-centered therapy. Social Service Review, 24.

Rogers, C. R. (1961). On becoming a person. Boston: Houghton-Mifflin.

Rutter, M., & Schopler, E. (Eds.). (1978). Autism: A reappraisal of concepts and treatment (pp. 9-11). New York: Plenum Press.

Sabatino, D. (1987). Preventive discipline as a practice in special education. Teaching Exceptional Children, 19(4), 8-11.

Salend, S., & Allen, E. (1985). Comparative effects of externally managed and self-managed response-cost systems on inappropriate classroom behavior. The Journal of School Psychology, 23, 59-67.

Schloss, P. J., Schloss, C. N., & Harris, L. (1984). A multiple baseline analysis of an interpersonal skills training program for depressed youth. Behavioral Disorders, 9(3), 182-188.

Schloss, P. J., Schloss, C. N., Wood, C. E., & Kiehl, W. S. (1986). A critical review of social skills research with behaviorally disordered students. Behavioral Disorders, 12(1), 1-13.

Schubert, M. A., & Glick, H. M. (1981). Least restrictive environment programs: Why are some so successful? Education Unlimited, 3, 11-14.

Schulz, J. B., & Turnbull, A. P. (1984). Mainstreaming handicapped students: A guide for classroom teachers (2nd ed.). Boston: Allyn & Bacon.

Schumaker, J. B., & Deshler, D. D. (1988). Implementing the regular education initiative in secondary schools: A different ball game. Journal of Learning Disabilities, 21(1), 36-41.

Sherman, B. (1985). The directory of residential treatment facilities for emotionally disturbed children. Phoenix, AZ: Onyx Press.

Simon, D. J., Vetter-Zemitsch, A., & Johnson, J. C. (1985). On campus: Systemic/behavioral interventions for behaviorally disordered adolescents. Behavioral Disorders, 10(2), 183-190.

Skrtic, T. M. (1988). Response to the January executive commentary: No more noses to the glass. Exceptional Children, 54, 475-476.

Skrtic, T. M. (1986). The crisis in special education knowledge: A perspective on perspective. Focus on Exceptional Children, 18(7), 1-16.

Spodek, B., Sarach, D. N., & Lee, R. C. (1984). Mainstreaming young children. Belmont, CA: Wadsworth.

Stainback, W., Stainback, S., Elscherat, S., & Daud, J. (1986). A non-intrusive intervention for acting out behavior. Teaching Exceptional Children, 19(1), 38-41.

Steinberg, Z. (1991). Pandora's children. Beyond Behavior, 2(3), 10-12.

Stephens, T. M., Blackhurst, A. E., & Magliocca, L. A. (1982). Teaching mainstreamed students. New York: Wiley.

Strayhorn, J., & Rhodes, L. A. (1985). The shaping game: A teaching tool. The Pointer, 29(4), 8-11.

Swan, W. W., Brown, C. L., & Jacob, R. T. (1987). Types of service delivery models used in reintegration of severely emotionally disturbed/behaviorally disordered students. Journal of the Council for Children with Behavioral Disorders, 12(2), 99-103.

Szymanski, L. S. (1980). Psychiatric diagnosis of retarded persons. In L. W. Szymanski & P. E. Tanguay (Eds.), Emotional disorders of mentally retarded persons (pp. 61-81). Baltimore: University Park Press.

Tanguay, P. E. (1980). Early infantile autism and mental retardation: Differential diagnosis. In L. W. Szymanski & P. E. Tanguay (Eds.), Emotional disorders of mentally retarded persons (pp. 101-109). Baltimore: University Park Press.

Tilley, B. K., Gross, J. C., & Cox, L. A. (1982, September). Administrative issues in educating emotionally disturbed students in public schools. In M. M. Noel & N. G. Haring (Eds.), Progress or change: Issues in educating the emotionally disturbed. Vol. 1, Identification and Progress Planning (pp. 135-164). Seattle: University of Washington, Program Development Assistance System.

Tomalesky, M., & Jackson, R. (1984). The safety harbor exceptional students center: Multiphasic academic/therapeutic program model. In S. Braaten, R. B. Rutherford, Jr., & C. A. Kardash (Eds.), Programming for adolescents with behavior disorders (Vol. 1, pp. 52-58). Reston, VA: Council for Exceptional Children, Council for Children with Behavioral Disorders.

Tompkins, J. R. (1978, April). A primer on therapeutic milieu: An historical review and implications for children in institutions and schools. Unpublished manuscript.

Turnbull, A. P. (1982). Preschool mainstreaming: A policy and implementation analysis. Educational Evaluation and Policy Analysis, 4, 281-291.

Vaughn, S. (1987). TLC--teaching, learning and caring: Teaching interpersonal problem-solving skills to behaviorally disordered adolescents. The Pointer, 31(2), 25-30.

Wang, M. C., Reynolds, M. C., & Walberg, H. J. (1987). Learner characteristics and adaptive education. In Handbook of special education: Research and Practice, Vol. 1. (pp. 61-65). Elmford, NY: Pergamon Press.

White, R. (1985). Increasing school competence: A new curriculum for BEH teachers in North Carolina. North Carolina Council for Children with Behavioral Disorders Newsletter, 5(1), 17-18.

Wineman, D. (1961). Early clinical experiences at Pioneer House. Unpublished master's thesis. University of Michigan Institute of Social Work, Ann Arbor.

Wood, F. H., Spence, J., & Rutherford, R. B. (1982). An intervention program for emotionally disturbed students based on social learning principles. In R. L. McDowell, G. W. Adamson, & F. H. Woods (Eds.), Teaching emotionally disturbed children (pp. 240-243). Boston: Little, Brown.

AUTHOR INDEX

230

Author's Backgrounds

James R. Tompkins, Ph.D.

James R. Tompkins received his Ph.D. in Educational Psychology from the Catholic University of America in Washington, D.C. in 1971. He was the Coordinator at the Unit of Education of Emotionally Disturbed Children, Division of Training Programs, Bureau of Education for the Handicapped, HEW, Washington, D.C. from 1965-1971. He has been Director of the Governor's Child Advocacy Council in North Carolina and an adjunct professor at the University of North Carolina, Chapel Hill. He has also worked as a consultant in public and parochial elementary schools and in residential treatment of emotionally disturbed children. He currently teaches Special Education for the Emotionally Disturbed at Appalachian State University in Boone, N.C.

David Wineman, Elton B. McNeil, and Nicholas Long have been major contributors to understanding theoretical and practical issues associated with therapeutic milieu. All of these personalities were associated with the University of Michigan Fresh Air Camp (FAC) during the same time as Tompkins (1960-1965), who was a student at Fresh Air Camp during the summers of 1960 and 1961 and was invited as faculty/staff at FAC during the summers of 1962-1965. At the Fresh Air Camp, the use of therapeutic milieu practices was explored in the treatment of highly aggressive acting out children and adolescents. In the years 1962-65, Tompkins teamed with Dr. Long in Washington D.C. to create a nationally recognized residential program for emotionally disturbed children; Hillcrest Children's Center. The implementation of therapeutic milieu practices and the Life Space Interview in the treatment and education of children at the center were essential to the program's success.

Dr. William Morse of the University of Michigan is a notable proponent of implementing therapeutic milieu practices in schools and institutions. He and Tompkins collaborated at conferences, Bureau of Education for the Handicapped panels, on the Joint Committee on Mental Health of Children, and in other professional activities. Morse's influence on Tompkins has been markedly significant in the understanding of the importance of therapeutic milieu practices for troubled children.

Patricia Tompkins-McGill, Ph.D.

Patricia Tompkins-McGill received her Masters Degree in Social Work from the Catholic University of America in 1965 and her Ph.D. in Special Education from The University of Texas at Austin in 1980. Since the early 1960s she has been committed to the welfare of children. She trained at the Fresh Air Camp at the University of Michigan with David Wineman and Nicholas Long and wrote her master's thesis on the use of the Life Space Interview in an elementary school as a project collaborated with Dr. Long.

She has had extensive experience in public child welfare and in private day and residential treatment of emotionally disturbed children. Among her work experiences have been Hillcrest Children's Center in Washington, D.C. and San Antonio Children's Center in Texas. She has also taught social work at The University of Texas in Austin and the College of Santa Fe in New Mexico. In both these experiences, she attempted to integrate concepts of therapeutic milieu into social work curricula. She is interested in the integration of these concepts into mainstreamed situations and into situations serving individuals with developmental disabilities. She is particularly committed to concepts and techniques which facilitate the provision of services for children and youth in their own communities.

For the past fifteen years, Dr. Tompkins-McGill has studied and researched stress in various situations, including stress among teachers of handicapped and non-handicapped students, public child welfare workers, and other human service personnel. She is also interested in and committed to relieving the stress which parents of children with handicaps experience.

From 1982-1991, Dr. Tompkins-McGill was the Executive Director of Las Cumbres Learning Services, Inc., a private non-profit agency serving people of all ages with developmental disabilities throughout rural northern New Mexico. In this role she utilized concepts of therapeutic milieu and Life Space Interviewing techniques in expanding services. She currently lives near Dallas, Texas, where she writes and consults.